PL/I PROGRAMMING

PL/I PROGRAMMING

A Structured, Disciplined Approach

EDWARD L. LAMIE
CALIFORNIA STATE COLLEGE, STANISLAUS

WADSWORTH PUBLISHING COMPANY
BELMONT, CALIFORNIA
A DIVISION OF WADSWORTH, INC.

Production Editor: Hal Lockwood, Bookman Productions
Designer: Paula Schlosser
Copy Editor: Aidan Kelly
Technical Illustrator: Barbara Hack

Library of Congress Cataloging in Publication Data

Lamie, Edward L.
PL/I programming.
Includes index.
1. PL/I (Computer program language)
2. Structured programming. I. Title. II. Title:
PL/one programming.
QA76.73.P25L35 001.64'24 81-14718
AACR2

ISBN 0-534-01067-9

Printed in the United States of America

2 3 4 5 6 7 8 9 10—86 85 84 83

ISBN 0-534-01067-9

Contents

A mes ancêtres québecois

Preface

The primary purpose of this book is to present an introduction to computer programming and PL/I (Programming Language/ One). Although several versions of PL/I are currently in use, the version emphasized here is the American National Standards Institute (ANSI) standard for PL/I adopted in August 1976. Consequently, this book is intended for use in an ANSI PL/I, IBM PL/I, or PL/C environment.

There are literally hundreds of computer programming languages available. Many of these languages are oriented toward the solution of a certain class of problems and cannot be effectively used for any other types of problems. However, PL/I is a high-level, multipurpose computer programming language that can be effectively utilized in a wide variety of applications, including commercial and scientific problems. PL/I has tremendous capability, is a massive language, and can be used by both novice and expert.

The approach taken in this book is to use problem-solving techniques in conjunction with each new PL/I concept introduced. For example, the three-step problem-solving process is presented in Chapter 1 and is consistently used throughout the book to develop complete solutions to problems. The first two chapters deal with preliminary concepts and provide a quick overview of programming concepts and PL/I. Chapters 3 through 14 introduce new PL/I concepts as well as classes of problems that can be solved with each new concept. Furthermore, new concepts are presented in a logical but gradual sequence. For example, a working knowledge of several of the more important data types is presented in Chapter 3, but detailed coverage of the fine points of these data types is deferred until Chapter 12.

Because this is an introductory book on programming and the PL/I language, only a subset of PL/I is discussed. The subset presented contains those features that are easily grasped by the beginning programmer and that can be used to solve many useful and interesting problems. Furthermore, the subset of PL/I discussed in the book is relatively machine-independent. Few (if any) changes are necessary to run the programs presented in this book on most IBM, DEC, CDC, Univac, Burroughs, or Honeywell computer systems that have PL/I compilers.

Starting with the very first chapter, structured programming techniques are emphasized throughout this book. In fact, every example presented uses only structured programming methodologies. Both pseudocode and flowcharts are used in the first five chapters as methods to develop computer solutions to problems, but only pseudocode is used exclusively in Chapters 6 through 14. The advantage of pseudocode is that it is both a clear, concise method of program development and a form of program documentation. Pseudocode is similar to PL/I and is more likely to be used as a program-development tool.

PL/I can be used in either batch or interactive mode and this book does not place special emphasis on either mode of operation. It is assumed that the mode of operation will be determined by the available facilities of the local computer installation and that instructions and procedures for running PL/I programs will also be provided.

Appendices E through K contain information about restrictions on PL/I compilers as well as other general information. Following is a brief summary of considerations for selected PL/I compilers.

IBM PL/I

Especially with PL/I-F, DOS PL/I Optimizer, OS PL/I Optimizer, and PL/I check-out, no changes are necessary to run any of the programs displayed in this book.

PL/C

Basically, PL/C is a subset of IBM PL/I, and most of the topics discussed in this book are available with PL/C. All the differences between the PL/I in this book and PL/C are indicated in footnotes or other discussion.

ANSI Subset G

As its name suggests, Subset G is a subset of ANSI PL/I. Differences between this book and Subset G are indicated in footnotes or other discussion.

Burroughs PL/I

Burroughs PL/I is based on IBM PL/I and is also compatible with this book.

CDC PL/I

CDC PL/I is based on a subset of ANSI PL/I but has many of the restrictions of Subset G.

Data General PL/I

Data General PL/I is based on Subset G.

DEC CPL
DEC CPL is based on ANSI PL/I but has a number of restrictions.

DEC VAX-11 PL/I
DEC VAX-11 PL/I is based on Subset G.

Digital Research PL/I-80
Digital Research PL/I-80 is based on Subset G.

Honeywell PL/I
Honeywell PL/I is based on ANSI PL/I and is compatible with this book.

IBM Series 1 PL/I
IBM Series 1 PL/I is based on a subset of ANSI PL/I.

Prime PL/I
Prime PL/I is based on Subset G.

Univac PL/I
Univac PL/I is based on ANSI PL/I and is compatible with this book.

Wang PL/I
Wang PL/I is based on Subset G.

An instructor's manual is available with this book. It contains sample course outlines and answers to selected problems. It also contains a complete set of transparency masters that can be used to help effectively teach the course.

Except for two years of high school mathematics, this book does not require any special background on the part of the reader. No previous programming background is assumed, and this book can be used in a one-semester or one-quarter introductory programming course. It can also be used in a second programming course if the first course is a FORTRAN or BASIC programming course.

I thank my sweet wife, Mary Ellen, for her understanding and support during the 11 months that I worked on this book. I am grateful to Bob Cook, Freeman Moore, and Dean Sanders for contributing several problems used at the end of selected chapters. I also thank Sophie Lashuay, who typed most of the manuscript.

I have enjoyed working on this book and welcome any comments or suggestions. I can be reached through Wadsworth Publishing Co., Belmont, California 94002.

Edward Louis Lamie

PL/I PROGRAMMING

1 Programming Fundamentals

1.1. INTRODUCTION

Computer programming is a problem-solving process that involves writing a series of instructions or statements in a particular computer-programming language, such as PL/I. The development of these instructions or statements can be a complex task and is often quite error-prone, because many humans are not accustomed to working at the level of exactness required by the computer. Consequently, the actual writing of a computer program is preceded by several problem-solving phases, which are discussed in the next section.

There are several terms and concepts which must be understood in order to grasp the fundamentals of computer programming. Some of these terms and concepts are more easily defined by means of an example, such as Program 1.1, which is a complete PL/I program. (The line numbers on the left in Program 1.1 are not part of the program; they are used only to label the lines so that they can be referred to in a discussion.)

PROGRAM 1.1.

```
1    JOB.
2    USER(LAMIE,PWORD)
3    CHARGE(CPS,D0001)
4    PLI,GO.
5    --EOR--
6    /*PROGRAM TO DISPLAY A MESSAGE*/
7    DISPLAY:  PROCEDURE OPTIONS(MAIN);
8                  PUT LIST ('HI THERE');
9              END DISPLAY;
10   --EOR--
11   --EOI--
```

Program 1.1 is complete because no additional information is needed to process this program on a computer, such as the Control Data Corporation Cyber 172. The PL/I program appears in lines 6 through 9, and all the other lines are special statements that are unique to the Cyber 172 computer system and are called *job-control language* (JCL) statements. The term "job" refers to the processing of a computer program, and the various JCL statements provide information about that program to the computer. For example, line 4 indicates that the program is written in the computer-programming language PL/I. If a different language were used, then line 4 would be appropriately changed. However, every computer system has its own unique set of JCL statements; for example, if this PL/I program were to be processed on an IBM or a Burroughs computer system, then different JCL statements would be required. See Appendix A for samples of JCL statements for various computer systems.

The only purpose of Program 1.1 is to display or print the message "HI THERE" on an interactive terminal, a line printer, or some equivalent output device. The information that is displayed or printed by a program is defined to be the *output* generated by that program. The only statement that produces output in this program is line 8, the PUT statement.

Note that a PL/I program is composed of a series of statements arranged in a particular order. Except for the comment (line 6), every PL/I statement is terminated with a semicolon (;). Comments are ignored by the computer and are used to make programs more readable for humans. Statements are processed in sequential order unless the computer is directed to do otherwise by control statements, such as IF statements or DO statements, which are discussed in Chapter 2.

The only language that any computer "understands" is its own machine language, which uses only binary digits to represent the various instructions and operations. Hence PL/I programs must be translated or *compiled* into machine language before they can be processed or executed by the computer. This translation process is performed by a *compiler*, which is actually a computer program that translates other computer programs into machine language. Line 4 in Program 1.1 is a JCL statement that directs the PL/I compiler to compile and execute the PL/I program. The machine-language program generated by the compiler is called the *object program;* whereas the PL/I program (lines 6 through 9) is called the *source program*. The compiler, under the control of the computer, transforms the source program into the object program; then the computer executes the machine-language statements in the object program.

1.2. PROBLEM-SOLVING FUNDAMENTALS

Problem solving by means of the computer requires several phases to ensure systematic development of a solution. The three phases in the problem-solving process are:

1. Problem definition
2. Algorithm design
3. Algorithm implementation

Basically, *problem definition* is the method by which the problem to be solved becomes clearly understood by the programmer. *Algorithm design* is the method by which the logical solution to the problem is developed and expressed in some intermediate form, such as pseudocode or flowcharts. (The term "algorithm" is defined in Section 1.2.2.) *Algorithm implementation* is the method by which the intermediate form of the solution is translated into a computer program, and that program is then tested and debugged.

1.2.1. Problem Definition

The most important criterion for problem solving is that the computer program correctly solve the intended problem. This may appear to be a trivial statement, but without precise problem definition one might easily develop a computer program that either solves a different problem or only partially solves the intended problem.

The problem-definition phase of problem solving requires that every aspect of the problem be precisely defined. One effective technique is to identify the major elements of a problem, so that the problem can be subdivided into smaller, simpler subproblems, which are easier to define. Another important requirement of this phase is that one must clearly understand what data are needed by the problem. That is, both the data to be manipulated and the data to be produced or displayed must be precisely defined.

This phase of the problem-solving process is important not only to ensure solution of the intended problem, but also to make less work of the subsequent phases. For example, algorithm design is generally easier when a precise problem definition is available, because in that definition a good portion of the solution has already been developed. In other words, a complete understanding and documenting of a problem represents a significant portion of the solution to that problem.

1.2.2. Algorithm Design

An *algorithm* is defined as a collection of instructions that will lead to a solution to some problem. An algorithm must also satisfy the following criteria:

1. Each instruction is unambiguous.
2. The instructions can be mechanically carried out.
3. The algorithm always terminates after a finite number of instructions are applied.

An algorithm is similar to a computer program in that the statements that make up a computer program must satisfy these same criteria. For example, each statement in a computer program is completely unambiguous; there is only one possible meaning for that statement. Each statement in a computer program is mechanically carried out, or executed, by the computer. Finally, computer programs that successfully solve a problem always stop after a finite number of statements have been executed.

The purpose of the algorithm-design phase is to take the problem definition and produce a logical solution to the problem in question. This logical solution is actually an algorithm, and it is passed on to the algorithm-implementation phase, where it is then transformed into a computer program. Algorithms can be represented in a variety of ways: as flowcharts, pseudocode, Chapin charts, decision tables, or even as a series of well-written English sentences. Later in this chapter, pseudocode and flowcharts are discussed, and several examples are presented.

1.2.3. Algorithm Implementation

The algorithm-implementation phase of the problem-solving process uses the algorithm produced by the algorithm-design phase to develop a computer program that correctly solves the intended problem. This phase involves the writing (or coding) of a computer program from an algorithm, followed by testing and removal of errors from (or *debugging*) that program. The amount of time spent in this phase can be significantly reduced if the two preceding phases have been completed in a thorough, accurate manner. In fact, the algorithm-implementation phase should be fairly mechanical, because the logical solution to the problem is developed in the preceding phases.

The writing of a computer program requires knowledge of a computer-programming language, such as PL/I, because the computer program must accurately represent the algorithm to be implemented. After the program is written, it is compiled; and during compilation it is checked for *compile-time errors* (also called *syntax errors*). Syntax errors arise when PL/I statements are incorrectly constructed. The compiler displays appropriate error messages if errors are found.

After the program is successfully compiled, one attempts to execute the program. If the program fails to execute correctly, then execution or *run-time errors* result. These errors are more difficult to find and correct, because sometimes no error messages are displayed and the program seems to terminate normally; yet it produces incorrect output. When execution-error messages are displayed, they sometimes seem confusing or meaningless. Execution errors often arise because of incorrect algorithms or incorrect implementation of algorithms. After all execution errors are removed, the program must be tested to make certain that it satisfactorily processes the various combinations of allowable data. The testing process can lead to the detection of additional execution errors, which must be corrected.

After the three phases of the problem-solving process have been completed, the resulting computer program should be able to solve the intended problem. However, the problem-solving process does not necessarily stop here, because future needs might require changes in or additions to the program. Modification of a computer program to accommodate changing needs and requirements is called *program maintenance*, and it is a major activity of many computer installations, because many programs are constantly being changed. How maintainable a program is depends on how well the program is written as well as on the quality of the supporting information (the *documentation*) about that program (for example, the problem definition, the algorithm, the program listing, the program tests, etc.). When properly applied, the problem-solving process can significantly facilitate both the development and the maintenance of programs.

1.3. THE PSEUDOCODE APPROACH

The second phase of the problem-solving process is algorithm design. There are many ways to represent algorithms, and each has its own advantages and disadvantages. The two algorithm representations discussed in this book are *pseudocode* and *flowcharts*. Basically, pseudocode is a series of English-like statements that represent a solution to a particular problem. Flowcharts are graphical representations of algorithms; they use symbols that depict various actions, connected by directed line segments. The pseudocode approach is discussed in this section, and the flowchart approach is discussed in section 1.5.

The purpose of pseudocode is to clearly represent the logical solution to a particular problem. After the pseudocode has been properly developed, the process of writing the computer program should be straight-forward and perhaps even mechanical. Depending on the complexity of the problem to be solved, pseudocode can be developed in one step or in several steps, by starting with a general solution and by refining each succeeding step until an appropriate amount of detail has been achieved.

There are very few rules which specify how pseudocode statements can be constructed; so great individual freedom and initiative is possible. One convention that is almost universally accepted is that indentation defines the scope of statements within the pseudocode. However, precisely three control structures are permitted in writing pseudocode statements. This fact is not really restrictive, because any computer-oriented problem can be solved by using these three structures. Furthermore, discipline and clear style are encouraged when only these control structures are used. Once this pseudocode approach is mastered, one can quickly develop solutions that are clearly readable by most other programmers. The three control structures that are allowed are as follows:

Sequence a series of sequential statements that appear at the same level of indentation and do not affect the order in which other statements are processed.

Alternation (also called the *IF statement*): a condition or test that results in a true or false answer. It is evaluated and, depending on whether the answer is true or false, one of two specified groups of statements is processed. Each such group can contain some or all of the three control structures. One of the statement groups may be empty (or null).

Repetition (also called the *DO statement*): one group of statements is specified, and the number of times this statement group is processed depends on a condi-

```
______________________________
______________________________
DO condition
    ______________________________
    ______________________________
    ______________________________
    IF condition
        THEN______________________________
            ______________________________
            ______________________________
        ELSE______________________________
            ______________________________
            ______________________________
IF condition
    THEN DO condition
         ______________________________
         ______________________________
         ______________________________
    ELSE ______________________________
         ______________________________
         ______________________________
______________________________
```

Figure 1.1. *A "skeleton" pseudocode structure.*

tion that is evaluated each time the group is processed. The statement group could be processed zero, one, two, or more times, and it can also contain some or all of the three control structures.

Pseudocode is composed of a series of statements that use only these three control structures. Each of the control structures may be used as often as needed throughout the program. For example, consider the "skeleton" pseudocode in Figure 1.1 in which each of the control structures is used more than once.

Each of the lines in Figure 1.1 represents some statement or action to be performed. It is easy to spot the sequence statements; they are scattered throughout the program, and here there are seven different such groups. There are two alternation (IF) statements; one is part of a repetition (DO) statement, and the other contains a DO statement. Note that the THEN and ELSE groups of statements are parts of the IF statement. If the specified condition in the IF statement is true, the THEN statement group is processed; otherwise, the ELSE statement group is processed. There are also two DO statements in the program; the first contains an IF statement, and the second is contained within an IF statement. The use of indentation should make clear the scope of each of these statements.

The pseudocode in Figure 1.1 can also be classified as a structured program because of its organization and its reliance on the three basic control structures.

If a PL/I program were written based on this pseudocode, and if only the three basic control structures were used, then it too could be classified as a structured program.

1.4. PSEUDOCODE EXAMPLES

The development of pseudocode and the writing of computer programs is best learned by practice. In this section, a series of examples is presented to illustrate the fundamental principles of the pseudocode approach. These examples are intended to be representative of problems which would typically be solved on a computer, and they should provide insight and understanding in writing pseudocode. In Chapter 2, complete PL/I programs are developed for each of these examples.

1.4.1. The Addition of Two Numbers

One of the simplest examples which can be studied is the problem in which the input consists of two integer numbers and the output consists of their sum. The term *input* is used here to describe the process by which information, such as numbers, is obtained by the computer. These numbers could actually be represented by holes in a punched card, by values typed in at a computer terminal, or by a variety of other methods. Similarly, the term *output* is used to describe the process used by the computer to display or present desired information, usually by means of line printers or computer terminals.

The term *variable* is also used extensively in the development of both pseudocode and PL/I programs. A *variable* is simply a programmer-defined symbolic name for a location in computer memory where data is stored. The programmer can choose any arbitrary name for a variable, but it is wise to select names that are meaningful for the problem being solved. Variables are important in algorithm design and implementation, because they are usually needed to describe input, data manipulation, and output. Variables can be used to acquire new values or modify current values at any time. Even for this simple problem, variables are essential in order to describe a solution.

The first two phases of the problem-solving process for this example are presented as Program 1.2.* The algorithm-implementation phase for this example appears in Chapter 2.

The numbers to the left of the pseudocode statements are not actually part of the pseudocode, and are used only as reference labels. Line 1 of the pseudocode represents the input of two numbers, and that these two numbers are to be stored in variables A and B. The word GET signifies input; this convention is used throughout the book.

*The term "program" is usually used to refer to only the final stage of the programming process, that is, to the statements executed by the computer. However, for learning purposes, we will usually be using the term "program" in this book to refer to the entire programming process, which begins with problem solving.

PROGRAM 1.2.

PROBLEM DEFINITION

The problem is to find the sum of two numbers. Input is to consist of any two integer numbers, which can be positive, negative, or zero. The output is to consist of one integer number, which is the sum of the two input numbers.

Sample input: 46 50

Sample output: 96

ALGORITHM DESIGN

Variables to be used

A, B	storage of data values (input)
SUM	storage of computed sum

Pseudocode

```
1 GET A, B
2 SUM = A + B
3 PUT SUM
4 END
```

Line 2 adds together the contents of variables A and B, and places this sum into the variable SUM. An equals sign (=) and a plus sign (+) are used in this line to perform these operations. The use of the plus sign is self-explanatory, but the equals sign means literally "is replaced by." That is, the equals sign signifies an assignment or replacement operation, rather than equality. Specifically, the old value of the variable on the left of the equals sign is replaced by the value of whatever is on the right side of the equals sign.

Line 3 specifies that the value stored in variable SUM is to be output. The word "PUT" signifies output; this convention is used throughout this book.

Line 4 simply indicates the end of the pseudocode. The pseudocode in Program 1.2 is classified as "straight line" pseudocode, because the statements are all processed in sequential order from the top to the bottom. There are no DO or IF statements to cause any deviation from this strict sequential order. However, very few nontrivial problems are this simple, and each of the following examples is more complex.

1.4.2. Find the Smaller of Two Numbers

This problem is a little more complex than the preceding one because it illustrates the concept of alternation. The first two phases of the problem-solving process are presented here, and the third phase, algorithm implementation, appears in Chapter 2.

PROGRAM 1.3.

PROBLEM DEFINITION

The problem is to find the smaller of two numbers. Input is to consist of any two integer numbers, which can be positive, negative, or zero. The output is to consist of whichever one of these numbers is algebraically smaller than the other. If the two numbers are equal, the output is to consist of the second number.

Sample input: 652 197

Sample output: 197

ALGORITHM DESIGN

Variables to be used

A, B storage of data values (input)

Pseudocode

```
1 GET A,B
2 IF A < B
3    THEN PUT A
4    ELSE PUT B
5 END
```

Line 1 of this pseudocode represents the input of two numbers, and that these two numbers are to be stored in variables A and B. Line 2 compares the contents of these variables with the condition "A < B," which uses the "less than" (<) operator. If the condition is true, the THEN clause is executed. If the condition is not true, the ELSE clause is executed. In other words, if the value of variable A is less than the value of variable B, then the output consists of the contents of variable A. If the value in variable A is greater than or equal to the value in variable B, then the output consists of the contents of variable B. Note the use of indentation, which implies that the THEN and ELSE clauses are part of the IF statement.

1.4.3. Find the Average (Mean) of a Group of Numbers

This problem is longer and more complex than the previous examples, and the concept of repetition (DO loops) is illustrated. The first two phases of the problem-solving process are presented here, and the algorithm-implementation phase appears in Chapter 2.

PROGRAM 1.4.

PROBLEM DEFINITION

The problem is to find the mean of an unknown number of positive values. Input is to consist of an arbitrary number of positive integer values, followed by a negative integer number, called a "sentinel value," which is used to mark the end of the data to be processed. The mean is computed by dividing the sum of the positive values by the number of input items that have positive values. The sentinel value is not used in the computation of the mean; its only use is to stop the input of any more values. The output is to consist of every positive value in the input (called the "echo check") and the mean of the positive numbers.

Sample input: 26 32 18 43 28 −1

Sample output: 26 32 18 43 28 29.4

ALGORITHM DESIGN

Variables to be used

X	storage of data values (input)
N	count the number of positive values
SUM	maintain subtotal of positive values
MEAN	computed mean

Pseudocode / **Comments**

```
 1  N, SUM = 0            initialization
 2  GET X                 get first value
 3  DO WHILE X >= 0       input until negative value
                            encountered
 4     PUT X              "echo check"
 5     SUM = SUM + X      compute the subtotal
 6     N = N + 1          increment the counter
 7     GET X              get the next value
 8  END                   end of the DO loop
 9  MEAN = SUM/N          compute the mean
10  PUT MEAN              display the mean
11  END                   end of pseudocode
```

The essence of this program is the group of statements controlled by the DO statement in line 3 (this construct is often called a DO loop). The statements inside the DO loop are processed repeatedly until the specified condition ("$X \geq 0$" in this case) is no longer true. This condition is evaluated initially when the

DO loop is first encountered and, if the condition is not true, then no statements within the DO loop (lines 4 through 7) are processed. However, if the condition is initially true, the DO loop is entered; each time the END of the DO loop (line 8) is encountered, the condition is evaluated; and if it is true, the statements within the DO loop are processed again. If the condition is false, the DO loop is exited; and the first statement (here, line 9) following the END of the DO loop is processed.

PROGRAM 1.5.

PROBLEM DEFINITION

Given information about a loan, the problem is to compute all the monthly balances until the loan is paid in full. The final month's payment must also be computed. The input consists of the initial balance or amount of the loan, the amount of the monthly payment, and the annual interest rate expressed as a percentage. The output consists of all monthly loan balances, as well as the final month's payment.

Sample input: 1000 100 15

Sample output: 1000 912.50 823.91 . . .

Here the loan is for $1,000, the monthly payment is $100, and the annual interest rate is 15 percent. The interest rate must be converted to a decimal value and divided by 12 so that it can be used to compute monthly interest.

ALGORITHM DESIGN

The algorithm must be able to properly handle all legitimate forms of input. In this example, a serious problem would arise if the first month's interest exceeded the monthly payment. The algorithm must be able to detect such a situation and not attempt to compute any monthly balances.

Variables to be used

BALANCE	initial and subsequent monthly balances
PAYMENT	monthly payment
RATE	interest rate
LAST_PAY	final month's payment

Note that there are two identical GET statements in this program: one immediately before the DO loop (line 2), the other as the last statement in that loop (line 7). This may seem redundant, but it is necessary because of the manner in which the condition of the DO statement is evaluated. This is also consistent with the way that PL/I evaluates conditions in a DO loop.

Be sure you understand this example thoroughly before you proceed to the next example. As an exercise, take the sample input, step through the pseu-

---

Pseudocode

```
GET BALANCE, PAYMENT, RATE
Convert RATE to monthly interest rate expressed
  as a decimal
IF PAYMENT is greater than first month's interest
  THEN compute the PUT all monthly balances
       compute and PUT the final month's payment
  ELSE PUT an error message
END
```

This algorithm contains all the major elements needed to solve the problem, but it does not contain very much detail. The advantage of writing a nondetailed algorithm as a first step is that you will be much less likely to become confused by details and can arrive at a solution in a short time. The next algorithm is a refinement of the previous one. It contains the same logic but is much more detailed.

Pseudocode

```
GET BALANCE, PAYMENT, RATE
RATE = RATE/12 * 0.01
IF PAYMENT > BALANCE * RATE
  THEN DO WHILE BALANCE > PAYMENT
           PUT BALANCE
           INTEREST = BALANCE * RATE
           BALANCE = BALANCE + INTEREST
                     - PAYMENT
       END
       LAST_PAY = BALANCE + BALANCE * RATE
       PUT LAST_PAY
  ELSE PUT 'ERROR--INVALID INPUT DATA'
END
```

TABLE 1.1. Trace Table for input 50, 85, −10.

Line number	N	SUM	X	MEAN	OUTPUT
1	0	0			
2			50		
3					
4					50
5		50			
6	1				
7			85		
8					
4					85
5		135			
6	2				
7			−10		
8					
9				67.5	
10					67.5
11					
Final values	2	135	−10	67.5	

docode, and produce the sample output. Tracing through the pseudocode is much easier if you use a table of variables to keep track of changes in each of these variables. For example, Table 1.1 records the actions of the pseudocode statements on a line-by-line basis for another set of input. Each time a GET statement is encountered, the next value in the input is crossed off. Whenever a statement causes the contents of a variable to change, the new value is recorded in the table. This provides a complete history of the pseudocode performance for a particular set of input and is an effective testing technique.

Finally, programs should be designed so that all legitimate forms of input can be properly handled. There is one bug (error) in the preceding pseudocode, since a circumstance can arise that cannot be properly handled. What would happen if the only data value in the input were a negative number? Table 1.2 illustrates what would happen in such a situation.

Note that none of the statements inside the DO loop are processed, because the condition "X ≥ 0" is not true. Nevertheless, the mean is supposed to be computed in line 9; but division by zero occurs because variable N contains zero. One can correct this erroneous situation by inserting an IF statement immediately after the first GET statement. The IF statement would contain the condition "X ≥ 0," and further processing would occur only if the condition were true. If the condition were false, an error message could be displayed.

1.4.4. Find Monthly Balances for a Loan (Program 1.5)

This problem illustrates the use of sequence, alternation, and repetition. The concept of refinement is demonstrated in the pseudocode development. The first two phases of the problem-solving process are presented here, and the algorithm-implementation phase appears in Chapter 2.

TABLE 1.2. Trace Table for input −25.

Line Number	*N*	*SUM*	*X*	*MEAN*	*OUTPUT*
1	0	0			
2			−25		
3					
9				???	

Note that multiplication and division are represented by the symbols * and /. Although this is arbitrary for pseudocode, it is consistent with PL/I and many other programming languages. Consequently, it is good practice to use this convention, because the conversion from pseudocode to PL/I is made easier.

1.5. THE FLOWCHART APPROACH

In this section we will describe the flowchart approach, another method by which algorithms can be represented. Flowcharts are sometimes a good alternative to pseudocode because they provide visual, or graphical, representations of algorithms.

A flowchart consists of a collection of symbols connected by directed line segments. The symbols have predefined meanings and contain statements about the actions to be performed (see Figure 1.2). The directed line segments represent the flow of control, that is, which symbol is to be processed next.

Flowcharts are effective graphical representations of algorithms. They are in widespread use and are easily understood. The actions depicted by flowcharts are easy to follow, because the directed line segments always specify the next action to occur. The symbol inscribed with the word START indicates the beginning of the flowchart, and the symbol with the word END indicates

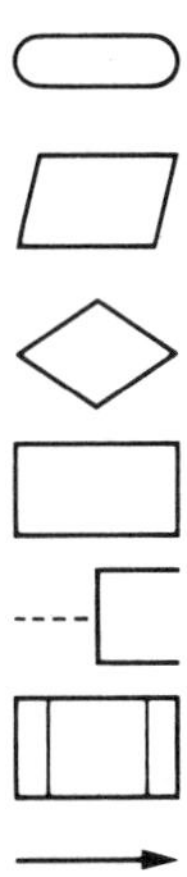

Indicates the beginning or end of a flowchart; either the word START or the word END is written inside this symbol.

Indicates input or output; GET and PUT statements both use this symbol.

Indicates a decision; a condition is written inside this symbol, and one of two paths leaving this symbol is selected, depending on the outcome of the evaluation of this condition.

The process symbol; used for computations and data manipulations.

The annotation symbol; used for making comments or providing other useful information (to be discussed later).

The predefined-process symbol; used to represent invocations to subprograms (to be discussed later).

Flow of control

Figure 1.2. *American National Standards Institute (ANSI) flowchart symbols.*

the end of the flowchart. The symbols between these two are encountered in the order specified by the directed line segments.

Flowcharts have a great deal in common with pseudocode, because both approaches are used to implement the same constructs of sequence, alternation, and repetition. The primary difference between these two algorithm representations is that pseudocode uses English statements to describe actions to be performed, whereas flowcharts use a pictorial representation of actions and manipulations.

1.6. FLOWCHART EXAMPLES

Section 1.4 contains problems in which pseudocode is used as a logical solution. Those same problems are used here to illustrate the basics of flowcharting. A brief description of each problem is included; and, for comparison, the pseudocode and the flowchart are displayed next to each other.

1.6.1. The Addition of Two Numbers

The symbol in the shape of a parallelogram is used to represent either input or output; the words GET or PUT designate which action is to be taken.

PROGRAM 1.6 (restating 1.2).

Input: Two integer numbers

Manipulation: Compute the sum of these two numbers

Output: The computed sum

PSEUDOCODE

```
GET A,B
SUM = A + B
PUT SUM
END
```

FLOWCHART

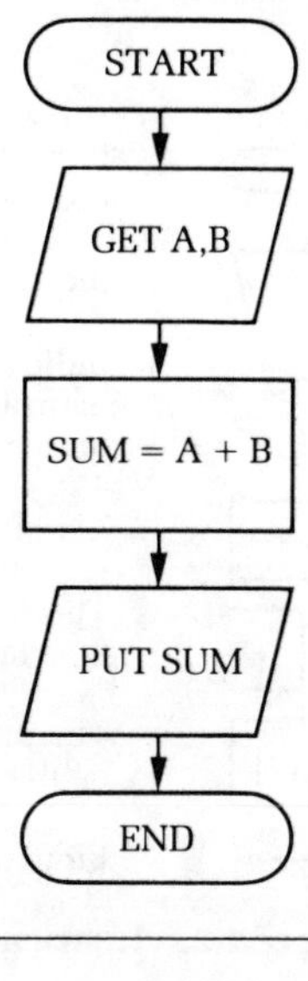

The rectangle is used to specify a computation, and the two oval-shaped symbols indicate the beginning and the end of the flowchart. The directed line segments specify the sequence of operations to be performed from beginning to end.

1.6.2. Find the Smaller of Two Numbers

The diamond-shaped symbol is used to represent decisions. A question that can be answered "yes" or "no" is written in this symbol, and two lines leave this symbol, corresponding to the two possible answers to this question. The decision symbol permits conditions or tests to be evaluated and closely corresponds to the IF statement in pseudocode.

PROGRAM 1.7 (restating 1.3).

Input: Two integer numbers

Manipulation: Decide which of these numbers is smaller

Output: The smaller number

PSEUDOCODE

```
GET A,B
IF A < B
  THEN PUT A
  ELSE PUT B
END
```

FLOWCHART

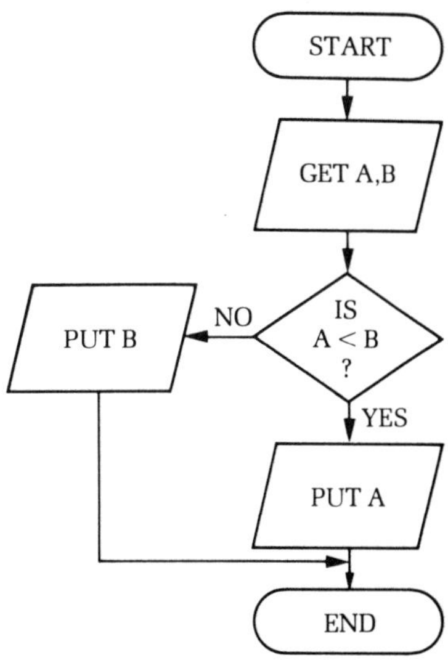

PROGRAM 1.8 (restating 1.4).

Input: A group of positive integer numbers

Manipulation: Compute the mean of these numbers

Output: Each number and the mean of all these numbers

PSEUDOCODE

```
N,SUM = 0
GET X
DO WHILE X ≥ 0
   PUT X
   SUM = SUM + X
   N = N + 1
   GET X
END
MEAN = SUM/N
PUT MEAN
END
```

FLOWCHART

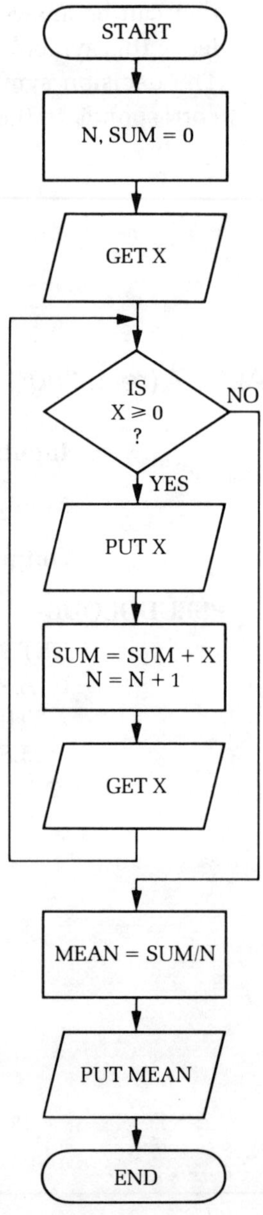

1.6.3. Find the Average (Mean) of a Group of Numbers

The diamond (also called the decision symbol) is used to represent alternation as well as the loop-control construct. Note that the decision symbol is used to begin the loop and evaluates the condition that appears in the DO WHILE statement. The looping condition is evaluated each time the loop is executed. If the looping condition is false when the loop is encountered, then none of the symbols in the loop are entered, and control passes to the first symbol following the end of that loop.

1.6.4. Find Monthly Balances for a Loan

All but two of the flowchart symbols introduced earlier appear in Programs 1.6 to 1.9. These two symbols are not appropriate for these examples, but they are effectively used in Chapter 5 where subprocedures are discussed.

Pseudocode and flowcharts both have their own sets of advantages and disadvantages for representing algorithms. Modification is cumbersome for both approaches, and changing the indentation might require rewriting or recopying a major portion of the pseudocode. This is not a difficult task, but it can be time consuming if the pseudocode is long. However, pseudocode is more concise and has the advantage of more closely resembling PL/I programs; it encourages programmers to employ the problem-solving process rather than immediately start coding (writing) the program. Flowcharts have the advantage of being a pictorial representation of operations to be performed and can be easily read, even by nonprogrammers. Flowcharts are probably more widely used in commercial programming, but acceptance of pseudocode is steadily increasing.

Deciding which of these two approaches to use is not really crucial, because algorithms can be completely represented by either method. For the sake of clarity, both approaches are used to represent many algorithms throughout the first five chapters of this book.

1.7. SUMMARY

Many terms and concepts have been introduced in this chapter. Here we will briefly review them. Every chapter in the book has a similar section which serves as a review of the topics discussed as well as a quick reference to important concepts.

1.7.1. Key Concepts

1. Every computer system has its own unique job-control language (JCL) statements that control the processing of computer programs.
2. A compiler translates PL/I statements into machine-language statements, because the only language any computer "understands" is its own machine language.

PROGRAM 1.9 (restating 1.5).

Input: Loan balance, monthly payment, annual interest

Manipulation: Compute all monthly balances and final payment

Output: All monthly balances and final payment

PSEUDOCODE

```
GET BALANCE, PAYMENT, RATE
RATE = RATE/12 * 0.01
IF PAYMENT > BALANCE * RATE
  THEN DO WHILE BALANCE > PAYMENT
            PUT BALANCE
            INTEREST = BALANCE*RATE
            BALANCE = BALANCE + INTEREST − PAYMENT
        END
        LAST_PAY = BALANCE + BALANCE*RATE
        PUT LAST_PAY
  ELSE PUT 'ERROR — INVALID INPUT'
END
```

FLOWCHART

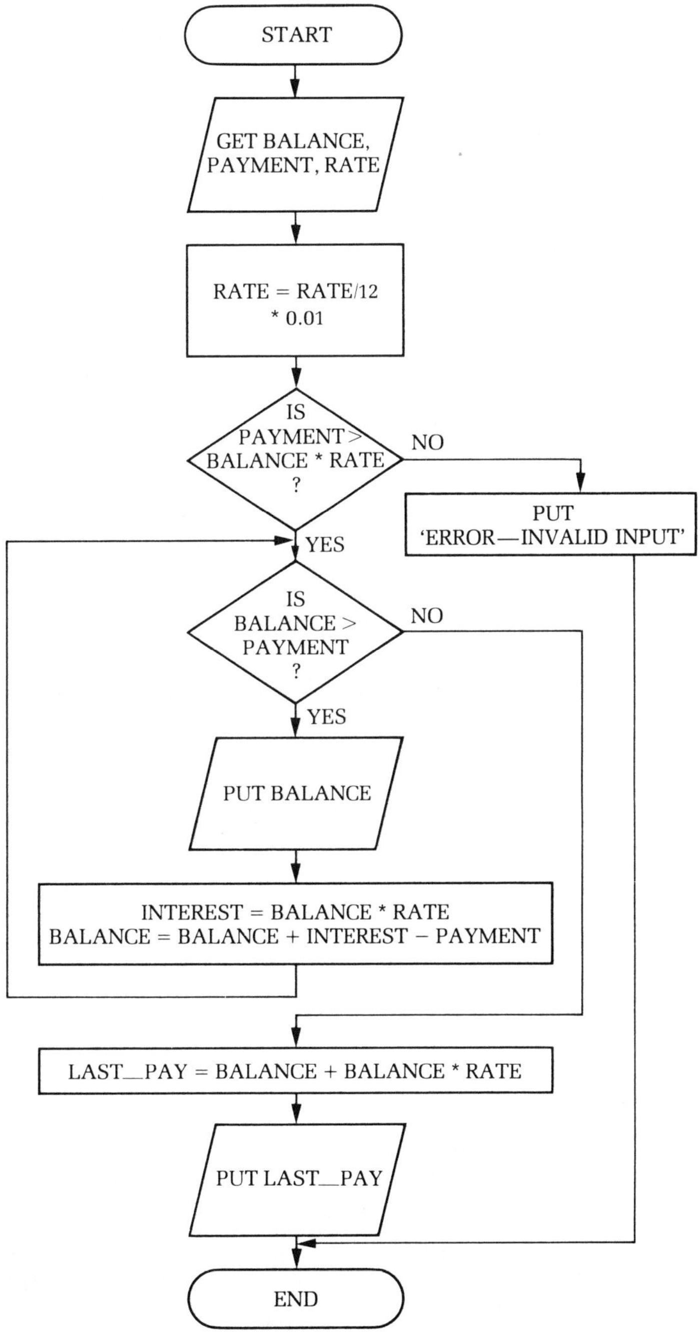
START
GET BALANCE, PAYMENT, RATE
RATE = RATE/12 * 0.01
IS PAYMENT > BALANCE * RATE ?
NO
PUT 'ERROR—INVALID INPUT'
YES
IS BALANCE > PAYMENT ?
NO
YES
PUT BALANCE
INTEREST = BALANCE * RATE
BALANCE = BALANCE + INTEREST − PAYMENT
LAST_PAY = BALANCE + BALANCE * RATE
PUT LAST_PAY
END

3. The three phases of problem solving using the computer are:
    a. problem definition
    b. algorithm design
    c. algorithm implementation
4. The problem-definition phase of problem solving requires that every aspect of the problem be precisely defined.
5. The algorithm-design phase requires that a logical solution to the problem be developed and expressed as pseudocode or as a flowchart.
6. The algorithm-implementation phase requires that the logical solution be translated into a computer program and that the program then be tested and debugged.
7. Pseudocode overview:
    a. A clear representation of the logic used in the solution to a particular problem.
    b. A series of English-like statements that resemble PL/I.
    c. Only three control structures are permitted:
        1. sequence
        2. alternation (IF)
        3. repetition (DO)
8. Flow of control for alternation (IF). If the condition in the IF statement is true, the block of statements under THEN is processed. If the condition is false, the block of statements under ELSE is processed. Whether the THEN or the ELSE block was processed, the next statement to be processed is the one immediately following the group of statements controlled by the IF statement.

```
______________________________
______________________________
IF condition
    THEN______________________________
        ______________________________
    ELSE______________________________
        ______________________________
______________________________
______________________________
```

Figure 1.3.

9. Flow of control for repetition (DO). When the DO statement is first encountered, the condition is immediately evaluated. If the condition is false, no statements within the DO loop are processed, and the next statement to be processed is the one that immediately follows the END of the DO loop (see Figure 1.4). If the condition is initially true, the DO loop is entered, and statements within the loop are processed. After this, the con-

```
____________________
____________________
____________________
DO condition
        ____________________
        ____________________
        ____________________
        ____________________
END
____________________
____________________
____________________
```

Figure 1.4.

dition is evaluated each time the END is encountered; as long as it is true, the statements within the DO loop are repeatedly processed. When the condition becomes false, then control passes to the first statement following the END of the loop.

10. A flowchart is a graphical representation of the solution to a problem. The ANSI flowchart symbols used are shown in Figure 1.2.

1.7.2. Terms and Phrases

Write out definitions and/or descriptions of the usage of each of these terms. Check your definitions against the text.

algorithm design
algorithm implementation
alternation
ANSI
arithmetic operations (+ − * /)
condition
control structures
debugging
DO
ELSE
END
flowchart
GET
IF
initialization
input
job-control language (JCL)
loop
output
PL/I
problem definition
programming
pseudocode
PUT
refinement
relational operators (< > =)
repetition
replacement operator (=)
sentinel value
sequence
statement processing
THEN
trace table
variable

PROBLEMS

Problem 1.1. Develop pseudocode programs and flowcharts for each of the following and provide sample input and output.

a. Get any three numbers in any order; display these same numbers in ascending order.

b. Get two numbers that represent an amount to be deposited and the annual interest rate. Display annual balances for the first ten years.

c. Get two numbers that represent the lengths of two sides of a right triangle; then compute and display the length of the hypotenuse, where the hypotenuse is the square root of the sum of the squares of the two sides.

d. Get one number which represents a temperature reading in Celsius; compute and display the equivalent reading in Fahrenheit (°F = °C * 1.8 + 32).

Problem 1.2. Show the output generated by each of the following pseudocode programs. (Hint: use trace tables; see section 1.4.3.)

a.
```
A = 1
B = 1
DO WHILE B < 10
    PUT A
    C = A + B
    A = B
    B = C
END
```

b.
```
A = 1
B = 2
DO WHILE B < 5
    IF A < 3
       THEN PUT A,B
            A = B
            B = B + 1
       ELSE B = 6
END
```

c.
```
A = 1
B = 1
DO WHILE A ≤ 5
    IF A = B
       THEN B = B + 2
       ELSE A = A + B − 1
    PUT A,B
END
```

d.
```
A = 2
B = 10
C = A + (10/B)
DO WHILE C < 10
    A = A + 2
END
PUT A,B,C
END
```

Problem 1.3. Develop the flowchart for each of the following and provide sample input, when needed, and output.

a. Compute and display this sequence:

   1, 4, 7, 10, . . . , 301.

b. Compute and display the sum of all values in the sequence in (a).

Problem 1.4. Match each of the following words with the one phrase that is most correct.

a. object program
b. output
c. DO
d. IF-THEN-ELSE
e. syntax errors
f. debugging
g. sentinel value
h. variable

1. information displayed by a program
2. execution errors
3. repetition
4. compile-time errors
5. alternation
6. pseudocode
7. removal of errors from a program
8. machine language
9. used to mark the end of input
10. sequence
11. programmer-defined symbolic name

Problem 1.5. Name and describe the phases of the problem-solving process.

Problem 1.6.

a. List the advantages and disadvantages of the pseudocode approach to representing the algorithms.
b. List the advantages and disadvantages of the flowchart approach to representing algorithms.

2 Introduction to PL/I

2.1. PL/I FUNDAMENTALS

Although PL/I has a tremendous number of features, it can be effectively used by the beginning programmer almost immediately. PL/I is simple to use, and the method of constructing program statements is consistent throughout the language. As an example of this simplicity, four complete programs are presented in this chapter; they are easily understood without detailed discussion of PL/I.

Before we study these programs, several important PL/I fundamentals should be understood. First, every PL/I program consists of one or more *procedures*. One of these procedures is declared to be the *main procedure*, and the others (if any) are called *subprocedures*. This feature makes it possible to subdivide one program into several smaller and more understandable subprograms. However, this feature is not studied until Chapter 5. Until then, every PL/I program will be a main procedure with no subprocedures. Furthermore, the term "procedure" can usually be used interchangeably with the term "program."

The general form of every main procedure is as shown in Figure 2.1. Although the procedure name is arbitrary, the programmer should make up a name that suggests the purpose of that procedure. A procedure name usually consists of from one to seven letters (A–Z) or digits (0–9), but the first character must be a letter. However, the rules for creating other symbolic names vary for the different PL/I compilers. For example, Table 2.1 shows the various name-length requirements for selected compilers.

The characters that are available to make up symbolic names are restricted to a particular character set that is available at a computer installation. The three most common character sets are listed in Table 2.2.

Generally, symbolic names may consist of letters, digits, and the underscore character (_). Complete rules for creating these names appear in Chapter 3 and in Appendixes E through K. The other characters in the three character sets are used to construct the various program statements. For example, every PL/I statement must end with a semicolon (;), and the blanks are used to separate elements within a statement and to increase readability.

Individual statements can be written "free form" (that is, no column or spacing restriction), but they should follow a proper pattern of indentation so

```
____name____ : PROCEDURE OPTIONS (MAIN);
               _______________
               _______________
                                     program statements
               _______________
               _______________
               END;      (or END ____name____ ;)
```

Figure 2.1. *General form of a PL/I procedure.*

TABLE 2.1. Name-length requirements.

PL/I compiler	*Maximum length of name in characters*
Burroughs	63
CDC	40
DEC (CPL or VAX)	31
Honeywell	256
IBM Call/OS	8
IBM DOS	31
IBM OS	31
PL/C	31
Univac	63

TABLE 2.2. Characters available for creating PL/I programs.

Character description	*ANSI character set*	*60-character set*	*48-character set*
letters	A through Z	A through Z	A through Z
digits	0 through 9	0 through 9	0 through 9
dollar sign	$	$	$
blank			
equal sign	=	=	=
asterisk	*	*	*
slash	/	/	/
plus	+	+	+
minus	−	−	−
left parenthesis	(	(	(
right parenthesis	)	)	)
comma	,	,	,
period	.	.	.
single quote mark	'	'	'
semicolon	;	;	
colon	:	:	
underscore	_	_	
not	¬	¬	
ampersand	&	&	
vertical bar	|	|	
greater than	>	>	
less than	<	<	
percent sign	%	%	
pound sign		#	
at sign		@	
question mark		?	

that the logic and the structure of the program can be easily understood by other programmers. Every main procedure terminates with an END statement, and the procedure name may be included optionally.

2.2. PL/I EXAMPLES

In this section, four complete PL/I programs are presented. These programs are motivated by the corresponding pseudocode in Chapter 1 and have sample input included. They should be executed on a computer, assuming that appropriate job-control language (JCL) statements are used. This would provide an excellent exercise in accessing the computer and learning the various details necessary to have a program executed.

2.2.1. The Addition of Two Numbers

This is the problem for which a pseudocode solution was developed in section 1.4.1. Program 2.1 follows the pseudocode exactly.

PROGRAM 2.1 (continuing 1.2).

```
/* ADDITION OF TWO NUMBERS */
ADD: PROCEDURE OPTIONS (MAIN);
          DECLARE (A, B, SUM) FIXED;
          GET LIST (A, B);
          SUM = A + B;
          PUT LIST (SUM);
     END ADD;
```

Sample input: 46 50

Sample output: 96

The first line of this program is a comment that contains a brief description of the program. Comments are ignored by the computer and are used for information purposes only. There is no limit to the number of comments that can be used, and they can be placed anywhere in a program. The characters /* begin each comment, and the characters */ terminate each comment. A comment can share a line with another statement, appear on one line by itself, or span arbitrarily many lines.

Several statements are necessary to give information to the computer about the program. The second statement assigns a name to the program and informs the computer that this is a main procedure. Every main program must begin with such a statement, and the programmer must create a program name. The third line of the program describes the characteristics of the variables used in the program. Here the variables are declared to be FIXED; that is, they are integer variables. For now, all numeric variables are either FIXED (integer) or FLOAT (floating point or real). The next three statements are almost identical to the corresponding pseudocode statements, except that the term LIST is used to describe the input/output process. LIST means that input or output values are to appear as a sequential list of values, rather than in a strict formatting or editing order. (The subject of data-, list-, and edit-directed input/output is discussed in Chapter 4.) Finally, the last statement in the program is the END statement, which denotes both the logical and the physical end of the program.

2.2.2. Find the Smaller of Two Numbers

Program 2.2 follows the pseudocode program developed in section 1.4.2.

PROGRAM 2.2 (continuing 1.3).

```
/* FIND THE SMALLER OF TWO NUMBERS */
SMALL: PROCEDURE OPTIONS(MAIN);
           DECLARE (A,B) FIXED;
           GET LIST(A,B);
           IF A < B
              THEN PUT LIST(A);
              ELSE PUT LIST(B);
       END SMALL;
```

Sample input: 652 197

Sample output: 197

Program 2.2 is also very similar to its pseudocode representation. Here the program name SMALL is chosen because it suggests the purpose of this program. Only two variables are declared and used in this program, and they are both FIXED (that is, fixed-point variables or integer variables).

The purpose of this program is to get any two integers, then find and display the smaller number. The IF statement is used to compare the variables A and B, which obtained their values from the previous GET statement. In other words, if variable A contains a number less than variable B, then the value in variable A is output. If variable A contains a number greater than or equal to variable B, then the value of variable B is output. This program is general, since it can be used to compare any two values, not just the numbers that appear in the sample input.

2.2.3. Find the Average (Mean) of a Group of Numbers

Program 2.3 follows the pseudocode developed in section 1.4.3 and is somewhat more complex than Programs 2.1 or 2.2.

Compare Program 2.3 carefully with its pseudocode counterpart to be sure you understand the purpose of each individual statement. The only differences between the pseudocode and PL/I assignment statements are that the latter end with semicolons and that there is no reference in pseudocode to whether or not the variables are FIXED. However, the variable MEAN could likely be assigned a noninteger value; consequently, the variable MEAN is declared as FLOAT. If MEAN were declared as FIXED and a value such as 29.4 were then assigned to it, the digits to the right of the decimal point would be truncated and the value 29 would be stored. Also, notice that the condition in the DO WHILE statement

PROGRAM 2.3 (continuing 1.4).

```
/* FIND THE MEAN OF A GROUP OF NUMBERS */
AVG: PROCEDURE OPTIONS (MAIN);
        DECLARE (N,SUM,X) FIXED;
        DECLARE MEAN FLOAT;
        N = 0;
        SUM = 0;
        GET LIST (X);
        DO WHILE (X >= 0);
            PUT LIST (X);
            SUM = SUM + X;
            N = N + 1;
            GET LIST (X);
        END;
        MEAN = SUM/N;
        PUT LIST (MEAN);
    END AVG;
```

Sample input: 26 32 18 43 28 −1

Sample output: 26 32 18 43 28 29.4*

*This value actually appears as 2.94000E+01, because FLOAT values are always displayed in exponential form when they appear in a PUT LIST statement.

is enclosed in parentheses. In PL/I, the condition must always have the parentheses; otherwise the entire statement is incorrect and will not compile correctly.

There are two identical GET statements in both the pseudocode and the PL/I programs, as is necessary whenever an input operation is used to control the termination of a DO loop. What would happen if there was only one GET statement and it immediately followed the DO statement?

2.2.4. Find Monthly Balances for a Loan

There are two pseudocode programs in section 1.4.4 for this final example. One program contains very little detail, but the other is greatly refined. Pseudocode can be developed by means of a series of refinements, and the PL/I program is always written using the most highly refined pseudocode program. In fact, the second pseudocode program of section 1.4.4 is so refined that writing the corresponding PL/I program is quite simple. All that really needs to be done is to fill in details required by the PL/I compiler and to observe the proper syntax (grammatical rules) for constructing PL/I statements. Using this method of pseudocode refinement ensures that a program solution is quickly developed

PROGRAM 2.4 (continuing 1.5).

```
/* FIND MONTHLY BALANCES FOR A LOAN */
LOAN: PROC OPTIONS (MAIN);
      DCL (BALANCE, PAYMENT, RATE, INTEREST, LAST_PAY)
        FLOAT;
      GET LIST (BALANCE, PAYMENT, RATE);
      RATE = RATE/12.0*0.01;
      IF PAYMENT > BALANCE * RATE
         THEN DO;
                 DO WHILE (BALANCE > PAYMENT);
                    PUT LIST (BALANCE);
                    INTEREST = BALANCE * RATE;
                    BALANCE = BALANCE + INTEREST -
                      PAYMENT;
                 END;
                 LAST_PAY = BALANCE + BALANCE * RATE;
                 PUT LIST (LAST_PAY);
              END;
         ELSE PUT LIST ('ERROR — INVALID INPUT DATA');
      END LOAN;
```

Sample input: 1000 100 15

Sample output: 10000 912.50 823.91 . . .

and that the corresponding PL/I program is easily written and is relatively error-free.

Compare Program 2.4 with its pseudocode equivalent to be sure you understand the purpose of the individual statements. Program 2.4 differs from Programs 2.1 to 2.3 in several ways, starting with the first two statements where PROCEDURE and DECLARE are abbreviated to PROC and DCL. The next difference occurs in the IF statement where a "DO group" is used in the THEN clause. This DO group contains a DO loop and two assignment statements (on lines 15 and 16). Although the DO group may seem to be an unnecessary complication, it is needed in order to make clear the range of the THEN clause. The DO group would *not* be necessary here if the two assignment statements on lines 15 and 16 were not a part of the THEN clause. (DO groups and DO loops are discussed in more detail in Chapters 5 and 8). The final difference occurs in the ELSE clause where a message is output.

Both numeric and character data can be manipulated with PL/I, although numeric data has been emphasized in the four examples in this chapter.

2.3. SUMMARY

The purpose of this chapter is to briefly study four examples of PL/I programs of varying degrees of complexity. Many programming-language details are not fully covered until later chapters, but the inherent simplicity of PL/I should become apparent from these examples.

2.3.1. Key Concepts

1. A PL/I program consists of one main procedure and zero or more subprocedures.
2. The terms "program" and "procedure" are often used interchangeably.
3. Every program begins with a PROCEDURE statement and ends with an END statement.
4. Statements can be written in "free form," but indentation should be used for clarity and readability.
5. Input data may use "free form" if a GET LIST statement is used.
6. Both FIXED (integer) and FLOAT (real) variables may be used in a program.
7. A variable is a symbolic name for some location in computer memory. The contents of a variable can change frequently when the program is being executed.
8. PROC and DCL are allowable abbreviations for PROCEDURE and DECLARE.
9. A "DO group" must be used in THEN and ELSE clauses whenever the range of that clause includes two or more different types of control structures (i.e., IF, DO, sequence).
10. Both numeric and character data may be displayed with a PUT LIST statement.
11. Every PL/I statement ends with a semicolon.
12. Blank lines and comments may be inserted anywhere in a program.

2.3.2. Terms and Phrases

Write a definition and/or description of usage for each of these terms. Check your definitions against the text.

character data
compiler
DO groups and DO loops
FIXED
FLOAT
free form
IF-THEN-ELSE
job control language
list-directed input/output
main procedure (program)
numeric data
program execution
syntax
truncation
variables

PROBLEMS

Problem 2.1. Modify the PL/I program in section 2.2.2 so that for any three input values, the program finds and displays the smallest of the three. (Hint: assume that the first value is the smallest number.)

Problem 2.2. Modify the PL/I program in section 2.2.3 so that the program finds and displays the mean of a known number of data values, and where the first input value specifies how many data values follow. For example: 5 98 62 83 76 85. Here the program is to find the mean of five values, i.e., 98 to 85. (Hint: use DO WHILE (N > 0); where N is the number of input values.)

Problem 2.3. Modify the PL/I program in section 2.2.4 so that the BALANCE is displayed once every 12 months, rather than every month.

Problem 2.4. Write PL/I programs for the pseudocode programs developed in Problem 1.1.

Problem 2.5. Match each of the following terms with the one phrase which is most correct.

1. free form	a. ignored by the computer
2. FIXED	b. real
3. END	c. no column or spacing restriction
4. comment	d. the last statement of a program
5. FLOAT	e. symbolic name
6. variable	f. integer
	g. A PL/I statement must end with it

Problem 2.6. *True or false?* If false, explain why.

a. ____ The ANSI character set, the 48-character set, and the 60-character set are the three most common character sets.

b. ____ Using LIST requires that the input values follow a strict formatting order.

c. ____ The procedure name may be included on the last statement of that procedure.

d. ____ A comment cannot share a line with any other statement.

e. ____ The words OPTIONS(MAIN) may be omitted from the first statement of a program.

f. ____ If you are using an IBM OS compiler, VARIABLE is a valid symbolic name.

g. ____ If you are using a UNIVAC compiler, a symbolic name may be a combination of letters and digits, not exceeding the length of 63.

Problem 2.7. Which of the following are valid PL/I statements? If a statement is not valid, explain why.

a. SUM = A + B

b. END;

c. DO WHILE X < 0;

d. SAMPLE: PROC OPTIONS(MAIN);

e. GET LIST (X,Y);

Problem 2.8. Briefly explain the purpose of each of the following PL/I statements:

PROCEDURE (PROC)

END

DECLARE (DCL)

DO

IF

GET

PUT

Problem 2.4. PL/I is an abbreviation for ______________________________ .

Problem 2.10. What is the basic difference between "DO groups" and "DO loops"?

Problem 2.11. Which PL/I statements are used to represent the concepts of sequence, alternation, and repetition, respectively?

Problem 2.12. Which of the three phrases of the problem-solving process is related to the actual writing of a PL/I program?

3 Data Types and Assignment Statements

A great variety of data types is available in PL/I, because the language is designed to be general purpose. PL/I is able to handle many distinctly different applications in areas such as scientific, commercial, and character-string processing. For example, some of the data types available are *bit, character, complex, fixed, float,* and *picture.*

The beginning programmer can effectively use PL/I with only a rudimentary knowledge of three data types: FIXED, FLOAT, and CHARACTER. The purpose of this chapter is to acquaint the reader with the fundamentals of these data types, as well as of variables, constants, and the construction of assignment statements. Complete details about most of the various data types are presented in Chapter 12.

3.1. CHARACTER, FIXED, AND FLOAT DATA TYPES

Most data can be classified as either "numeric" or "character-string." Character-string data generally look like a string of characters, including letters, digits, and various special characters. Numeric data generally take the form of signed or unsigned whole numbers or fractional quantities.

Numeric data is subdivided into two major types, *FIXED* and *FLOAT*. FIXED data types represent integer values or whole numbers.* The FLOAT data type represents floating-point values or real numbers. In other words, a FIXED value has no decimal point, whereas a FLOAT value can have an embedded decimal point. Both data types can be signed or unsigned; consequently, all FIXED and FLOAT values are positive or negative numbers.

It is not always obvious which numeric data type should be used in a given situation. Here are some basic guidelines for making this choice.

1. For integer values where the only arithmetic operations are addition and subtraction, use FIXED.
2. For integer or real values where a mixture of arithmetic operations is used, such as addition, subtraction, multiplication, division, and exponentiation, use FLOAT.
3. Greater selectivity can be used when complete details of the data types are known (Chapter 12).

The CHARACTER data type, which can be abbreviated as CHAR, is used to represent character strings. Much useful information is in a character-string or non-numeric form, e.g., headings, labels, names, and addresses. The CHARACTER data type can be used to represent this form of variable-length data and make possible various character-string manipulations as well.

3.2 VARIABLES AND CONSTANTS

All data in a computer program is represented by either variables or constants. A constant is simply a quantity that does not change, and a variable represents

*This is not a complete definition of FIXED, but it is adequate as a working concept.

a quantity that can change during the execution (processing) of a program.

All constants are either numeric values or character strings. Here are some examples of each type:

FIXED;	45 −106 890 −2 0
FLOAT;*	8.5 −876.3 .00001 0.0 1.0E−5
CHARACTER;	'ABC' '123 OAK ST' '45' 'JANE''S HAT'

Note that all the FIXED examples are integers and that all the FLOAT examples are values which contain a decimal point. The last FLOAT example (1.0E−5) is in *scientific notation,* which uses exponents, and represents the quantity .00001. Commas are not permitted in either FIXED or FLOAT constants. Each of the CHARACTER examples is enclosed with quote marks, but the last two examples require extra consideration. The constant 45 is an integer, but the constant '45' is a character string because of the quote marks. The constant 'JANE''S HAT' represents the string JANE'S HAT, because two adjacent quote marks are used to represent a single quote mark within a CHARACTER constant.

All variables represent numeric values or character strings and take the appearance of symbolic names. A variable is a programmer-defined name which represents a position in computer memory where the data value is actually stored. The actual storage locations of variables are generally not known to the programmer, because such details are handled by the PL/I compiler. All the programmer needs to do is make up valid variable names and tell these variable names to the compiler by means of a DECLARE† statement. The rules§ for creating valid variable names are as follows:

1. A variable name is composed of one or more characters. See Section 2.1 for the limits of various compilers.
2. Each character can be a letter (A through Z), a digit (0 through 9), or an underscore (_).
3. The first character of the variable name must be a letter.
4. Embedded blanks are not permitted.

The DECLARE statement is used to define variable names and to specify whether numeric or character-string values are to be represented. The general form of the DECLARE statement is

DECLARE *variable name(s) attribute(s)* ;

*Technically, only the last example is a FLOAT constant. However, the convention used for numeric data types until Chapter 12 is that integer values are FIXED, and noninteger values are FLOAT.

†The DECLARE statement is classified as a nonexecutable statement, because its only purpose is to provide information to the compiler. This happens before the program is executed.

§These rules are compatible with all major versions of PL/I. See the appendixes for other variations with specific PL/I compilers.

3.2.1. Examples of FIXED Data Type Declaration

If symbolic names A, B, and C are to be used as FIXED variables, they could be declared as

```
DECLARE A FIXED;
DECLARE B FIXED;
DECLARE C FIXED;
```

However, these three variables could be declared with only one DECLARE statement:

```
DECLARE A FIXED,
        B FIXED,
        C FIXED;
```

This can also be written by using the *attribute factoring* feature, in which all the variables in parentheses take on the same attribute as in the following:

```
DCL (A, B, C) FIXED;
```

Note that DECLARE can be abbreviated DCL. The various abbreviated forms will be used throughout this book for their simplicity and ease.

If a variable is used in a PL/I program, but is not declared, the compiler automatically assigns it the attribute FIXED, which is called the *default attribute.** However, it is not wise to take advantage of this feature. Instead, all variables should be explicitly declared, which not only is good programming style, but also increases the computer-to-computer portability of the program, because most non-ANSI PL/I compilers have other than FIXED defaults (see the appendixes for other defaults).

3.2.2. Examples of FLOAT Data Type Declaration

If symbolic names A, B, and C are to be used as FLOAT variables, they could be declared as follows:

```
DCL (A, B, C) FLOAT;
```

Other forms of the DECLARE statement can also be used, but this one is preferable because of its conciseness. The DCL statement can specify initial values of the variables with the INITIAL or INIT attribute. For example, the following statements would initialize all the variables to zero:

```
DCL (A, B, C) FLOAT INITIAL (0.0);
DCL (D, E, F) FIXED INITIAL (0);
```

*All variable names must be explicitly declared with Subset G.

Only one value may appear in an INITIAL attribute. For example, the following declaration is invalid:

DCL (A, B, C) FIXED INIT (3, 4, 5);

3.2.3. Examples of CHARACTER Data Type Declaration

If symbolic names A, B, and C are to be used as character-string variables, and each contains exactly ten characters, then they could be declared as follows:

DCL (A, B, C) CHAR(10);

The size of the character string must be explicitly specified. In the preceding example, specifying only "CHAR" rather than "CHAR(10)" would result in a fatal error. Character-string variables can be initialized to a particular value in the same way that FIXED or FLOAT variables are:

DCL (A, B, C) CHAR(10) INIT ('GOOD GRIEF');

Note that the quantity in the INIT attribute is a character-string constant (i.e., enclosed by quote marks). However, the number of characters in the INIT attribute does not have to be the same as that specified in the declaration statement, as the following examples show:

DCL (A, B, C) CHAR(10) INIT ('ABCD');
DCL (A, B, C) CHAR(10) INIT ('ABCDEFGHIJKLM');

In both examples, all variables are initialized to character strings of precisely ten characters in length. In the first example, six blanks are added to the right of string 'ABCD' and the variables are initialized to 'ABCDbbbbbb', where the small "b" represents a blank. This process of placing significant data on the left and blank padding on the right is called *left justification*. In the second example, the character string is truncated to ten characters, and the string 'ABCDEFGHIJ' is placed into each of the three variables. These blank padding and truncation features also apply to assignment statements that assign to a character variable a value different from that in the variable's declaration.

Some situations require that a character variable be able to contain a character string of variable length, whereas in the previous examples the character variables contained fixed-length character strings. The following example illustrates the use of the "VARYING" or "VAR" attribute, which supports this variable-length feature for character strings.

DCL A_STRING CHAR(80) VARYING;

In this case, the variable A_STRING can contain a character string of from 0 to 80 characters. The VARYING attribute can be factored along with other attributes, but the factoring must be carried out carefully. Consider these two examples:

```
DCL (A, B, C) VAR CHAR(30);
DCL (A, B, C VAR) CHAR(30);
```

In the first example, all three variables are declared as character and varying in length. In the second example, although all three variables are declared as character, only C is declared as varying in length. The placement of the factoring parenthesis does affect the scope of the various attributes in the declaration of all variable types (not just of character variables).

Character variables with the VARYING attribute can be initialized somewhat as FIXED and FLOAT variables can. The following examples illustrate some of the variations of the INITIAL attribute for character strings.

```
1  DCL (A, B, C) CHAR(6) VAR INIT('');
2  DCL (A, B, C) CHAR(6) VAR INIT('ABCD');
3  DCL (A, B, C) CHAR(6) VAR INIT((2)'ABCD');
4  DCL (A, B, C) CHAR(6) VAR INIT ('(2)ABCD');
```

In these examples, the declaration of character variables is identical, except for the INITIAL attribute. That is, character variables A, B, and C can contain up to six characters. In example 1, each variable is initialized to the null character string (i.e., the character string of length zero). In example 2, each variable is initialized to the string 'ABCD'; note that here the variables would have been initialized to 'ABCDbb' if the VARYING attribute were not declared. In example 3, a replication factor* of 2 is used, and each variable is initialized to the string 'ABCDAB'; that is, the replication factor causes the string 'ABCDABCD' to be generated, but the last two characters are truncated in the initialization process, because six is the declared maximum length of the character variables A, B, and C. In example 4, each variable is initialized to the string '(2)ABC' because no replication factor is recognized. Replication factors must precede the strings that are to be replicated; they may also be used in other statements such as assignment statements and input/output statements.

3.3. ASSIGNMENT STATEMENTS

The primary purpose of an assignment statement is to store a particular value in a numeric or character variable. The value to be stored could be a constant, another variable, or the result of a numeric or character expression. The general form of assignment statements is:

variable = *expression* ;

*Replication factors for string constants are not permitted for either PL/C or Subset G.

When an assignment statement is encountered during the execution of a program, the expression is evaluated, and the result is placed in the variable which appears on the left side of the equals (=) sign. Remember that the equals sign is a replacement operator, not a statement of equality. It can be interpreted literally as "is replaced by"; i.e., the contents of the specified variables are replaced by the value of the expression appearing on the right side of the equals sign.

Several variables can be assigned the same value* of an expression by separating each of the variables with a comma. For example:

```
A,B,C = 0;
```

Variables A, B and C are each assigned the value zero as a result of the execution of this assignment statement.

Expressions are classified as being either numeric or character. In general, expressions take one of the following forms:

constant
variable
manipulations involving constants, variables, functions, and appropriate operators

Functions are discussed in later chapters, and most of the available operators are discussed in this chapter. There are numeric operators as well as character-string operators, and each is discussed in one of the following sections.

3.3.1. Numeric Expressions

Both FIXED and FLOAT variables and constants use the same numeric (or arithmetic) operators:

+	addition
−	subtraction
*	multiplication
/	division
**	exponentiation (raising a number to a power)

All of these arithmetic operators can operate on two *operands* (which here means a variable, constant, or subexpression). However, addition and subtraction operators can also be used as *unary operators;* i.e., each can operate on only one operand. Given these definitions, a numeric expression is composed

*In Subset G, only one variable may appear on the left side of an equals (=) sign.

of one of the following: constant, variable, unary operation, or arithmetic operation(s). Some examples of numeric expressions are:

45	constant
VARA	variable
A + B	simple arithmetic operation
− A	unary operation
A + B / C − D * E	several arithmetic operations

If more than one operator appears in an expression, then the order in which the operators are evaluated is important. An operator-precedence rule is used, in order to avoid any confusion about which operator is to be evaluated next. The precedence order for arithmetic operators is:

1.	**	exponentiation (highest precedence)
2.	* /	multiplication, division
3.	+ −	addition, subtraction (lowest precedence)

The precedence order requires all exponentiations to be performed before all multiplications and divisions, and all multiplications and divisions to be performed before any additions and subtractions. Here are several examples of the use of the precedence order:

1.	4 + 5 * 2	Result = 14
2.	(4 + 5) * 2	Result = 18
3.	2 + 4 ** 2	Result = 18
4.	2 ** 3 ** 2	Result = 512
5.	2 + 3 − 4	Result = 1
6.	3 * −2	Result = −6

Example 1 illustrates that multiplication is performed before addition, and example 2 demonstrates that parentheses may be used to alter the order in which operators are evaluated. Example 3 illustrates that exponentiation is performed before addition. Examples 4 and 5 show operators of the same precedence appearing in an expression. When this happens, the operators are evaluated from left to right, except for consecutive exponentiation operators, which are evaluated from right to left. Example 6 illustrates the use of a unary operator and the fact that parentheses are not required here, because two operators may appear immediately adjacent to each other only if one is a unary operator. The complete precedence rule used to determine the order of evaluation is as follows:

1. Evaluate operators inside a set of parentheses first. If nested sets of parentheses appear, evaluate the innermost set first, then expand outward, observing the order of step 2 through step 5 while performing this evaluation.
2. Evaluate all unary operators next.

3. Evaluate all exponentiation operators next. If more than one such operator appears, evaluate them from left to right, except for two or more consecutive exponentiation operators, which are evaluated from right to left.
   Left to right example: 2 ** 3 + 3 ** 2
   Right to left example: 2 ** 3 ** 2
4. Evaluate all multiplication and division operators next. If more than one such operator appears, evaluate them from left to right.
5. Evaluate all addition and subtraction operators last. If more than one such operator appears, evaluate them from left to right.

We have not distinguished between FIXED and FLOAT values in numeric expressions, because both types use the same operators and may be intermixed in an expression. If intermixing does occur, the final value of the expression is FLOAT. The following examples illustrate this point, as well as some situations to avoid.

1.	45 + 10 − 1.0	Result = 54.0
2.	1 / 2	Result = 0.5
3.	1.0 / 2.0 + 1.0 / 2.0	Result = 1.0
4.	(A + B) (C − D)	Invalid expression
5.	A − * 4	Invalid expression

Here example 2 is noteworthy because it results in what may be an unexpected value. Both of the operands are FIXED values (i.e., integers), but the result of the division operator (i.e., 0.5) is not an integer.* The expression in example 4 is invalid, because an operator is missing. All operators must explicitly appear even where an operator seems to be implied. Because side-by-side operators are not permitted, the expression in example 5 is invalid.

3.3.2. Character-String Expressions

In contrast to numeric operators, there is only one character-string operator, which is concatenation (||). Concatenation is simply the joining together of two character strings to produce a new character string. There are several character-string functions described in later chapters, which can be used in expressions. In this chapter, only the replication feature (which was previously discussed) and the concatenation operator are used in character-string expressions. Consider the following examples.

*FIXED values can actually be other than integer values, but this aspect is not discussed until Chapter 12. A good rule to follow is: Never divide one FIXED value by another FIXED value.

1. 'ABC' || 'DEF' Result: 'ABCDEF'
2. 'ABC' || '' Result: 'ABC'
3. (2)'XX' || (3)'Y' Result: 'XXXXYYY'
4. '' Result: '' (Null String)

The expressions in the first three examples illustrate the concatenation operator. The null string, replication feature, character-string constants, and character-string variables may all be used with this operator. However, if more than one concatenation operator appears in an expression, the operators are evaluated from left to right. Of course, parentheses may be used to alter this order of evaluation.

The expression in example 4 is simply a null character string, i.e., a character string of length 0. Null strings may also be used in the INITIAL attribute of the DECLARE statement.

3.4. SUMMARY

This chapter presents the reader with a working knowledge of three necessary data types, and of construction of assignment statements. Fundamentals of FIXED, FLOAT, and CHARACTER data types are presented in a way that allows the beginning programmer to effectively use the concepts immediately. Numeric and character-string expressions and their role in assignment statements are discussed.

3.4.1. Key Concepts

1. Most data can be classified as numeric or character string.
2. Numeric data can be classified as FIXED or FLOAT.
3. FIXED data can be regarded as integer data.
4. FLOAT data is floating point or real data.
5. CHARACTER data is non-numeric or string data.
6. All data is either variable or constant.
7. The DECLARE statement establishes attributes for variables.
8. All variables in a program should be declared.
9. DECLARE statements are non-executable; they are processed before the program begins execution.
10. Assignment statements are executable.
11. Assignment statements are used to place the value of an expression into a variable.
12. Automatic conversion from numeric to character and from character to numeric is often possible.

3.4.2. Terms and Phrases

Write a definition and/or description of usage for each of these terms. Check your definitions against the text.

assignment statements
attribute factoring
binary operators
blank padding
CHAR
CHARACTER
concatenation
constant
conversion
DCL
DECLARE
expressions
FIXED
FLOAT
INIT
INITIAL
null character string
numeric (arithmetic) operators
operator
operator precedence
replacement operator
replication
truncation
unary operators
VAR
variable
VARYING

PROBLEMS

Problem 3.1. For each of the following declaration statements, indicate whether or not the statement is valid. If the statement is not valid, suggest changes that would make the statement valid. If the statement is valid, discuss the meaning and effect of that statement.

a. DCL (A, B) FIXED;

b. DCL IMAGE CHAR VAR;

c. DCL (A, T) FLOAT INIT ('ABC');

d. DCL (A, B, C) FIXED INIT (20, 10, 18);

e. DCL CNAME CHAR(4) VAR INIT ('STRINGS');

f. DCL (A, B FIXED) FLOAT INIT (0.0);

g. DCL 8EIGHT FIXED;

h. DCL TYPE CHAR(10) INIT ('CLASS A');

Problem 3.2. Assume that the declaration here holds for each of the following assignment statements. State what value is stored in each variable after each assignment statement is executed.

```
DCL  (A, T) FIXED INIT (12),
     (B, U) FLOAT INIT (5.0),
     (C, V) CHAR(10) VAR INIT ('ABCD');
```

a. T = A * B + 0.6;

b. V = T;

c. T = 10 + A / 2;

d. U = ((B * 2) − A) + (A − 6);

e. V = C || 'XYZ';

f. V = (3) 'Q' || C || 'VALUE';

g. V = '';

h. T = (45 − 3 + A) + A / 4;

i. T = B;

j. U = A;

k. T = 15 / 16 + 18 / 19;

l. T = 4 / 5.0 + 4 / 5.0;

m. U = 4 / 5.0 + 4 / 5.0;

n. T = A ** 2;

o. T = A ** 0.5; (square root)

p. V = C || '=' || (5) '5';

Problem 3.3. Locate and, if possible, correct the error(s) in each of the following assignment statements. Assume that variables are properly declared.

a. A + B = C;

b. X = ($ * Y) (T − P);

c. R = 'ABC' + 45.6;

d. ((A * P) / ((W + L)) − 5));

e. T = (A + 4) * D);

f. N = B * − D * 5,600;

g. Z = (((X + 3)**(Y + 2)*7);

h. A + C = (**A − 22.9/M);

i. W = ('A' || U) + 'C';

j. A/B = B/A;

k. Z = ((N* − A) + 6/*M;

l. W = 'A' || 47;

m. M = (((A + Y)*C) − A/B);

Problem 3.4. Match each of the following words with the one phrase which is most correct.

1. CHAR
2. unary operator
3. attribute factoring
4. INIT
5. constant
6. symbolic names
7. DCL

a. one operator in an assignment statement
b. specifies what type of values can be stored in a variable
c. the number 5
d. Data Communication Language
e. variables
f. it operates on one operand

g. represents character strings
h. a variable that has the same value throughout the program
i. initializes variables in a DECLARE statement
j. all variables within parentheses take on the same attribute
k. DCL (A,B,C) FIXED INIT;

Problem 3.5. Give a one-statement declaration for each of the following:

a. A variable, A, which is an integer with the initial value of 27.
b. A variable, C, which is a character string of variable length. Initialize the value to 'ABCDEFG'.
c. Three variables, A, B, C, all of which are real.
d. Four variables, A, B, C, D, all of which are character strings. A, B, C are of a fixed length of 30 characters, but D can contain from 1 to 30 characters.
e. A variable, A, which is a real number initialized to the value of π.

Problem 3.6. *True* or *false*. If false, explain why.

a. ____ *AMT is a valid character name.
b. ____ A variable is a compiler-defined name which represents a position in memory where the data value is actually stored.
c. ____ Division may be used as either an arithmetic operator or a unary operator.
d. ____ If A is a FIXED variable, then A = 'A'; is a valid assignment statement.
e. ____ If character-string variable A contains the value '264' and C, B are FLOAT variables, then C = B/A is a valid assignment statement.
f. ____ Consecutive exponentiation operators are evaluated from left to right.
g. ____ FIXED and FLOAT variables may be intermixed in an expression.
h. ____ Unary operators are always evaluated before any other operators are evaluated in an expression.
i. ____ The equals sign in an assignment statement does not signify equality.
j. ____ To represent a quote mark in a character-string constant, two adjacent quote marks must be used.

Problem 3.7. Use the three phases of the problem-solving process to develop a solution to the following problem. The formula to compute interest compounded annually for an investment is:

$$\text{Amount} = \text{Principal times } (1 + \text{Interest rate})^{\text{YEARS}}$$

where

Amount	is the current amount or value of the investment.
Principal	is the amount of money originally invested.
Interest rate	is the annual rate of interest expressed as a decimal (e.g., 11% is .11).
YEARS	is the number of years that the principal has been invested.

Similarly, the formula to compute interest compounded daily for an investment is:

$$\text{Amount} = \text{Principal times} \left(1 + \frac{\text{Interest rate}}{365}\right)^{365 \times \text{YEARS}}$$

The problem here is to compute and display the current value of an investment compounded annually and compounded daily. The input consists of the amount originally invested, the interest rate, and the number of years invested.

Sample input: 5000, .11, 5

Sample output:

```
COMPOUND INTEREST PROBLEM
PRINCIPAL = ________
INTEREST RATE = ________
NUMBER OF YEARS = ________
AMOUNT(COMPOUNDED ANNUALLY) = ________
AMOUNT(COMPOUNDED DAILY) = ________
```

Hint: the statements

```
PUT SKIP LIST(A);
PUT SKIP LIST(B);
```

cause the values of variables A and B to each be displayed at the beginning of an output line. If A and B were FLOAT variables, then their values would be displayed in exponential form.

Problem 3.8. The following statements are all syntactically correct and can appear on one line.

```
DO WHILE(X=5);A=B*C;D=A;PUT LIST(A);X=X-1;END;
```

This method of representing PL/I problems saves a lot of space; so why does each statement appear on a separate line and follow a pattern of indentation throughout this book?

Problem 3.9. In this book, DECLARE statements are always placed at the beginning of a program. However, DECLARE statements can be validly placed anywhere within a program. Why is this possible?

Problem 3.10. Suppose that variables A, B, and C are declared as FIXED, FLOAT, and CHAR(10) VAR, respectively. Which of the following statements could result in an execution error because of a data-conversion problem? Give examples of initial values for these variables that would cause the problems:

a. A = B;

b. B = A;

c. A = C;

d. B = C;

e. C = A;

4 Input/Output Operations

Input/output operations enable a computer program either to acquire values for its variables from an external source or to transmit the values of expressions to an external source. This "external source" can be a programmer at an interactive terminal, a punched-card reader, or a line printer.

The ability of a computer program to acquire data from an external source is a powerful feature that enables the program to be more general and more useful. Rather than being restricted to only a single set of data, the program should be able to properly handle any set of data by using input operations. Similarly, the ability to transmit the contents of variables or the result of expressions to an external source is an important link in the human-computer communication process.

The three forms of input/output (I/O) operations discussed in this chapter are *data-directed* I/O,* *list-directed* I/O, and *edit-directed* I/O. (Some other forms of I/O are discussed in Chapter 14.) Data-, list-, and edit-directed I/O operations are easy to use and are adequate for most problems that the beginning programmer is likely to encounter. All these forms are *stream-oriented;* that is, all input or output data are viewed by the programmer as being a single, continuous stream of characters.

4.1. DATA-DIRECTED INPUT/OUTPUT

Data-directed I/O is the simplest form of I/O, because unformatted, self-identifying input and output data items are permitted. That is, the input data items are not placed in any specific positions or columns, but they must be separated by one or more blanks and/or a comma. On output, the data items are placed in predesignated regions or fields.

The general form for data-directed I/O statements is:

GET DATA (*variable(s)*);
PUT DATA (*variable(s)*);

Assume that the variables A, B, and C are declared FIXED, CHAR(20) VAR, and FLOAT, respectively. The following input statement gets values from the input stream.

GET DATA (A, B, C);
Input stream: A = 2500, B = 'CHARACTERS', C = 62.49;

When this GET statement is executed, variable A acquires the value 2500, variable B acquires the value 'CHARACTERS', and variable C acquires the value 62.49. Note that the items in the input stream are in the form

variable = value

*Data-directed I/O is not permitted with Subset G.

The variable names in the input stream also appear in the variable list of the GET statement. The semicolon signifies the end of a group of items which can be accessed by one GET statement. Note that character-string values in the input stream must be enclosed by quote marks.

Here are some examples that illustrate the use of the GET statement:

1. GET DATA (A, C, B);
2. GET DATA (A, B, C, D);
3. GET DATA;

Input stream: A = 2500, B = 'CHARACTERS', C = 62.49;

Example 1 shows that order is not important in the list of variable names in the GET statement; i.e., the order of the variable names in the GET statement do not have to correspond with the order of variable names in the input stream. Example 2 contains a variable name that does not appear in the input stream. This is a valid statement, because extraneous variable names can appear in the GET statement, but they do not acquire any values. However, extraneous variable names are not permitted in the input stream. Example 3 does not contradict the previous statement. The variable names in the GET statement are optional; if they are all omitted, all variables referenced in the input stream acquire values. However, if any variable name appears in the GET statement, then all variable names appearing in the input stream must also appear in the GET statement.

Output is similar to input in that the form of data items is:

variable = value

Each output data item is separated by blanks, and a semicolon signifies the end of a group of items displayed by one PUT statement. For example, assume that the variables A, B, and C, which are used in the previous examples, have the values 2500, 'CHARACTERS', and 62.42, respectively. The following PUT statement generates the indicated output.

PUT DATA (A, B, C);

Output: A = 2500 B = 'CHARACTERS' C = 62.49;

The data items are placed in predesignated fields that are chosen by the compiler. Note that character strings are enclosed by quote marks in the output stream.

Two additional forms of the PUT DATA statement are:

1. PUT SKIP DATA (A, B, C);
2. PUT DATA;

Example 1 shows that the SKIP option can be used with a PUT DATA statement. The SKIP option causes variable A to be placed in the first position of the next output line. If the SKIP option is not used, variable A is placed in the next available position, which could be on the same line as values from a previous PUT DATA statement. (The LINE and PAGE options may also be used; they are discussed later in this chapter.)

The statement in example 2 causes the values of all variables to be displayed. This statement should be used with caution, because every variable known to the program (at the time the PUT statement is executed) is displayed. This statement is often used for testing and debugging purposes. However, uninitialized variables can cause an execution error during the processing of a PUT DATA statement.

4.2. LIST-DIRECTED INPUT/OUTPUT

List-directed I/O is so named because both input data and output data are viewed as a list of data elements. This stream of data elements is free from formatting requirements such as specifying the size of each data element or the columns in which each item appears. For input, the data elements are separated by a comma and/or one or more blanks. For output, each data element is automatically placed in data fields, each of which is approximately 24 characters long. No two output data elements can share a field and, if needed, a data element can use more than one field.

Assume that variables A, B, and C have been declared FIXED, FLOAT, and CHAR(40) VAR, respectively. The following input statement would get data values from the input stream and place them into those variables.

```
GET LIST (A, B, C);
```

The following input data lists are equivalent, in that variables A, B, and C acquire the same values if the preceding GET statement is executed.

```
406   98.5   'A STRING'
406, 98.5, 'A STRING'
406   ,   98.5      'A STRING'
```

Note that character strings must be enclosed by a pair of quote marks, because the input list is unformatted; the quote marks flag the beginning and the end of a character string. If a quote mark is desired as an input character, then the "double quote" feature can be used as illustrated below.

The order of the variables appearing in the GET statement is important only to the extent that the variable type must agree with the type of the input data element. For example, a FIXED variable can get a FIXED data element but not an arbitrary character string.

The general form for both the GET and the PUT statements for list-directed I/O is:

GET LIST (*variable(s)*);
PUT LIST (*expression(s)*);

Note that input (GET) is restricted to variables, but output (PUT) can apply to expressions. The value of any numeric or character-string expression can be displayed; this includes constants, variables, and complex expressions as discussed in Chapter 3. For both GET and PUT statements, each variable or expression must be separated by a comma. Of course, blanks can always be inserted because PL/I statements are free-form.

Here are examples of various forms of the PUT LIST statement:

1. PUT LIST (A, B, C) ;
2. PUT LIST ('THE VALUE OF A IS', A) ;
3. PUT LIST (A + B * 0.5) ;
4. PUT SKIP LIST (A, B, C) ;
5. PUT SKIP(2) LIST (A, B, C) ;

In example 1, the contents of variables A, B, and C are displayed in adjacent fields. However, the contents of variable A will not necessarily appear in the first field of an output line. List-directed output is stream-oriented; so the contents of A are placed in the next available output field, which could be in the middle of an output line. The SKIP, LINE, or PAGE (which are discussed shortly) options could be used to force the contents of variable A into the first field of a new output line.

In example 2, literal text is used to label the contents of a variable. A numeric expression appears in example 3; this expression is evaluated, and the result is placed in the next available output field. Any valid numeric or character-string expression may appear in a PUT LIST statement. Examples 4 and 5 are identical to example 1, except that the SKIP option is used to place data in the first output field of the next output line—or in the second line to come for SKIP(2). If the next available field is already the first output field, then a blank line is displayed, because the first output field of the next line is used; so the SKIP(2) option would then cause two blank lines to appear.

The LINE or PAGE output options can be used in place of the SKIP option. These options are particularly useful for line-printer output. The PAGE option is used to specify the first field of the next page. The LINE option must have a line number included; for example, LINE(10) would use the first field of line number 10, where line number 1 is the top of the page. This would cause a page ejection if that line number has already been exceeded on the current page.

4.2.1. Example of List-Directed Input/Output

This example is identical to the "Addition of Two Numbers" problem discussed in Chapters 1 and 2. It shows what effects the GET and PUT statements have. The problem is simple: two integer numbers are acquired, and their sum is displayed along with identifying information. The complete PL/I program is shown in Program 4.1.

PROGRAM 4.1

```
ADD: PROC OPTIONS (MAIN);
        DCL (A, B) FIXED;
        GET LIST (A, B);
        PUT SKIP LIST ('ADDITION OF TWO NUMBERS');
        PUT SKIP(2) LIST ('THE NUMBERS ADDED ARE', A,B);
        PUT SKIP(2) LIST ('THE SUM IS', A + B);
    END ADD;
```

If the input values for variables A and B were 142 and 83, respectively, then the following output would appear on the line printer or interactive terminal:

```
ADDITION OF TWO NUMBERS
          (blank line)
THE NUMBERS ADDED ARE        142        83
          (blank line)
THE SUM IS                   225
```

All output fields are the same width, which is about 24 columns. In the output here, each character-string constant appears in the first field, and the contents of the numeric variables appear in the second (and third) field. Note that all the numeric values appear as integers, because the variables are declared as FIXED. If the variables were declared as FLOAT, then they would appear in exponential or scientific form. For example, the floating-point value 36.928 would appear as 3.69280E+01.

4.3. EDIT-DIRECTED INPUT/OUTPUT

Both list- and edit-directed I/O are stream-oriented. However, edit-directed I/O requires the programmer to specify precisely how the input and the output are to appear. Even though input and output are streams of data, the input stream can be regarded as a series of input lines, and the output stream can be regarded as a series of output lines. In practice, an input line is a line typed in at an interactive terminal, or data appearing on a punched card. Similarly, an output line could be a line displayed at an interactive terminal, or a line printed on a line printer.

The programmer can specify a position within an input or an output line, because the first character position in each is designated as column 1, the second as column 2, and so on. That is, any position in an input or output line can be located by specifying its column number. This character-position orientation of input/output lines is essential for edit-directed I/O.

The general form for edit-directed I/O statements is:

GET EDIT *(variable(s))* *(specification(s))*;
PUT EDIT *(expression(s))* *(specification(s))*;

The general form of the edit-directed I/O statements is similar to that of the list-directed I/O statements. The principal difference is that a set of specifications is required for each edit-directed I/O statement. These specifications state exactly how the data elements of the input or output lines are to appear. The specifications used in this chapter are as follows:

A(*n*)	Alphanumeric specification; used for character-string constants, variables, and expressions. Here *n* specifies the number of characters in the alphanumeric field; e.g., A(5), A(10).
F(*w*)	Fixed-point specification; used for FIXED constants, variables, and expressions. Here *w* specifies the total field width (number of columns) for an integer quantity; e.g., F(2), F(8).
F(*w*,*d*)	Fixed-point specification; used for FLOAT constants, variables, and expressions. Here *w* specifies the total field width (number of columns), and *d* specifies the number of digits to appear to the right of the decimal point; e.g., F(10,2), F(8,4).
X(*n*)	Space-skipping specification; for input it is used to ignore a certain number of characters, and on output it is used to display a certain number of blanks. Here *n* specifies the number of spaces; e.g., X(5), X(10).
COL(*n*) or COLUMN(*n*)	Designate a particular column as the next position in an input or output line. Here *n* is the column number; e.g., COL(1), COL(25).
LINE(*n*)	Designate column 1 of a particular line as the next position in an output line. Here *n* is the line number; e.g., LINE(5), LINE(40).
PAGE	Designate column 1 of line 1 of a new page as the next position in an output line.
SKIP(*n*)	Designate column 1 as the next position in an input or output line after skipping *n* lines; e.g., SKIP(0), SKIP, SKIP(2). SKIP is equivalent to SKIP(1).

Other available specifications, such as the "E" specification for FLOAT data, the "P" specification for PICTURE data, and the "B" specification for BIT data, are discussed in Chapter 12.*

The "next position" (or column number) for input and output lines is automatically maintained by the computer with the use of *stream pointers*. The programmer cannot directly access the stream pointer, but may alter the position of the stream pointers by using the various input/output specifications and

*One specification that is available but is not discussed in this book is the "C" specification for COMPLEX data.

options. There may be as many stream pointers as there are input/output devices and files. However, for convenience of discussion in this chapter, we will assume there is only one input stream pointer and one output stream pointer.

There are only a few rules governing the use of stream pointers, specifications, and options, but you must clearly understand them in order to use edit-directed I/O effectively. The most important rules are as follows:

1. Stream-pointer values are modified only by explicit use of the specifications and options. For example, stream pointers are not automatically set to column 1 when another GET EDIT or PUT EDIT statement is encountered.
2. A stream pointer is automatically set to column 1 of the next line whenever the last column of an input or output line is used.
3. If the stream pointer is already set to column 1 when the option "COL(1)" is encountered, there is no change in the stream pointer for the line being processed. However, one line is skipped and the stream pointer remains at column 1 if the option "SKIP" or "SKIP(1)" is encountered under the same circumstances.
4. A data-conversion error could occur if the specifications do not agree with the variables or expressions. For example, a problem could result if an "F" specification were used to display a character-string variable.
5. If there are fewer data specifications (i.e., "F" and "A") than variables or expressions, the specification list is automatically repeated until every variable or expression is represented by a data specification.
6. If there are more specifications than are needed for the variables or expressions, then all excess specifications are ignored.
7. For PUT EDIT statements, the "SKIP(0)" option can be used to repeatedly print on the same line (called "overprinting" when line printers are used).
8. Specifications and options can be freely intermixed in the specification list.

These rules are quite straightforward and are easy to remember once their applications have been studied in several programs. In each of the following examples, assume that the input and/or output stream pointer is set to column 1.

4.3.1. Edit-Directed Input: Example 1

Suppose that the following input line is processed by the following GET statement. Assume that variables A, B, and C are declared FIXED, FLOAT, and CHARACTER, respectively.

Input line: 123456789STRING (begins at column 1)
Input statement: GET EDIT (A, B, C) (F(3), F(6,2), A(6));

When this GET statement is executed, variable A acquires the integer value 123, variable B acquires the floating-point value 4567.89, and variable C acquires the character string value 'STRING'. Note that there is no decimal point in the input line; however, the "F(6,2)" specification implicitly creates a decimal point when variable B acquires its value, since it states that the input value is obtained from a field of six characters, and that there are to be two digits to the right of the implicit or explicit decimal point.

Immediately before this GET statement was processed, the stream pointer was set to column 1. Variable A acquires a value by using a specification "F(3)," and the stream pointer is then set to column 4. Variable B acquires a value by using specification "F(6,2)," and the stream pointer is then set to column 10. Variable C acquires a value by using specification "A(6)," and, if this is the end of this input line, the stream pointer is set to column 1 of the next input line; otherwise, it is set to column 16.

4.3.2. Edit-Directed Input: Example 2

Suppose that the following input line is processed by the following GET statement. Assume that variables A, B, and C are declared FIXED, FLOAT, and CHARACTER, respectively, and that the stream pointer is set to column 1.

Input line: 6−4.83298XAB624
Input statement: GET EDIT (A,B,C)(F(1),F(6,1),X(1),A(3));

When this GET statement is executed, variable A acquires the integer value 6, variable B acquires the floating-point value −4.832, and variable C acquires the character-string value '8XA'. Note that the value acquired by variable B does not agree with its specification in the input statement; i.e., the stored value is of the form F(6,3), but F(6,1) was specified. The reason for this difference is that the presence of an explicit decimal point in an input line always supercedes the specification in the input statement.

After this GET statement is executed, the stream pointer is set to column 12. The remainder of the input line could either be ignored or be processed by another GET EDIT statement.

4.3.3. Edit-Directed Output: Example 1

Suppose that the assumptions in the two previous examples are in effect, and variables A, B, and C contain the values 25, 19.62, and 'GOOD GRIEF', respectively. The following output statement would then produce the indicated output lines:

Output statement: PUT EDIT ('A=', A,B,C)
(COL(1),A(2),F(2),SKIP,F(4,1),A);

Output lines: A=25 (This line starts in column 1)
19.6GOOD GRIEF

No sign is displayed for positive numeric values, but negative values use one column for the sign, and this fact must be considered when field width is specified. Similarly, a decimal point requires one column, as is illustrated in this example. Note that the decimal point for variable B is displayed, but one digit is truncated,* because the output must conform to the F(4,1) specification. The contents of variable C are displayed by use of the "A" specification without a statement of the field width. This is a simplified version of this specification and is applicable only to PUT EDIT statements. When it is used, a field is automatically created that is the same size as the expression being displayed.

4.3.4. Edit-Directed Output: Example 2

Suppose that the assumption in the previous examples are in effect, and that variables A, B, and C contain the value −196, 0.4632, and 'STRING', respectively. The following output statement would then produce the indicated output lines:

Output statement:
```
PUT EDIT ('C=',C,(3)'ABC',A,B,C)
        (COL(1),(2)A(2),COL(1),A,F(4),
         COL(2),F(6,4),X(2),A);
```

Output lines:
```
C=ST
ABCABCABC-196
 0.4632  STRING
```

The first two expressions in the PUT EDIT statement are displayed with a specification that contains a repetition factor, i.e., "(2)A(2)," which is equivalent to "A(2),A(2)." Because of this, only the first two characters of variable C are displayed. The next expression in the output list contains a replication factor that causes the string 'ABC" to be replicated three times. The column option is used three times in the specification list, changing the value of the stream pointer and generating a new line each time. The "X" specification is used to separate the contents of variables B and C. The column specification can also be used to space out data items on an output line. In this example, the specification "X(2)" could be replaced with the option "COL(10)," thus producing the same output line.

4.3.5. Edit-Directed Output: Example 3

Suppose that the artwork in Figure 4.1 is to be generated by a PUT EDIT statement. The display is obtained with only one PUT EDIT statement, which

*In PL/C, values are rounded rather than truncated in order to conform to an output F specification.

```
***************
*             *
*   0     0   *
*      A      *
*   <----->   *
*             *
***************
```

Figure 4.1.

```
***************
***************
***************
***************
***************
***************
***************
```

(a)

(b)

Figure 4.2.

produces a total of seven lines of output. The most difficult part of this problem is counting the columns in which the various characters are to appear. The counting process is greatly simplified by generating a field of asterisks (in Figure 4.2a) by means of the following statements, where variable X is properly declared.

```
X = '***************';
PUT EDIT (X, X, X, X, X, X, X)
         (COL(1), A);
```

The desired artwork is then drawn by hand over the field of asterisks, as shown in Figure 4.2b. The column for each character is then easily located, and the following PUT EDIT statement that produces this artwork is quickly developed.

```
PUT EDIT ((15)'*', '*', '*', '*','0','0','*',
          '*','A','*', '*','<----->','*', '*','*',
          (15)'*')
          (COL(1),A,
          COL(1),A,COL(15),A,
          COL(1),A,COL(5),A,COL(11),A,COL(15),A,
          COL(1),A,COL(8),A,COL(15),A,
          COL(1),A,COL(5),A,COL(15),A,
          COL(1),A,COL(15),A,
          COL(1),A);
```

Producing larger and more complex displays is not particularly difficult, but it is quite tedious and time-consuming. In general, the position of each character must be counted, and each position must be used in the corresponding PUT EDIT statement. Simplifications are sometimes possible; for example, the artwork in Figure 4.1 is also produced by the following statement.

```
PUT EDIT ('***************', '*             *',
          '*  0   0   *', '*      A      *',
          '*  <------>  *', '*             *',
          '***************')
          (COL(1),A);
```

4.3.6 Remote-Format Specifications

The same list of specifications can be used by many GET or PUT EDIT statements if a remote-format statement is also given. The general forms for the input/output statements and the remote statement are:

GET EDIT (*variable(s)*) (R(*label*));
PUT EDIT (*expression(s)*) (R(*label*));
label: FORMAT (*specification(s)*);

The remote format is a nonexecutable statement and can be placed anywhere within the program. It can be accessed by both GET and PUT EDIT statements. For example, Program 4.2 contains several references to the same remote-format statement.

Given the following input line, Program 4.2 would produce the indicated output line.

```
Input line:  798−6.4359A SHORT STRING
Output line: 798     −6.4359      A SHORT STRING
```

PROGRAM 4.2.

```
TESTRF: PROC OPTIONS (MAIN);
           DCL (A, N) FIXED INIT(0),
               B FLOAT,
               C CHAR(40) VAR;
 SPECS: FORMAT (COL(1),F(3), X(N),F(7,4),X(N),A(14));
 /* BLANK LINES MAY BE FREELY INSERTED */

           GET EDIT (A,B,C) (R(SPECS));
           N = 5;
           PUT EDIT (A,B,C) (R(SPECS));
        END TESTRF;
```

The specification "X(N)" is used in the remote-format statement to separate the values in the output line by several spaces. The variable N has the value 0 when the input operation is performed; this specifies that no input columns are to be skipped. During output, variable N has the value 5, causing five spaces to be output between each of the data elements.

All specifications and options may use numeric expressions* rather than constants. This feature applies to remote-format statements and specification lists that are part of GET and PUT EDIT statements and is especially useful with the "X" specification, the column option, and repetition factors.

There are no restrictions for a remote-format statement on what specifications and options can be used. The statement is simply a way to create a specification list that can be accessed by multiple input/output statements.

Blank lines and comments may be placed anywhere within a program to improve readability. Comments may begin or end anywhere a program statement could be placed.

4.4. THE ENDFILE CONDITION

Computer programs are often designed to process an unknown quantity of input data; so there must be a way to tell them when all that data has been used. PL/I has the ON statement, which can detect several different conditions, including the end of input data. Specifically, the ENDFILE condition can detect the end-of-file condition that occurs when an input operation is attempted after the end of the input data stream has been reached.

Data files are not discussed until Chapter 14; so only the version of the ENDFILE condition that pertains to detecting the end of input data streams

*Expressions in format lists are not permitted with Subset G.

supplied by the programmer is discussed here. The input data supplied by the programmer often uses the default input file, called SYSIN on most systems. The general form of the ON ENDFILE statement most often used in this book is:

ON ENDFILE (SYSIN) *assignment statement or PUT statement*;

The ON ENDFILE statement is an instruction that means, if the end of file is detected, the indicated statement is to be executed. Some examples are:

```
ON ENDFILE (SYSIN) FLAG = 1;
ON ENDFILE (SYSIN) PUT LIST ('EOF ENCOUNTERED');
```

In the first example, an assignment statement is executed when the end of input data is detected. This is the most common use of this condition, because it is readily handled by the control structures discussed in the next chapter. The second example shows that a message could be displayed whenever this condition arises.

When punched data cards are used for input, the end-of-file condition arises when the program attempts to perform an input operation after all data cards have been input. If data is being entered from an interactive terminal, the end-of-file condition can usually be created by typing a special sequence of characters or by depressing only the "return" key when input data is expected from the terminal.

The ON ENDFILE statement is executable, and is often placed at the beginning of a program. The end-of-file detection mechanism is not activated until the ON statement is executed.

4.5. SUMMARY

This chapter deals with three important methods of performing input/output operations. Data-directed I/O is unformatted, and all input and output lines contain a series of data items that resemble assignment statements. List-directed I/O allows data to be handled in an unformatted manner, whereas edit-directed I/O requires data to be formatted. All methods are stream oriented; i.e., all input and output data are regarded as a continuous stream of characters. A frequent combination of these methods is GET LIST utilized for input and PUT EDIT utilized for output. The ON ENDFILE statement can be used to detect the end of input data.

4.5.1. Key Concepts

1. Only variables can appear in a GET statement, but expressions may appear in a PUT statement; for example:

```
GET LIST(A,B,C);
PUT LIST(A+B*C);
```

2. The PAGE, LINE, and SKIP options can be used with data-, list-, and edit-directed output statements, but of these only the SKIP option can be used with input statements.
3. The column (COL) option is applicable only to edit-directed I/O.
4. An input or an output line may contain a combination of data-, list-, and edit-directed data items.
5. The edit-directed specifications discussed in this chapter are A(*w*), F(*w*), F(*w*,*d*), and X(*n*).
6. The "A" specification is used to specify character-string values. The two "F" specifications are used for fixed-point and floating-point values.
7. If an output "A" specification is larger than needed, blanks are added on the right. If an output "A" specification is smaller than needed, characters are truncated on the right (left-justified).
8. If the field width of an output "F" specification is larger than needed, blanks are added on the left. If it is too small, digits are truncated on the left (right-justified).
9. Stream pointers keep track of the current position in input and output data streams.
10. Both GET EDIT and PUT EDIT statements can access a remote-format statement.
11. The ON ENDFILE statement is used to detect the end of input data.

4.5.2. Terms and Phrases

Write out definitions and/or usage descriptions of these terms. Check yourself against the text.

A(*w*)	list-directed I/O
COL(*n*)	ON ENDFILE
data-directed I/O	PAGE
edit-directed I/O	remote format
F(*w*)	SKIP(*n*)
F(*w*,*d*)	stream-oriented data
input/output (I/O)	stream pointer
LINE (*n*)	X(*n*)

PROBLEMS

Problem 4.1. Show the exact output resulting from the execution of Program P4.1.

Problem 4.2. Show the exact output resulting from the execution of Program P4.2, given input of:

```
46   983.2   -89
```

PROGRAM P4.1.

```
TCHAR: PROC OPTIONS (MAIN);
        DCL A CHAR(1) INIT('*');
        PUT EDIT ((10)'A',(10)'A',A||'OUTPUT'||A,
          (10)'A',(10)'A')
                 (COL(1),A);
    END TCHAR;
```

PROGRAM P4.2.

```
LE: PROC OPTIONS (MAIN);
        DCL (X1,X3) FIXED,
          X2 FLOAT;
        GET LIST (X1,X2,X3);
        X1 = 2 * X1;
        X2 = X2 / 10;
        PUT EDIT ('X1=',X1,'X2=',X2,'X3=',X3)
                 (COL(1),A,F(4),X(5),A(2),F(7,3),A,F(3));
    END LE;
```

PROGRAM P4.3.

```
MIX: PROC OPTIONS (MAIN);
        DCL BETA CHAR(3),
            QUEBEC FLOAT,
            XRAY FIXED;
        GET EDIT (BETA,QUEBEC,XRAY)
                 (COL(3),A(3),X(2),F(3,2),X(3),F(2));
        PUT EDIT (QUEBEC,BETA,XRAY)
                 (COL(1),F(4,1),COL(6),A(3),X(1),F(3));
    END MIX;
```

Problem 4.3. Show the exact output resulting from the execution of Program P4.3, given an input line beginning in column 1:

ALPHA$19.16*496STRING

Problem 4.4. Given an input line, beginning in column 1:

68$4.398SOLD−824

write a declaration statement and a GET statement so that variables A, B, C, and D acquire the values '$4.39', 6, −8, and 'OLD', respectively.

Problem 4.5. Describe and give an example of each of the different ways in which a variable can acquire a value. Hint: at least three different ways have been discussed in this book so far.

Problem 4.6. Write one PUT statement which produces the following heading:

```
                    STUDENT TESTS
NAME          SOCIAL SECURITY #          SCORE
```

Problem 4.7. Given the declarations:

```
DCL A FIXED,
    (C,D VAR) CHAR(20),
     B FLOAT;
```

show the output for each of the following program segments where ƀ represents a blank.

a.
```
A = 16;
D = 'STRING';
PUT EDIT('A=',A,'THE STRING ISƀ',D)
         (COL(10),X(5),A(2),F(5),X(2),A(20),A(20)),
```

b.
```
C = 'A'
D = 'NUMBER';
B = 26.32;
PUT EDIT(B,'ƀISƀ',C,D)
         (COL(5),F(3,1),A,A,A);
```

c.
```
A = 12;
B = 14.0;
C = 'ABC';
D = 'ƀ';
PUT EDIT(A,'+',B,C||D,C)
         (COL(10),F(1),A,F(3,0),SKIP,A,A);
```

d.
```
A = 2;
B = 1.5;
PUT EDIT(A+B)(COL(A+3),F(4));
```

e.
```
C = '';
D = '';
PUT EDIT('THIS IS IT'||C||D,'NOW')
        (COL(3),A,A);
```

f.
```
A = 3;
D = 'STRINGb̸';
PUT EDIT(D)(COL(A),A(A));
```

Problem 4.8. Use the following input line and declarations for each problem. Show the values acquired by the specified variables after each GET statement is executed.

```
Input line—starts in column 1
    −649.2THIS IS A STRING49AB73.6CD
DCL(A,B) FIXED,
    (C,D) FLOAT,
    (E,F VAR) CHAR(20);
```

a. GET EDIT(F,D)(COL(1),A(1),F(5,1));

b. GET EDIT(A,F,D,E)(COL(2),F(3),COL(14),A(13),
F(3,0),X(2),A(10));

c. GET EDIT(C,E,A)(COL(1),F(6,1),X(16),A(3),COL(27),F(2));

d. GET EDIT(E)
(COL(32),A(1),A(6));

e. GET LIST(C); What happens when this statement is executed?

f. GET EDIT(C,F,A)(COL(2),F(2),COL(7),A(4),X(12),F(1));

Problem 4.9. Explain the purpose of each of the specifications for edit-directed I/O, and give an example of each.

Problem 4.10. Explain the concept of stream pointers. How can the pointer be changed? How can the end of an input stream be detected?

5 Control Structures

This is a particularly important chapter, because the concepts discussed here form the basis for developing complete, meaningful programs. The topics presented in the previous chapters are integrated by means of the control structures discussed in this chapter, and all future programming development is based on topics contained in these first five chapters.

For example, Chapter 1 introduced the notions of problem solving, pseudocode, and flowcharts, which are used throughout this book. Chapter 2 introduced the idea of a PL/I program and illustrated the relationship between PL/I programs, pseudocode, and flowcharts. Chapter 3 introduced the various data types, as well as the assignment of values to variables in a PL/I program. Chapter 4 presented three important methods of data input and output, including techniques by which the end of an input data stream can be detected. In Chapter 5, structures are presented that control the execution of statements introduced in previous chapters. Two of these control structures, introduced in Chapters 1 and 2, are the DO statement and IF statement, which are used to implement the concepts of repetition and alternation. Repetition is often called looping, and involves the repeated execution of a group of statements as long as a certain specified condition is met. Alternation refers to the selection of a group of statements to be executed based on the outcome of some specified conditions. The third control structure discussed in this chapter permits the creation and use of *subprocedures*. Subprocedures are procedures "owned" by a main procedure. This feature makes it possible to break a large, complex problem down into several smaller, simpler problems.

In this chapter, relational expressions are discussed first, because many conditions for both DO statements and IF statements are relational expressions. Next we will consider the two simple forms of DO loops that are most commonly used. Then we will discuss the primary form of IF statements, followed by the DO group, which is very useful in conjunction with IF statements.

5.1. RELATIONAL AND LOGICAL EXPRESSIONS

Many conditions used in DO and IF statements are actually comparisons of two or more data elements. For example, a condition involving numeric data elements could be a test to decide whether one data element was arithmetically larger than the other. Similarly, character data elements can be compared, but the comparison is based on each element's position in the *collating sequence* (alphabetical order) of the character set, rather than on the magnitude of each data element.

Data elements in a relational expression are compared by a relational operator. There are eight such operators, listed in Table 5.1.

5.1.1. Simple Relational Expressions

Simple relational expressions involve a comparison between two data elements or data expressions, whereas compound relational expressions involve several such comparisons joined together by logical operators.

TABLE 5.1. PL/I relational operators.

Operator	*Meaning*
>	greater than
<	less than
=	equal
<=	less than or equal
>=	greater than or equal
¬=	not equal
¬>	not greater than
¬<	not less than

TABLE 5.2. Values of selected relational expressions.

Expression	*Value*
B < C	true
A > B + C	false
C ¬= 10.5	true
B <= A	true
A + 10 > C	false
X > Z	false
Y = 'JEAN'	false
X < Y	true
X > 'AA' || Y	true
X ¬= 'AB'	true
X ¬< Z	false

The two primary forms of simple relational expressions are:

numeric expression *relational operator* *numeric expression*
character expression *relational operator* *character expression*

Every relational expression has a value of either true or false, depending on whether or not the specified condition is met. For example, suppose numeric variables A, B, and C contain the values 45, 18.5, and 56.82, respectively, and suppose character variables X, Y, and Z contain the values 'ABC', 'JOHN', 'B', respectively. Table 5.2 shows some relational expressions using these variables and their corresponding values.

Note that both FIXED and FLOAT data types may be used within a relational expression. In some circumstances both numeric and character data types may be used within a relational expression, because the PL/I compiler will attempt to convert the data types so that they are compatible. However, this mixing of data types is highly error-prone; so data conversion will not be discussed further until Chapter 12.

The list of examples in Table 5.2 is not exhaustive, of course, because any valid numeric or character expression—including any that could appear on the right-hand side of the equals sign in an assignment statement—may be used in a relational expression. For now, the major restriction is that the rela-

TABLE 5.3. PL/I logical operators.

Operator	*Meaning*
| (OR)	The OR operator compares two expressions, and has the value "true" if either or both of these expressions is true. Otherwise, it has the value "false."
& (AND)	The AND operator compares two expressions, and has the value "true" only if both expressions are true. Otherwise, it has the value "false."
¬ (NOT)	The NOT operator negates the value of a logical expression.

tional operator must compare either two numeric expression or two character expressions.

5.1.2. Logical Expressions

There are many situations in which simple relational operations are not adequate to fully state a condition. For example, suppose a condition were needed that would have the value "true" if numeric variable A contained a value greater than 5 but less than 10. This condition could be stated mathematically as:

$$5 < A < 10$$

Although the mathematical condition looks like a relational expression, it does not correctly represent the desired condition in PL/I. Consequently, additional operators are needed to join together simple relational expressions to form compound relational expressions. These compound relational expressions are quite powerful and can represent a large variety of logical conditions.

The additional operators needed are called *logical operators*, and expressions which contain them are called *logical expressions*. In fact, the terms "logical expression" and "compound relational expression" are equivalent and are used interchangeably. Table 5.3 describes three of these additional operators. The solution to the problem of writing a PL/I condition that would be true if numeric variable A contained a value greater than 5 but less than 10 is therefore:

$$A > 5 \;\&\; A < 10$$

There is a temptation to write this condition as $A > 5 \;\&\; < 10$, but that is incorrect, because a logical operator should operate on expressions, not parts of expressions.

Suppose numeric variables A, B, and C contain the values 16.25, 82, and 5, respectively, and suppose that character variables X, Y, and Z contain the values 'ALPHA', 'BETA', and 'ABC', respectively. Table 5.4 contains some logical expressions and their corresponding values. Note that the NOT (¬) operator

TABLE 5.4. Selected logical expressions and values.

Expression	*Value*
$A < 20 \vert C > 10$	true
$\neg (B > 100)$	true
$A > 100 \vert B > 90 \& C < 10$	false
$\neg (A > 100 \vert B > 90) \& C < 10$	true
$X > \text{'A'} \& Y < \text{'C'}$	true
$Y > \text{'D'} \vert A = 10$	false

can be used in logical expressions also. However, it differs from the AND and OR operators, in that it operates on only one expression and has the effect of "reversing" the value of that expression. In other words, the NOT operator does not perform any comparison; it simply changes a true value to a false value, or a false value to a true value. Note also that a logical expression can contain any number of NOT, AND, and OR operators. In the absence of parentheses, the NOT operators are evaluated first, then the relational operators, then the AND operators, and finally the OR operators.

5.2. THE DO STATEMENT

The concept of repetition was introduced in Chapter 1 and is a key component in the structured programming approach. Briefly, repetition allows a group of statements to be repeatedly executed as long as a certain specified condition is met. This is an important concept, because it gives tremendous power to the programming process, yet maintains conciseness and simplicity in the actual program statements.

Three variations of the DO statements are discussed in this section, and two of them are used for repetition. The three forms of the DO control structure discussed here are:

1. the DO WHILE loop
2. the Iterative DO loop
3. the DO group

The DO WHILE loop appears in several programs in Chapter 2. The iterative DO loop is another form of repetition, because it specifies the number of times a loop is repeated. The DO group is not really a form of repetition, because the statements in this group are executed only once.

5.2.1. The DO WHILE Loop

The following PL/I statements appear in a program in Section 2.2.4:

```
DO WHILE (BALANCE > PAYMENT);
    PUT LIST (BALANCE);
    INTEREST = BALANCE * RATE;
    BALANCE = BALANCE + INTEREST - PAYMENT;
END;
```

```
DO WHILE (condition);
    ____________
    ____________
    ____________          statement(s)
    ____________
    ____________
END;
```

Figure 5.1. *The DO WHILE loop.*

This is an example of a DO WHILE loop. There are three statements between the DO and the END statements. The number of times that these three statements are executed is determined by the condition that appears in the DO statement. The contents of variable BALANCE are changed each time the loop is executed; eventually the condition BALANCE > PAYMENT will no longer be true, and the loop will be exited.

The general form of the DO WHILE loop is shown in Figure 5.1.

The purpose of the DO WHILE loop is to control the number of times the statements between the DO and the END statements are executed. The DO statement specifies a condition to be met, and the END statement marks the end of the DO loop. The condition contained in the DO WHILE statement can be a simple relational expression or an extremely complex logical expression. Although PL/I is free form, the words DO and WHILE must be separated by one or more blanks, so that the compiler can properly identify and process that statement. There can be any number of statements between the DO WHILE and the END statements.

When the DO WHILE statement is initially encountered, the condition is evaluated. If it is false, no statements in the loop are executed, and control passes to the first statement after the END statement. If the condition is initially true, the statement(s) inside the DO loop are executed. Each time the END statement is encountered, the condition in the DO WHILE statement is evaluated; if it is still true, the statements inside the DO loop are executed again. When the condition becomes false, control then passes to the first statement after the END statement.

Program 5.1 is a complete program designed to illustrate the DO WHILE loop. It is sometimes called the "millionaire" problem, because looping is performed until an invested amount equals or exceeds one million.

The two statements inside the DO WHILE loop are repeatedly executed as long as AMOUNT remains less than one million. Note that the contents of variable AMOUNT are changed each time the loop is executed. Eventually AMOUNT will exceed one million, and control then passes to the PUT EDIT statement, which immediately follows the DO WHILE loop. Also note the use of the INITIAL or INIT "attribute" for initialization and the use of blank lines to

DO *numeric variable* = *numeric expression 1* TO *numeric expression 2* BY *numeric expression 3;*

____
____
__________ statement(s)
____
____

END;

Figure 5.2. *The iterative DO loop.*

improve program readability. Blank lines, like comments, can be inserted anywhere in a program.

5.2.2. The Iterative DO Loop

Another form of repetition is the iterative DO loop. The number of times statements in this type of loop are executed depends on a clause that specifies the initial and final values of a particular variable. The amount by which that variable changes at the end of each iteration is also specified, and looping stops when the variable exceeds its final value.

The general form of the iterative DO loop is shown in Figure 5.2.

The purpose of the iterative DO loop is to control the number of times the statements between the DO and the END statements are executed. The first numeric expression specifies the initial value of the numeric variable (also called the index variable), and the second numeric expression specifies the final value of the numeric variable. The BY clause is optional; it is used to indicate the amount by which the numeric variable changes at the end of each loop. If the BY clause is omitted, the amount of change is 1.

When the iterative DO statement is first encountered, the numeric variable is initialized to the first numeric expression. Each time the END statement is encountered, the numeric variable is incremented by 1 (or by numeric expression 3, if it is present). If the numeric variable then contains a value less than or equal to the second numeric expression, the loop is executed again; otherwise, the loop is exited. Consider the following example:

```
DO I = 1 TO 4;
    PUT LIST(I);
END;
```

Here the variable I acquires an initial value of 1 and is incremented by 1 each time the END statement is encountered. The output for this example consists of the values 1, 2, 3, 4. When this loop is exited, variable I contains the value 5.

In the preceding example, variable I could be declared either FIXED or FLOAT, because only integer values were involved. In the following example,

PROGRAM 5.1.

PROBLEM DEFINITION

$1000 is invested at 11 percent, compounded annually. The problem is to find the number of years required for the value of this investment to reach one million dollars. There is no input, and the output consists of several lines that indicate the final amount and the number of years.

Sample input: None

Sample output:
INITIAL AMOUNT IS $1000
ANNUAL INTEREST RATE IS 11 PERCENT
FINAL VALUE IS ________
NUMBER OF YEARS IS ________

ALGORITHM DESIGN

Variables to be used:

AMOUNT	initial and subsequent amounts
RATE	annual interest rate
N	number of years

PSEUDOCODE

```
Initialize AMOUNT,RATE,N
DO WHILE AMOUNT < 1,000,000
    add current year's interest to AMOUNT
    increment N by 1
END
PUT AMOUNT,N
END
```

FLOWCHART

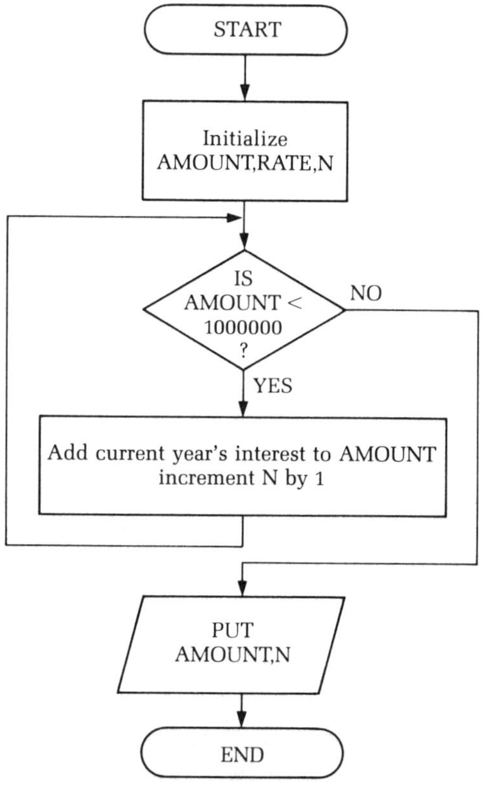

ALGORITHM IMPLEMENTATION

```
/* THE MILLIONAIRE PROGRAM */
MILLION: PROC OPTIONS (MAIN);
            DCL AMOUNT FLOAT INIT (1000.0),
                RATE FLOAT INIT (0.11),
                N FIXED INIT (0);
            DO WHILE (AMOUNT < 1000000.0);
               AMOUNT = AMOUNT + AMOUNT * RATE;
               N = N + 1;
            END;
            PUT EDIT ('INITIAL AMOUNT IS $1000',
                      'ANNUAL INTEREST RATE IS 11 PERCENT',
                      'FINAL VALUE IS  ', AMOUNT,
                      'NUMBER OF YEARS IS  ', N)
                     (COL(10),A,COL(10),A,COL(10),A,F(8),
                      COL(10),A,F(3));
        END MILLION;
```

however, variable X must be declared as FLOAT, because it acquires fractional values:*

```
DO X = 0.0 TO 1.0 BY 0.2;
    PUT EDIT (X) (COL(1), F(3,1));
END;
```

Here variable X acquires an initial value of 0.0 and is incremented by 0.2 each time the END statement is encountered. The output consists of the values 0.0, 0.2, 0.4, 0.6, 0.8, 1.0; and when this loop is exited, the value 1.2 is stored in variable X.

Both of the preceding examples have a positive increment, but negative increments (or decrements) are permitted, as we can see in the following:

```
DO J = 9 TO 2 BY −2;
    PUT EDIT (J) (COL(1), F(2));
END;
```

Here variable J acquires an initial value of 9 and is reduced by 2 each time the END statement is encountered. The output consists of the values 9, 7, 5, 3; and the value 1 is stored in J when this loop is exited. If the BY clause in this example were omitted, the PUT statement in the loop would not be executed at all, and control would immediately pass to the first statement after the END statement, because the initial value of variable J exceeded the specified final value.

Variables, constants, and complex expressions can be used to specify the initial value, final value, and increment in an iterative DO loop. However, temporary variables are used by the compiler to store these values during execution of the DO loop. Consequently, changing the values of variables used in these expressions during execution of the DO loop will have no effect on the number of times the DO loop is executed, as the following example shows:

```
I = 4; F = 5; C = 6;
DO K = I−2 TO F+3 BY C−4
    PUT LIST (K);
    I = I+1; F = F+1; C = C+1;
END;
```

Although the contents of variables I, F, and C are explicitly altered during each execution of the loop, the number of times the loop is executed is not affected, because the compiler uses only the initial values of these expressions, which are stored in temporary variables known only to the compiler. In other words, the DO statement "DO K = 2 TO 8 BY 2;" is equivalent to the one in the

*Fractional values in iterative DO statements are not permitted with Subset G.

preceding example, and the output consists of the values 2, 4, 6, 8. However, explicitly changing the value of variable K within the loop would affect the number of times the DO loop is executed. Note that more than one statement can appear on a line; however, this is generally not advisable, because it reduces the readability of the program.

Program 5.2 provides a good illustration of the use of the iterative DO loop. The problem here is to approximate the value of π (about 3.14159265) by performing a specific number of computations.

The statements inside this DO loop are executed 20 times; when the loop is exited, the value 21 is stored in variable I. This program is an excellent example of the use of the iterative DO loop, because the loop must be executed a specific number of times. In general, the iterative DO loop is used whenever the exact number of iterations required is known, and the DO WHILE loop is used whenever the number of iterations required depends on the evaluation of some logical or relational expression.

PROGRAM 5.2.

PROBLEM DEFINITION

The value of π can be computed by using Leibnitz's formula:

$$\pi = 4\left(1 - \frac{1}{3} + \frac{1}{5} - \frac{1}{7} + \frac{1}{9} - \frac{1}{11} + \ldots\right)$$

The purpose of this problem is to approximate the value of π by computing the first 20 terms of Leibnitz's formula. The current term and the current value of π are displayed each time the loop is executed.

Sample input: None

Sample output:

ITERATION	TERM	PI
1	4.0000	4.0000
2	−1.3333	2.6666
.	.	.
.	.	.
.	.	.
.	.	.
20	.	.

ALGORITHM DESIGN

Variables to be used:

PI	current value of π
TERM	current term
I	counter
ODD	values: 1, 3, 5, 7, 9, 11, . . .
SIGN	alternating sign (+1 or −1)

PSEUDOCODE

```
Initialize variables PI, TERM, ODD, SIGN
PUT Column headings
DO I = 1 TO 20
    PUT I, TERM, PI
    compute next TERM
    add TERM to PI
END
END
```

ALGORITHM IMPLEMENTATION

Each successive TERM is computed by adding 2 to ODD, changing the sign of SIGN, and assigning SIGN/ODD to TERM.

```
/* APPROXIMATING THE VALUE OF PI */
COMPUTE: PROC OPTIONS (MAIN);
            DCL (PI, TERM, I, ODD, SIGN) FLOAT INIT(1);
            PUT EDIT('ITERATION', 'TERM', 'PI') /*HEADINGS*/
                  (COL(5), A, COL(15), A, COL(25), A);
            DO I = 1 TO 20;
               PUT EDIT(I, 4*TERM, 4*PI)
                     (COL(9),F(2),COL(14),F(7,4),COL(23),F(6,4));
               /* COMPUTE NEXT TERM */
               SIGN = -1 * SIGN;
               ODD = ODD + 2;
               TERM = SIGN/ODD;
               /* ADD TERM TO PI */
               PI = PI + TERM;
            END;
         END COMPUTE;
```

FLOWCHART

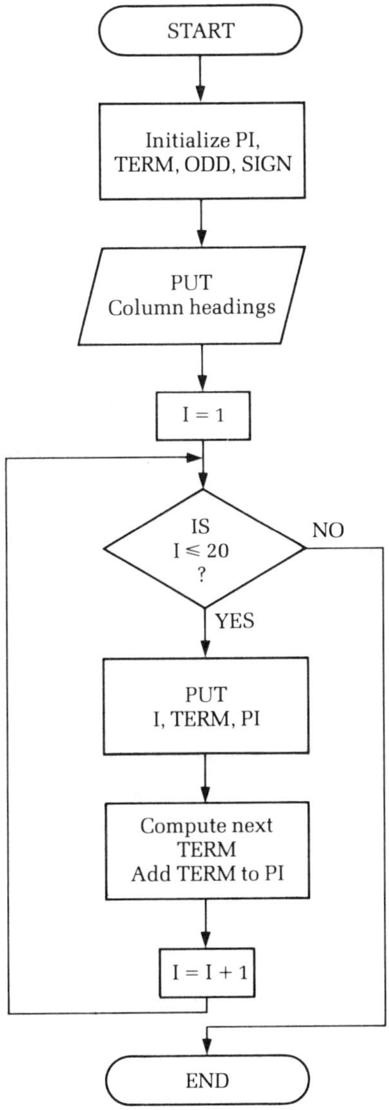

Note: Initialize values of variables

PI	1
TERM	1
ODD	1
SIGN	1

```
DO;
    __________
    __________
    __________            statement(s)
    __________
END;
```

Figure 5.3. *The DO group.*

5.2.3. The DO Group

The two previous variations of the DO statement are used to implement two forms of repetition. However, the DO group is not actually a form of repetition, because the statements in this group are executed only once. The general form of the DO group is shown in Figure 5.3.

The DO group is principally used in THEN or ELSE clauses of IF statements. It is particularly valuable when two or more statements are required in such clauses. Without this construct, a THEN or ELSE clause could not easily accommodate more than one statement, as is illustrated in the program segment shown as Program 5.3.

In this segment, all the statements contained in one of the DO groups will be executed once, depending on the evaluation of the condition in the IF statement. Note that any executable statement, including DO and IF statements, DO WHILE loops, and iterative DO loops, can be placed within a DO group.

5.3. THE IF STATEMENT

The concept of alternation was introduced in Chapter 1 and is another key component in the structured programming approach. Briefly, alternation allows a condition to be evaluated and, depending on the outcome of that evaluation, one of two groups of statements to be executed. The IF statement is used to

PROGRAM 5.3.

```
IF A = B + C
   THEN DO;
            X = 25;
            PUT SKIP LIST ('THEN CLAUSE');
        END;
   ELSE  DO;
            X = 12;
            DO I = 1 to 15;
                PUT LIST (I);
            END;
        END;
```

implement the alternation concept. Several examples of it were presented in Chapter 2.

Unlike the DO statement, there is only one form of the IF statement, although several variations are permitted. The general form of the IF statement is:

```
IF condition
  THEN statement(s);
  ELSE  statement(s);
```

The condition in the IF statement can be any logical or relational expression. When the IF statement is encountered, this condition is evaluated. If it is true, the statement(s) in the THEN clause are executed. If the condition is false, the statement(s) in the ELSE clause are executed. After one of these two actions is performed, control passes to the first statement immediately after the IF statement. Any executable statement may be included in a THEN or an ELSE clause, including another IF statement. If more than one statement must be executed in a THEN or ELSE clause, then a DO GROUP or DO loop is usually required. An excellent example of the usefulness of DO groups and DO loops in an IF statement appears in section 5.2.3.

In the following example, assume that FIXED variables A, B, and C contain arbitrary, distinct values. The following IF statement will decide which of these variables contains the smallest value, and then display that value.

```
IF A < B
  THEN IF A < C
          THEN PUT LIST (A);
          ELSE PUT LIST (C);
  ELSE IF  B < C
          THEN PUT LIST (B);
          ELSE PUT LIST (C);
```

Note that an IF statement is used in a THEN clause and in an ELSE clause and that these IF statements in turn could have IF statements in their THEN and ELSE clauses, and so on. However, IF statements become difficult to read and understand when this process of containing IF statements in other IF statements is carried very far.

Not every IF statement needs to have complete THEN and ELSE clauses. Either clause may be null; that is, a clause need not have any statements associated with it. The following examples illustrate the use of null THEN and null ELSE clauses.

```
1. IF A = B
      THEN PUT SKIP LIST ('A EQUALS B');
      ELSE;
2. IF A = B
      THEN PUT SKIP LIST ('A EQUALS B');
```

```
3. IF A = B
      THEN;
      ELSE PUT LIST ('A IS NOT EQUAL TO B');
```

Examples 1 and 2 are logically equivalent; the only difference between these examples is that example 1 contains a null ELSE clause, but the ELSE clause is completely missing in example 2. Both examples are valid, although the null ELSE is mainly used in more complex situations, such as IF statements contained in other IF statements. If the ELSE clause is missing, or is null, no action is taken when the condition is false, and control then passes to the first statement after the IF statement. A null THEN clause appears in example 3. Null THEN clauses are valid, but not particularly useful.

Program 5.4 illustrates the use of the IF statement. The problem here involves sorting three character values.

Program 5.4 contains several features not found in previous programs. For example, character values can be used in relational or logical expressions. However, for character values, relational operators such as "less than" (<) refer to the alphabetical order or collating sequence of the character set, rather than to arithmetic or numeric magnitude. The sorting technique used in this program is commonly called the "bubble" or "exchange" sort method. The sort loop is executed twice because three variables need to be sorted. A trace table using the suggested sample input would verify that two passes through the loop are required. The temporary variable TEMP is needed for the exchange operation to maintain the contents of the variables.

5.4. SUBROUTINES

The stuctured programming approach involves the proper use of sequence, repetition, and alternation in the design and implementation of algorithms. These concepts have been discussed in this and previous chapters. In this section, we present a new concept, *subroutines,* that can be an effective tool for algorithm design and implementation.

There are three types of procedures in PL/I: main procedures, subroutine procedures, and function procedures. Main procedures have already been presented, and function procedures will be discussed later. Only the rudiments of subroutine procedures (or simply subroutines) are presented in this section; more complete information appears in Chapter 10. The goal here is to impart a basic working knowledge of subroutines.

A subroutine is simply a collection of statements associated with a programmer-defined procedure name (one to seven letters and digits, where the first character must be a letter). A subroutine is subordinate to another procedure, because it is activated only by an explicit instruction, as illustrated in Figure 5.4.

In Figure 5.4, the main procedure calls (or invokes) the subroutine at two different locations. The main procedure invokes the subroutine with a "CALL" statement, which causes control to pass to the subroutine. The statements

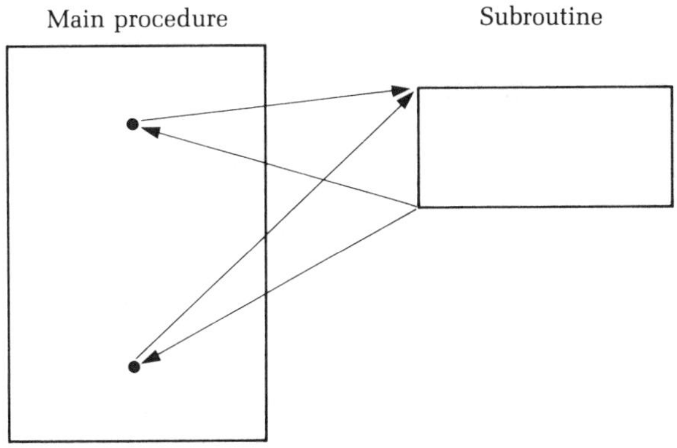

Figure 5.4. *Main procedure and subroutine.*

```
subroutine name: PROC;   or PROC (parameter(s));
                    ____
                    ____
                    ____         statement(s)
                    ____
                    ____
                    RETURN;
                 END;   or END subroutine name;
```

Figure 5.5. *General form of the subroutine.*

within the subroutine are executed, and then control passes back to the first statement after the CALL statement in the main procedure. As Figure 5.4 shows, the subroutine can be invoked a second time (or any number of times), and the entire process repeated.

Subroutines are valuable because they can shorten programs when the same set of statements is to be executed repeatedly. Subroutines can also aid in the problem-solving process, because the problem can be broken down into several parts, and each part can be solved with a subroutine, presumably by starting with the simplest part first.

A subroutine is called or invoked by means of the CALL statement. The CALL statement has two forms:

CALL *subroutine name*;
CALL *subroutine name (argument(s))*;

The primary difference between these two forms of the CALL statement is that the second form explicitly provides for the passing of numeric or character expressions to and from the subroutine, whereas the first form does not. The reasons for using each of these forms will be clarified by the examples in this section.

The general form for subroutines is shown in Figure 5.5. The form of the PROC (PROCEDURE) statement used also determines the form of the CALL

PROGRAM 5.4.

PROBLEM DEFINITION

The input for this problem consists of three character values which represent names of three persons. These three character values are to be sorted in ascending alphabetical order. The output consists of these three values in alphabetical order. Relational expressions can be used to compare two character values. For example, the relational expression 'A' < 'B' is true, but the relational expression 'GRAND' < 'GARDEN' is false.

Sample input: 'SMITH MARY'
'JONES HARVEY'
'ADAMS CHRIS'

Sample output: 'ADAMS CHRIS'
'JONES HARVEY'
'SMITH MARY'

ALGORITHM DESIGN

Variables to be used:

NAME1, NAME2, NAME3	character strings for 3 persons
TEMP	temporary character variable
I	loop counter

PSEUDOCODE

```
GET NAME1, NAME2, NAME3
Sort NAME1, NAME2, NAME3
    in ascending order
PUT NAME1, NAME2, NAME3
```

FLOWCHART

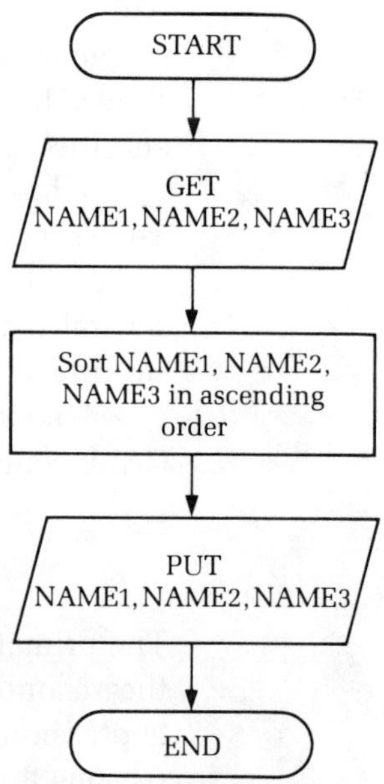

Neither the pseudocode nor the flowchart contains enough detail for a PL/I program to be developed; so further refinement is necessary.

PSEUDOCODE, REFINED

```
GET NAME1, NAME2, NAME3
DO the following twice
    IF NAME1 > NAME2
        THEN exchange NAME1 and NAME2
    IF NAME2 > NAME3
        THEN exchange NAME2 and NAME3
END
PUT NAME1, NAME2, NAME3
END
```

FLOWCHART, REFINED

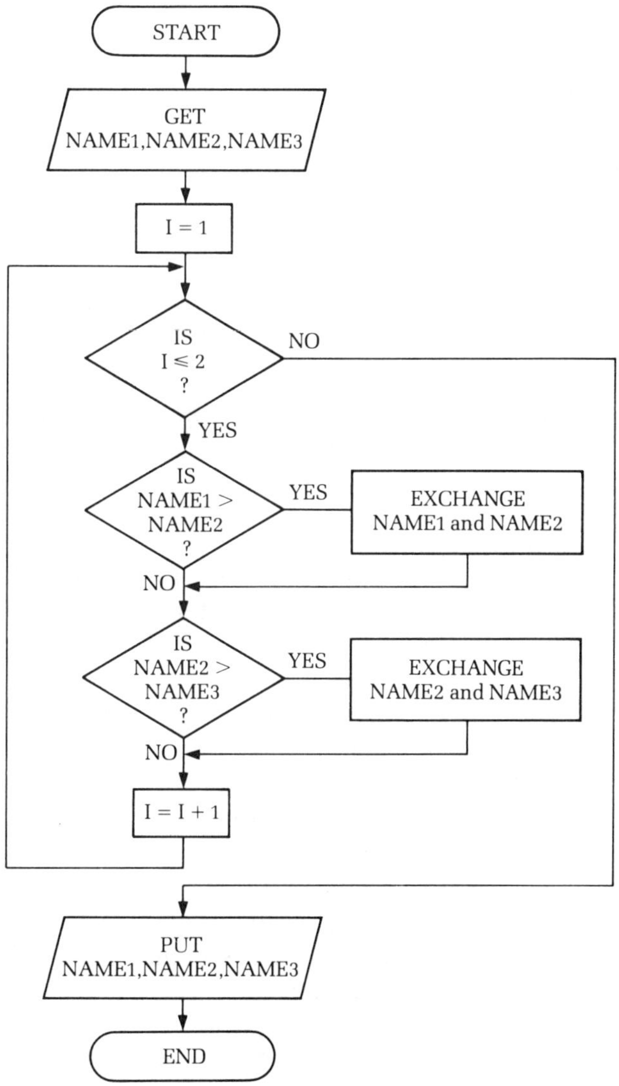

ALGORITHM IMPLEMENTATION

```
/* SORT 3 CHARACTER STRINGS IN ASCENDING ORDER */
SORT: PROC OPTIONS (MAIN);
          DCL (NAME1, NAME2, NAME3, TEMP) CHAR(30) VAR,
               I FIXED;
          GET LIST (NAME1, NAME2, NAME3);
          DO I = 1 TO 2;          /* BEGIN SORT LOOP */
             IF NAME1 > NAME2
                THEN DO;          /* EXCHANGE */
                        TEMP = NAME1;
                        NAME1 = NAME2;
                        NAME2 = TEMP;
                     END;
             IF NAME2 > NAME3
                THEN DO;          /* EXCHANGE */
                        TEMP = NAME2;
                        NAME2 = NAME3;
                        NAME3 = TEMP;
                     END;
          END;
          PUT SKIP LIST(NAME1);
          PUT SKIP LIST(NAME2);
          PUT SKIP LIST(NAME3);
      END SORT;
```

statement that can be used to invoke the subroutine. The RETURN statement is optional; it specifies that control is to be passed to the first statement after the CALL statement that invoked the subroutine. If the RETURN statement is omitted, the END statement serves as a RETURN statement.

We will consider several examples of subroutines, but first a brief review of terminology is in order. The calling procedure is the procedure which invokes or calls a subroutine with a CALL statement. A calling procedure can be any of the three types of procedures, but in this book it is usually a main procedure. *Arguments* can appear in the CALL statement of a calling procedure, and *parameters* appear in subroutines. An argument can be a numeric or character expression (recall that constants and variables are defined as expressions), but a parameter is always a numeric or character variable that should be declared in the subroutine.

Program 5.5 uses a subroutine without parameters. This is a simple addition problem, but it does illustrate the most important feature of subroutines.

Subroutine GETADD is physically contained inside the main procedure and is thus classified as an internal subroutine. All subroutines are assumed to be internal until Chapter 10, where a complete description is presented. An internal subroutine without a DECLARE statement has access to all variables used in the main procedure, and conversely, the main procedure has access to all variables used in the subroutine. For example, the variable SUM is computed in subroutine GETADD, and is used in the main procedure.

If an internal subroutine does contain a DECLARE statement, then the variables appearing in that DECLARE statement are accessible only by that subroutine and not by the calling procedure. The subroutine still has access to all variables used in the calling procedure, but the calling procedure has access to only those variables used in the subroutine which do not appear in a DECLARE statement. Program 5.6 gives an example of this situation.

In Program 5.5 the subroutine GETADD physically follows the IF statement in the main procedure. Could the subroutine be unintentionally invoked after the IF statement is executed? No, because subroutines must be explicitly invoked and cannot be accidentally invoked because of their placement in the main procedure. The compiler stores subroutines in such a way that they are invisible to the statements in the calling procedure. Consequently, the END ADDPROB statement is encountered after the IF statement is executed.

Two somewhat unfamiliar flowchart symbols are used here to represent subroutines; they were defined in Figure 1.2. The annotation symbol is connected to the flowchart with a dashed line and is used here to specify whether the flowchart represents a main procedure or a subroutine. This symbol can also be used to make comments about various aspects of the flowchart. The predefined-process symbol is used to specify the invocation of a subroutine.

Program 5.6 uses a subroutine with parameters. This is a variation of the sort problem in section 5.3, except that numeric rather than character values are sorted.

The primary difference between Programs 5.5 and 5.6 is that the sort procedure passed arguments to a subroutine, but the addition procedure did not. The subroutine in the addition problem always manipulates variables A, B, and C, but the sort problem must be able to handle different pairs of variables, such as A, B and B, C. For example, there are two calls to subroutine SWAP in the sort problem:

```
CALL SWAP(A,B);
CALL SWAP(B,C);
```

However, the parameter list in subroutine SWAP consists of the variables VALUE_1 and VALUE_2. The arguments do not have to have the same names

PROGRAM 5.5.

PROBLEM DEFINITION

Input consists of two sets of three integer numbers. The sum of each of these sets is computed, and output consists of the larger of the 2 sums.

Sample input: 46 89 32
23 42 17

Sample output: THE LARGER SUM IS 167

ALGORITHM DESIGN

A subroutine is used to handle the input and the addition of each set of numbers.

Variables to be used:

A, B, C	set of integer values
SUM1, SUM2	sums of the two sets of values
SUM	sum computed by subroutine

PSEUDOCODE

Main Procedure:

```
CALL GETADD
Store SUM in SUM1
CALL GETADD
Store SUM in SUM2
IF SUM1 > SUM2
  THEN PUT SUM1
  ELSE PUT SUM2
END
```

GETADD Subroutine:

```
GET A,B,C
SUM = A + B + C
RETURN
```

FLOWCHART

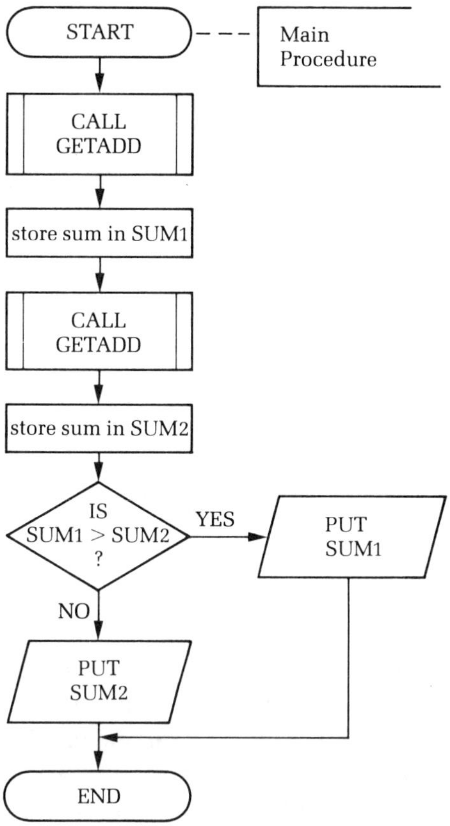
START
Main
Procedure
CALL
GETADD
store sum in SUM1
CALL
GETADD
store sum in SUM2
IS
SUM1 > SUM2
?
YES
PUT
SUM1
NO
PUT
SUM2
END

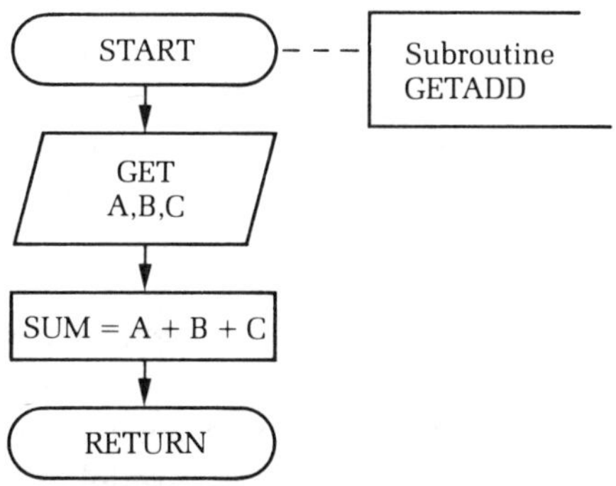
START
Subroutine
GETADD
GET
A,B,C
SUM = A + B + C
RETURN

ALGORITHM IMPLEMENTATION

```
/* ADDITION PROBLEM USING SUBROUTINE GETADD */
ADDPROB: PROC OPTIONS (MAIN);
            DCL (A,B,C, SUM, SUM1, SUM2) FIXED;
            CALL GETADD;
            SUM1 = SUM;
            CALL GETADD;
            SUM2 = SUM;
            IF SUM1 > SUM2
               THEN PUT SKIP LIST ('THE LARGER SUM IS', SUM1);
               ELSE PUT SKIP LIST ('THE LARGER SUM IS', SUM2);
GETADD:  PROC;   /* SUBROUTINE TO GET AND ADD 3 VALUES */
               GET LIST (A,B,C);
               SUM = A + B + C;
               RETURN;
           END GETADD;
           END ADDPROB;
```

as the variables in the parameter list, because arguments can be expressions. However, arguments and parameters should agree in number and in the data type of corresponding arguments and parameters. For example, the parameter list of subroutine SWAP consists of two integer (FIXED) variables, and the argument lists of both calls to SWAP consist of two integer variables.

When subroutine SWAP is invoked with the statement "CALL SWAP (A,B);", the variable VALUE_1 represents the variable A and the variable VALUE_2 represents the variable B. When subroutine SWAP is invoked with the statement "CALL SWAP (B,C);", the variable VALUE_1 represents the variable B and the variable VALUE_2 represents the variable C. That values can be named differently in the subroutine is an important feature, because subroutines can therefore be very flexible and useful. For example, one can develop a "library" of subroutines to be used by programmers who would need to know only the names of the subroutines and the number and data types of the arguments to be used.

Both pseudocode and flowcharts have been used to represent algorithms in Chapters 1 through 5. However, from Chapter 6 on, only pseudocode will be used to represent algorithms. Those who wish to continue using flowcharts should find it easy to do so because of the parallel development of pseudocode and flowcharts. I prefer pseudocode, because of its conciseness and closeness to the PL/I language, but I acknowledge that flowcharts are widely used.

PROGRAM 5.6.

PROBLEM DEFINITION

The input for this problem consists of three integer values, which are to be sorted in ascending order (smallest first). The output consists of these three values in ascending order.

Sample input: 19 36 −45

Sample output: −45 19 36

ALGORITHM DESIGN

A subroutine is used to exchange the values of two variables that are not in ascending order.

Variables to be used:

A,B,C	integer values to be sorted
VALUE_1,VALUE_2	values to be swapped in the subroutine
TEMP	temporary integer variable
I	loop counter

PSEUDOCODE

Main Procedure:

```
GET A,B,C
DO the following twice
    IF A > B
       THEN CALL SWAP(A,B)
    IF B > C
       THEN CALL SWAP(B,C)
END
PUT A,B,C
END
```

Subroutine SWAP:

```
Exchange the 2 values
RETURN
```

FLOWCHART

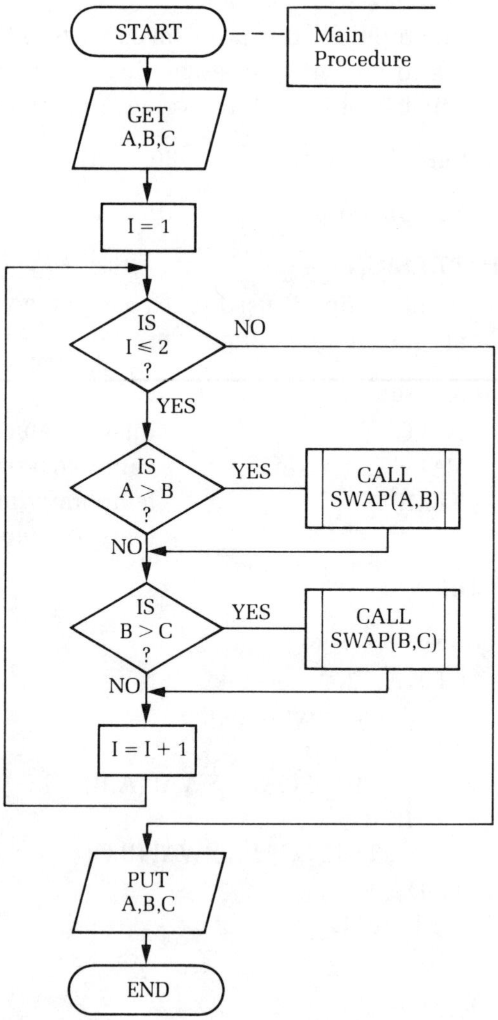
START
Main
Procedure
GET
A,B,C
I = 1
IS
I ≤ 2
?
NO
YES
IS
A > B
?
YES
CALL
SWAP(A,B)
NO
IS
B > C
?
YES
CALL
SWAP(B,C)
NO
I = I + 1
PUT
A,B,C
END

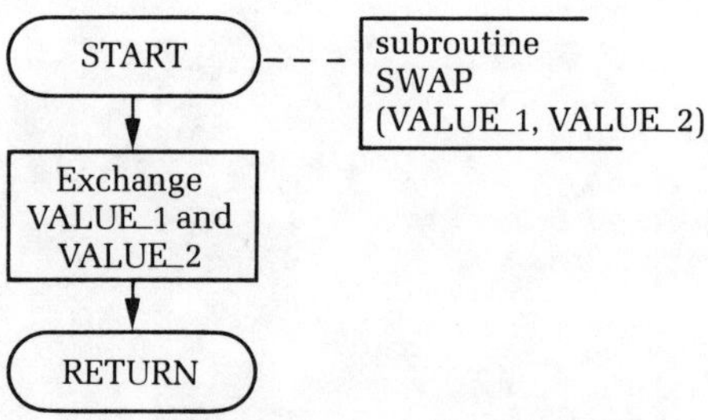
START
subroutine
SWAP
(VALUE_1, VALUE_2)
Exchange
VALUE_1 and
VALUE_2
RETURN

ALGORITHM IMPLEMENTATION

```
/* SORT 3 INTEGERS                              */
/* EXCHANGE PERFORMED BY SUBROUTINE SWAP */
SORT: PROC OPTIONS (MAIN);
            DCL (A, B, C, I, TEMP) FIXED;
            GET LIST (A, B, C);
            DO I = 1 TO 2;
                IF A > B
                  THEN CALL SWAP(A, B);
                IF B > C
                  THEN CALL SWAP(B, C);
            END;
            PUT SKIP(2) LIST (A, B, C);
SWAP: PROC (VALUE_1, VALUE_2);
            DCL (VALUE_1, VALUE_2) FIXED;
            TEMP = VALUE_1;
            VALUE_1 = VALUE_2;
            VALUE_2 = TEMP;
            RETURN;
        END SWAP;
        END SORT;
```

5.5. SUMMARY

Relational and logical expressions have been discussed in this chapter, with an emphasis on how they are used to establish conditions for alternation and repetition. The three forms of the DO statement are presented, and the IF statement is discussed. A working knowledge of subroutines is presented. Detailed procedures will be thoroughly covered in Chapter 10.

5.5.1. Key Concepts

1. Relational expressions are used to compare the values of two numeric or character-string expressions.
2. The logical operators are AND, OR, and NOT.
3. Logical expressions consist of one or more relational expressions operated on by logical operators.
4. The iterative DO loop and the DO WHILE loop are forms of repetition.
5. The statements within a DO WHILE loop are repeatedly executed as long as the specified condition is true.
6. The condition in a DO WHILE statement or an IF statement can be a rela-

tional expression or a logical expression. (It can also be a variable or constant, as will be discussed in Chapter 12.)

7. If the condition in the DO WHILE statement is false when the DO WHILE loop is first entered, then no statements within that loop are executed.
8. Each time the END statement of a DO WHILE loop is encountered, the specified condition is evaluated; if it is true, the statements within the loop are executed again. If it is false, the loop is exited, and control passes to the first statement after the END statement.
9. The statements within an iterative DO loop are repeatedly executed as long as the value in the index variable does not go beyond a specified limit.
10. If a "BY clause" is not present in an iterative DO statement, an increment of +1 is added to the index variable each time the END statement is encountered. The BY clause can be used to specify an increment which is positive or negative and which is integer or floating point.
11. In this chapter, all variables and expressions in an iterative DO loop are assumed to be numeric. However, later chapters (especially Chapter 8) will discuss additional forms of the iterative DO loop.
12. The IF statement is a form of alternation.
13. If the condition in an IF statement is true, the statements in the THEN clause are executed. If the condition is false, the statements in the ELSE clause are executed. However, if the ELSE clause is missing when the condition is false, or if the THEN clause is missing when the condition is true, control passes to the first statement after the IF statement.
14. DO groups or DO loops are often used when a THEN or ELSE clause requires more than one statement to be executed.
15. Null THEN or ELSE clauses are permitted, i.e., THEN; or ELSE;
16. For character-string values, relational operators refer to the alphabetical or collating sequence of the character set, rather than to arithmetic or numeric magnitude.
17. A subroutine is a collection of statements associated with a procedure name. Statements in a subroutine are executed only when another procedure explicitly invokes (calls) that subroutine.
18. The CALL statement is used to invoke (call) a subroutine.
19. Arguments can appear in the CALL statement, and parameters can appear in a subroutine.
20. An internal subroutine is one that is contained within another procedure, such as a main procedure.
21. Variables declared in a main procedure are accessible by all the procedures it contains. However, variables declared in a subroutine are known only to that subroutine.

5.5.2. Terms and Phrases

Write out definitions and/or usage descriptions of these terms. Check yourself against the text.

AND operator (&)
argument
BY
CALL
DO group
DO WHILE loop
index variable
internal subroutine
invocation
iterative DO loop
logical expression
NOT operator (¬)
null ELSE (ELSE;)
null THEN (THEN;)
OR operator (|)
parameter
relational expression
RETURN
sort
subroutine

PROBLEMS

Problem 5.1. *True or false?* Evaluate each logical expression, assuming:

A = 41.6, B = 'ABC', C = 'AB', D = '91'

a. ____ B < 'CD' & A < 50
b. ____ (B||C = 'ABCAB')|(B < 'A' & D < 100)
c. ____ D + A < 100|¬(B||C < 'Z' & (A = 41))
d. ____ 10 < A|D − A + D¬ = D
e. ____ ¬(¬(¬(B = C)))
f. ____ A = 41.6|B < C
g. ____ (B < 'MN'|C < 'AB'|¬(B||C < 'MNAM')
h. ____ A¬ < 100 & D¬ > 100

Problem 5.2. Show the exact output produced by each of the following program segments, where the declaration used for each segment is:

```
DCL (I,J,K) FIXED,
    (A,B) FLOAT;
```

a.
```
K = 0;
I = 1;
DO WHILE (I < 10);
    K= K + I;
    I = I + 1;
    PUT LIST(I,K);
END;
```

b.
```
K = 0;
I = 1;
DO WHILE (I < 10);
    I = I + 1;
    K = K + I;
    PUT LIST(I,K);
END;
```

c.
```
DO I = 1 TO 10;
    I = I + 1;
    PUT LIST(I);
END;
```

d.
```
K = 1;
I = 1;
DO WHILE(I + K < 10);
    IF I = K
      THEN DO;
               I = I + 1;
               K = K + 2;
           END;
      ELSE DO;
               K = K + 1;
               I = I + 1;
           END;
    PUT LIST(I,K);
END;
```

e.
```
DO A = 1.3 TO 2.7 BY .3;
    B = A + A;
    PUT LIST(A,B);
END;
```

f.
```
DO I = 5 TO 1 BY -1;
    DO J = 1 TO 5;
        PUT LIST(I,J);
    END;
END;
```

Problem 5.3. Use the problem-solving process to develop a solution for this problem. Compute the sums of two "adjacent" numbers from a list of any eight numbers, as indicated by the sample input and output.

Sample input: 24 16 28 72 9 8 12 70

Sample output:

ADJACENT NUMBERS	SUM
24 16	40
28 72	100
9 8	17
12 70	82

Problem 5.4. Modify Program 5.2 to compute the first 50 items instead of 20, but to display the term for every fifth computation of that term.

Problem 5.5. Modify Program 5.2 to use a subroutine to compute the next term.

Problem 5.6. Use the problem-solving process to compute the sum of an arbitrary number of values. The first input value is the number of values, which is followed by the data values to be added.

Sample input: 5 6 2 9 3 7

Sample output:

```
NUMBERS
  6
  2
  9
  3
  7
27 IS THE SUM
```

Problem 5.7. *True or false?*

a. ____ The following relational expression is equivalent to the statement "A is greater than or equal to B":

```
A >| = B
```

b. ____ The following is a valid relational expression:

```
A + B < C − D
```

c. ____ The PUT statement in the following DO loop is executed six times:

```
DO I = 1 TO 10 BY 2;
    PUT LIST(I);
END;
```

d. ____ The PUT statement in the following DO loop is executed four times:

```
I = 1;
DO WHILE(I < 10);
    PUT LIST(I);
    I = I*2;
END;
```

e. ____ Immediately after executing the following DO loop, variable I contains the value 25:

```
DO I = 1 TO 24;
    PUT LIST(I);
END;
```

f. ____ The PUT statement in the following DO loop is executed once:

```
K = 10;
DO I = 2 TO K;
    PUT LIST(I);
    K = 0;
END;
```

g. ____ The terms "DO group" and "iterative DO loop" are used interchangeably.

h. ____ An IF statement can appear in the THEN or ELSE clause of another IF statement.

i. ____ The ELSE clause of an IF statement can be omitted or may appear as:

```
ELSE;
```

j. ____ If the RETURN statement of a subroutine is missing, the last END statement of that subroutine serves as a RETURN statement.

k. ____ Parameters can be expressions, but arguments must be variables.

Use the problem-solving process to develop solutions for the following problems.

Problem 5.8. The Indians sold Manhattan Island for $24 in the year 1627. Suppose the Indians had invested this money at 7 percent interest compounded annually. What would the value of this investment be today? Display the initial and final amounts, as well as the amount every ten years.

Sample input: None

Sample output: THE MANHATTAN PROBLEM
INITIAL AMOUNT: $24
ANNUAL INTEREST RATE: 7%

YEAR	AMOUNT
1627	24.00
1637	.
1647	.
.	.
.	.

Problem 5.9. An unknown number of two-digit exam scores appear on an arbitrary number of input lines. There are exactly ten scores on each input line; the smallest score is 00 and the largest score is 99. Compute and display the following:

a. total number of exam scores
b. average of all the scores
c. the number of scores between 60 and 80 (inclusive)

Sample input: 68928743758299817183
.
.
.

Sample output: ANALYSIS OF EXAM SCORES
TOTAL NUMBER OF SCORES IS ______
OVERALL AVERAGE ______
SCORES BETWEEN 60–80 ______

Problem 5.10. A drone is flying a straight, level course at an altitude of 40,000 feet. A surface-to-air missile (SAM) is launched to destroy the aircraft. The SAM has a homing device that enables it to change direction continuously and to always head directly toward the drone. If the SAM gets within 1,500 feet of the drone, then the aircraft is considered destroyed, as shown in Figure 5.6.

The speed of the drone is 600 feet per second, and the speed of the SAM is 1,500 feet per second. The problem is to simulate the positions of the drone and the SAM and to calculate where the drone is destroyed. For convenience, simulate the positions of the SAM and the drone at one-second intervals. Computing the drone's X, Y-coordinates at each interval is easy:

DX = DX + 600
DY = 40,000 (stays constant)

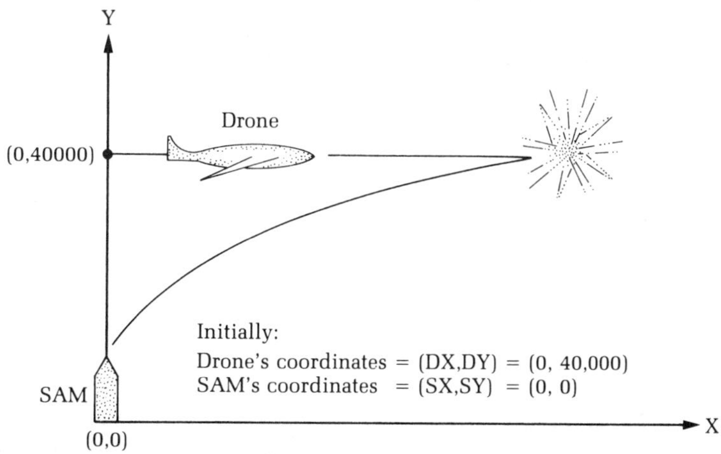

Figure 5.6.

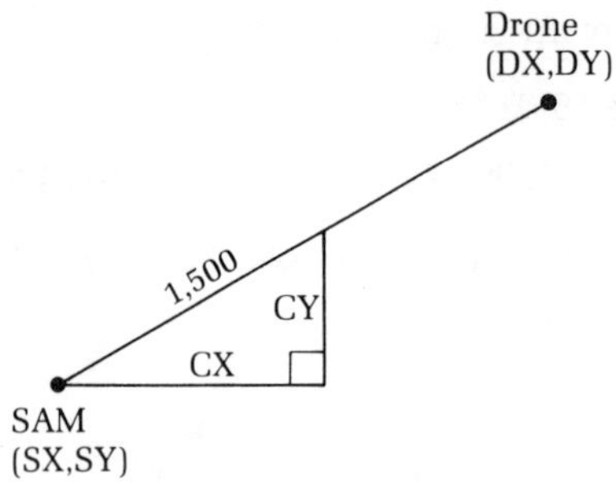

Figure 5.7.

Computing the SAM's new X, Y-coordinates requires the use of a right triangle to simulate the homing capability of the SAM, as shown in Figure 5.7.

The distance between the SAM and the drone at any instant in time is:

$$\text{Distance} = \sqrt{(DX - SX)^2 + (DY - SY)^2}$$

In Figure 5.7, CX and CY represent the amount of change to the SAM's X, Y-coordinates every second. Using trigonometric relationships,

$$CX = 1500 * \left(\frac{DX - SX}{\text{distance}}\right)$$

$$CY = 1500 * \left(\frac{DY - SY}{\text{distance}}\right)$$

Thus, the SAM's new coordinates every second are:

$$SX = SX + CX$$
$$SY = SY + CY$$

Compute and display each simulated second of time, the coordinates of the drone, and the coordinates of the SAM. This tabulation continues until the distance between the SAM and the drone is less than 1,500 feet.

Sample input: None

Sample output:

DRONE—SAM PROBLEM

TIME	DX	DY	SX	SY
0	0	40000	0	0
1	600	40000	.	.
2	.	.	.	.
.	.	.	.	.
.	.	.	.	.
.	.	.	.	.

6 Numeric Computation

This chapter deals with problems that require much numeric data manipulation and computation. Both fixed- and floating-point data are used, although the latter is emphasized. Many of these problems require the use of common operations, such as square root, truncation, absolute value, or trigonometric values. Consequently, one goal of this chapter is to survey some of the available numeric functions. Another goal is to solve several numerically oriented problems that demonstrate the computational capability of PL/I.

6.1. NUMERIC DATA TYPES

The numeric data types used in this chapter are FIXED and FLOAT. As before, FIXED is used to represent integer quantities, and FLOAT is used to represent all other numeric quantities.

The advantage of the FLOAT data type is that very large or very small numbers can be represented, because exponential notation is used to establish or "float" the decimal point to the desired position. For example, the value $3682*10^{35}$ would be difficult to represent as a FIXED value, but is easily represented as a FLOAT value, as:

```
3.682E+38
```

Here the exponent E+38 specifies that the actual decimal point is 38 places to the right of the decimal point shown. If the exponent were E−38, then the actual position of the decimal point would be 38 places to the left of the position shown.

Exponential notation can be used to conveniently describe floating-point values. The following examples of assignment statements illustrate several forms of floating-point constants:

```
A =  34.89E+45;
B =  .9E-2;
C =  45678E8;
D = -1.45E+16;
E =  1.45E-16;
```

Floating-point values described with exponential notation are not restricted to assignment statements; they can be used in any statement where numeric constants are allowed. Although the programmer has considerable freedom in using exponential notation in statements such as the assignment statement, the output form for exponential notation is rigid. Figure 6.1 shows how a FLOAT value would appear if displayed by a PUT DATA, PUT LIST, or a PUT EDIT statement with an E specification.*

*The general form for the E specification is E(w,d), where w is the total field width and d is the number of fractional decimal digits. Note that $w \geq d + 7$.

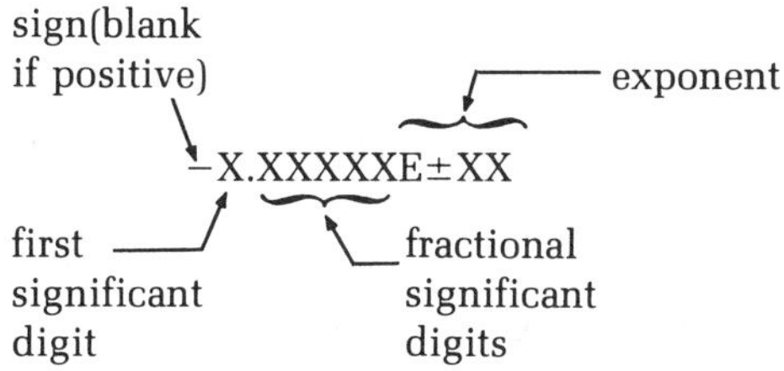

Figure 6.1. *Format for exponential notation.*

For example, the following PUT statement:

```
PUT EDIT (93214.6, −0.000045)(COL(1),E(12,5),COL(1),E(8,1));
```

produces the output:

```
 9.32146E+04
−4.5E + 05
```

The maximum size of the exponent for floating-point values differs for the various PL/I compilers. For example, IBM S/370 compilers permit an exponent range of about −78 to +75, i.e., 10^{-78} to 10^{+75}. By contrast, CDC Cyber 172 compilers allow an exponent range of about −294 to +322, i.e., 10^{-294} to 10^{+322}. The number of significant digits allowed also varies, but the programmer can partially control this by use of declaration statements, as will be discussed in Chapter 12.

The size of FIXED data values also differs for the various PL/I compilers. For example, many IBM PL/I compilers permit integer values in the range of −99,999 to +99,999. By contrast, CDC Cyber 172 compilers permit integer values in the range of −281,474,976,710,656 to +281,474,976,710,655. The programmer can partially control the size and form of FIXED data values, as will be discussed in Chapter 12.*

6.2. BUILT-IN FUNCTIONS

A built-in function is a function procedure supplied by the compiler. These functions are easy to use, and there are generally many of them; only a few are discussed here. These functions can be timesavers and can help the programmer avoid "reinventing the wheel" whenever a common task needs to be handled.

Functions are invoked by referring to the function name and a list of argument(s); recall that a subroutine is invoked with a CALL statement. Function invocations can appear in any statement where an expression can appear,

*For example, integer values in the range of −2,147,483,648 to +2,147,483,647 are also possible with IBM PL/I compilers.

TABLE 6.1. Built-in numeric functions.

Typical function invocation	*Value returned*	*Restrictions on arguments*
ABS(X)	absolute value of X	
ACOS(X)	arccosine of X (in radians)	$\|X\| \leq 1$
ASIN(X)	arcsine of X (in radians)	$\|X\| \leq 1$
ATAN(Y)	arctangent of Y (in radians)	
ATAN(Y,X)	arctangent of $\frac{Y}{X}$ (in radians)	$X > 0$
ATAND(Y)	arctangent of Y (in degrees)	
COS(X)	cosine of X	X in radians
COSD(X)	cosine of X	X in degrees
DATE	current date: 'YYMMDD' (See Summary)	
EXP(X)	e^X	
LOG(X)	natural logarithm (base e) of X	$X > 0$
LOG10(X)	common logarithm (base 10) of X	$X > 0$
LOG2(X)	base 2 logarithm of X	$X > 0$
MOD(X,Y)	X modulo Y $\left(\text{remainder of } \frac{X}{Y}\right)$	
ROUND(X,N)	X rounded to N decimal places	
SIGN(X)	1 if $X > 0$, 0 if $X = 0$, -1 if $X < 0$	
SIN(X)	sine of X	X in radians
SIND(X)	sine of X	X in degrees
SQRT(X)	square root of X	$X \geq 0$
TAN(X)	tangent of X	X in radians
TAND(X)	tangent of X	X in degrees
TIME	current time: 'HHMMSS' or 'HHMMSSTTT' (See Summary)	
TRUNC(X)	integer portion of X	

and more than one function invocation can appear in a statement. For example, consider the *square root* function SQRT, which computes the square root of some number that is an argument to the SQRT function. The value returned by SQRT can be used as part of an expression. For example:

```
X = 15.5 + SQRT(25);
```

Here the SQRT function computes the square root of 25 and returns the value 5 (actually, it returns the floating-point value 5.00000E+00). This returned value is used in the expression, and the value 20.5 is stored in variable X. All the functions are similar to SQRT, because each requires one or more arguments to supply the data to be manipulated, and all the functions then return one value.

Table 6.1 gives brief descriptions of some built-in numeric functions. Other functions are commonly available as well, but those in Table 6.1 are adequate to solve many computationally oriented problems. The arguments to these functions can be expressions, and some of the arguments have restrictions. Failing to observe these restrictions will result in an error condition that might terminate execution of the program. The best way to become familiar with these built-in functions is to use them to solve problems; so we will devote the next section to solved problems that use some of these functions.

6.3. EXAMPLES

Each of the three problems in this section requires use of one or more built-in functions. In fact, these problems would be much more difficult to solve if these functions were not available.

6.3.1. Plotting the Sine Curve

The sine curve is to be plotted (graphed) by means of a line printer or computer terminal. Although a typical line printer has about 132 horizontal print columns, only the first 80 columns will be used. For convenience, the X-axis of the sine curve will be *vertical* in the output. In other words, the X values increase with each successive line of output.

The offset adjustment is necessary to place the graph in the center of the output area. The amplitude computation is necessary because the actual value returned by the sine function ranges between −1 and +1, but the shape of the curve is more easily seen when many columns (for example, 72) are used.

Many other curves can be plotted by using the approach in Program 6.1. An axis can be plotted and overprinted on curves by use of the SKIP(0) feature in the PUT EDIT statement.

6.3.2. Finding Prime Numbers

A prime number is defined as a positive integer that cannot be factored into the product of any two positive integers which are each greater than 1. In other words, a prime number *N* has exactly two *divisors* (positive integers that evenly divide it): 1 and *N* itself. The first five prime numbers are 2, 3, 5, 7, and 11.

The problem here is to find all the prime numbers from 1 to 200. Even numbers are all divisible by 2; so, except for 2 itself, even numbers cannot be prime. Therefore only the odd numbers following 2 need to be checked.

There are two built-in functions that can be used in this problem, the TRUNC function and the MOD function. Suppose *N* is being checked as a potential prime, and *D* is a positive integer, where $1 < D < N$. If *D* evenly divides *N*, then *N* cannot be a prime number. One way to implement this test is with the TRUNC function:

Is N = D* TRUNC(N/D)?

If the answer to this question is yes, then *N* cannot be a prime number, because *N* is evenly divisible by *D*. The TRUNC function takes the integer portion of the quotient and this value is multiplied by *D*, producing *N* only if the original quotient was an integer.

Another way to find out whether *D* evenly divides *N* is with the MOD function, which returns the remainder in the division of two numbers. This function is easier to use, and the test can be implemented as follows:

Is MOD(N,D) = 0?

PROGRAM 6.1.

PROBLEM DEFINITION

Plot the sine curve from 0 degrees to 360 degrees. The output area consists of 80 horizontal columns and 40 vertical lines. The horizontal columns are used to represent Y-axis values, and the vertical lines are used to represent X-axis values.

Sample input: None

Sample output:

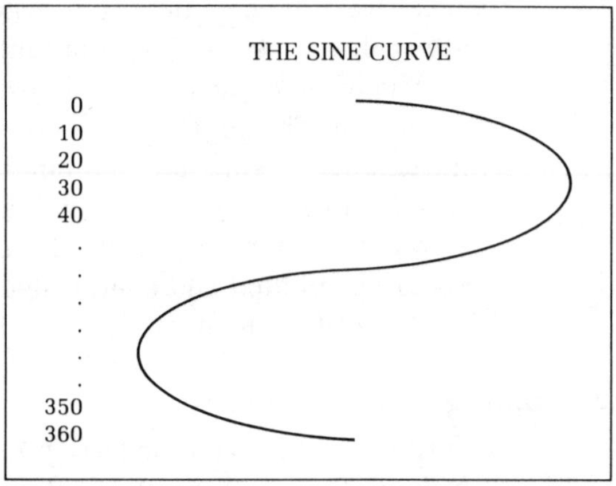

ALGORITHM DESIGN

The function SIND and the COLUMN feature of the PUT EDIT statement are quite useful in solving this problem.

Variables to be used:

X 0–360 degrees
S sine of X(adjusted)

If the answer to this question is yes, then *N* cannot be a prime, because *N* is evenly divisible by *D*. Basically, the MOD function returns the remainder of the expression *N*/*D*. If the remainder is zero, then *D* evenly divides *N*. If the remainder is not zero, then *D* does not evenly divide *N*, and further testing is probably necessary.

There are several interesting features in Program 6.2 that need additional clarification. For example, the CALL statement has two arguments associated with it. These arguments are not really necessary, because subroutine PRIME has access to all variables in the main procedure and because renaming of variables is not required for this problem. Note that the only potential divisors of *N* are the positive integers from 2 to the square root of *N*. If *N* has two or more divisors, then one of them must be less than or equal to the square root of *N*.

PSEUDOCODE

```
DO X = 0 TO 360
    Compute sine of X
    Compute offset (column 42 represents Y = 0)
    Compute amplitude of sine curve (SIND(X)*36)
    PUT 'S' at column 42 + SIND(X)*36
END
END
```

ALGORITHM IMPLEMENTATION

```
/* PLOT THE SINE CURVE */
PLOT: PROC OPTIONS (MAIN);
        DCL (X, S) FIXED;
        PUT EDIT ('THE SINE CURVE')(COL(33),A);
        PUT SKIP(2);
        DO X = 0 TO 360 BY 10;
            S = 42 + SIND(X)*36;
            PUT EDIT (X,'S')(COL(1),F(3),COL(S),A);
        END;
    END PLOT;
```

Notice that a WHILE clause is added to an iterative DO statement in subroutine PRIME. A WHILE clause can always be added to an iterative DO statement, to provide an additional method for terminating the DO loop. When the END statement of the DO loop is encountered, both the iteration count and the WHILE condition are checked. The loop is terminated when either the iteration count is exceeded or the WHILE condition becomes false (whichever occurs first).

6.3.3. Computing Sin X

The value for the sine of X can be obtained with the built-in functions SIN or SIND. However, we will not use these functions in this problem. Instead, we

PROGRAM 6.2.

PROBLEM DEFINITION

Find all prime numbers between 1 and 200. The output consists of a heading followed by the prime numbers.

Sample input: None

Sample output: THE PRIMES ARE 2 3 5 7 11 . . .

ALGORITHM DESIGN

The first prime number is 2, and only the odd numbers from 3 to 200 are possible prime numbers.

Variables used:

N	possible prime number
D	possible divisor of N
FLAG	set to 1 if D evenly divides N

PSEUDOCODE

Main Program

```
PUT heading and the value 2
DO N = 3 TO 200 BY 2
    CALL CHECK to find out whether N is prime
    IF FLAG = 0
       THEN PUT N
END
```

will compute the sine of X by computing terms in an infinite series where X is an angle measured in radians:

$$\sin X = X - \frac{X^3}{3!} + \frac{X^5}{5!} - \frac{X^7}{7!} + \ldots$$

The number of terms necessary to compute sin X depends on how much accuracy is desired. For example, if accuracy to ten decimal digits is required, then many terms would be computed. However, if only two decimal digits need to be accurate, then relatively few terms would be computed. The actual size of

Subroutine CHECK

```
FLAG = 0
DO D = 2 TO √N WHILE FLAG = 0
   IF D evenly divides N
      THEN FLAG = 1
END
RETURN
END
```

ALGORITHM IMPLEMENTATION

```
/* FIND ALL PRIME NUMBERS BETWEEN 1 AND 200 */
PRIME: PROC OPTIONS (MAIN); /* MAIN PROCEDURE */
          DCL (N, D, FLAG) FIXED;
          PUT SKIP LIST ('THE PRIMES ARE', 2);
          DO N = 3 TO 200 BY 2;
             CALL CHECK (N, FLAG);
             IF FLAG=0
               THEN PUT LIST(N);
          END;
CHECK: PROC(N,FLAG);          /* SUBROUTINE CHECK */
          DCL (N,FLAG) FIXED;
          FLAG=0;
          DO D = 2 TO SQRT(N) WHILE (FLAG = 0);
             IF MOD(N,D) = 0
               THEN FLAG = 1;     /* N IS NOT PRIME */
          END;
          RETURN;
       END CHECK;
       END PRIME;
```

the angle X will also affect the number of terms computed. In general, smaller absolute values of X will require fewer computed terms than larger absolute values of X.

The built-in functions ABS and MOD are used in Program 6.3 to help simplify the algorithm implementation. In the variation of the DO statement used here, a WHILE clause is appended to a portion of an iterative DO statement and provides the only means of exiting from the loop, because the iterative portion of the DO statement does not specify a maximum number of iterations. Note that individual factorials are not computed and that each suc-

PROGRAM 6.3.

PROBLEM DEFINITION

Compute the trigonometric sine of angle X for various input values of X. Each individual value of X should be less than or equal to $2*\pi$ (about 6.28) because $2*\pi$ radians equals 360 degrees. The input consists of an arbitrary number of values for X, and the output consists of a table showing each intermediate computation of the sine of X. The sine of X is computed to six decimal places.

Sample input: .45 1.3

Sample output:

```
SIN(X) FOR X = .45

TERM #  CURRENT TERM  CURRENT SIN(X)
  1
  2
  3
  4
  .
  .
  .
THE SINE OF .45 is .XXXXXXX

************************************

SIN(X) FOR X = 1.3

TERM #  CURRENT TERM  CURRENT SIN(X)
  1
  2
  .
  .
  .             etc.
```

cessive term is computed by performing several operations on the previous term. Finally, the built-in function SIN is used to compare the actual value of the sine of X to the computed value.

6.4. SUMMARY

The purpose of this chapter is twofold:

a. to introduce numeric built-in functions

ALGORITHM DESIGN

Each term in the sine computation uses a factorial as its divisor, i.e., 3!, 5!, 7!, etc. However, the factorial value becomes increasingly large for each succeeding term and is likely to become too large for the computer to handle. For example,

3! = 3*2*1 = 6
5! = 5*4*3*2*1 = 120
7! = 7*6*5*4*3*2*1 = 5040
9! = 9*8*7*6*5*4*3*2*1 = 362,880

Consequently, the algorithm must be designed to avoid the danger posed by the factorial computation. If the input angle X exceeds 2*π, then X must be adjusted by subtracting 2*π as necessary.

Variables used:

X	input angle in radians
SINE	computed sine of X
TERM	computed term (X^N/N!)
N	values of 1,3,5,7,9,11,...
SIGN	+1 or −1
I	counter
PI	π
FLAG	flag to signal end of input

b. to present techniques for solving numerically oriented problems

Many PL/I built-in functions are provided, and Table 6.1 is a partial listing of some of the ones most commonly used. These built-in functions are easy to use and provide considerable computational power.

Two of the built-in functions (DATE and TIME) require a few additional remarks. If used, these built-in functions must be declared as BUILTIN, so that the compiler does not consider them as variables. For example,

PSEUDOCODE

First approach:

```
Do while input data is available
    Get X, adjust if X > 2*π
    Initialize variables
    PUT heading
    Do while |TERM| > 0.0000005
        Compute next TERM and add to SINE
        PUT TERM#, TERM, SINE
    END
END
```

Refinement:

```
GET X
Do while input data is available
    IF X > 2*π
      THEN X = modulo (X,2*π)
    Initialize variables SIGN, SINE, TERM, and N to 1
    PUT heading
    Do I = 1 BY 1 WHILE |TERM| > 0.0000005
        N = N+2
        SIGN = −1*SIGN
        TERM = X^N/N!
        SINE = SINE + SIGN*TERM
        PUT I, TERM, SINE
    END
    PUT closing lines
    GET X
END
END
```

```
DCL (DATE,TIME) BUILTIN;
```

The other built-in functions may also be declared as BUILTIN, but it is not necessary to do so.

The value returned by the TIME function for IBM PL/I and PL/C compilers is the character string

'HHMMSSTTT'

The substring 'TTT' represents thousandths of seconds, and the rest of the string represents hours, minutes, and seconds.

ALGORITHM IMPLEMENTATION

```
/* COMPUTING THE SINE OF ANGLE X (IN RADIANS) */
TRIG: PROC OPTIONS (MAIN);
        DCL (X, SINE, TERM, N, SIGN) FLOAT,
            (I, FLAG) FIXED INIT(0),
            PI FLOAT INIT(3.14159265);
        ON ENDFILE (SYSIN) FLAG=1;
        GET LIST (X);        /* FIRST VALUE OF X */
        DO WHILE (FLAG = 0);
           IF X > 2*PI
              THEN X = MOD(X, 2*PI);
           SIGN, SINE, TERM, N = 1;
           PUT EDIT ('SIN(X) FOR X = ',X,        /* HEADING */
                     'TERM #', 'CURRENT TERM',
                       'CURRENT SIN(X)')
                     (SKIP(5),COL(10),A,F(9,6),
                     SKIP(2),COL(1),A,COL(10),A,COL(25),A);
           DO I = 1 BY 1 WHILE (ABS(TERM) > 0.0000005);
              N = N + 2;
              SIGN = -1*SIGN;
              TERM = TERM*X**2/(N*(N-1));
              SINE = SINE + SIGN*TERM;
              PUT EDIT(I, TERM, SINE)
                      (COL(2),F(3),COL(10),F(12,6),COL(23),F(8,6));
           END;
           PUT EDIT ('THE SINE OF',X,'IS',SINE,(30)'*')
                     (SKIP(2),A,F(8,6),A,F(8,6),SKIP(2),A);
           GET LIST(X);
        END;
    END TRIG;
```

6.4.1. Key Concepts

1. The FIXED data type is used to represent integer values, and the FLOAT data type is used to represent all other numeric values. (This statement is not complete, because the FIXED data type can represent noninteger values, as will be discussed in Chapter 12.)
2. The value stored in a FLOAT variable is always in exponential form.
3. If a FLOAT variable appears in a PUT DATA or PUT LIST statement, the value displayed is in exponential form. However, if a FLOAT variable appears in a PUT EDIT statement, the value displayed can be in fixed-point

form or floating-point form, depending on whether the "F" or the "E" specification is used.
4. A built-in function is a function procedure supplied by the compiler.
5. Functions are invoked by referring to the function name and a list of zero or more arguments.
6. Function references can be used in any statement where expressions are allowed.
7. The FLOAT data type is particularly useful in representing numbers that are extremely large or extremely small.
8. A WHILE clause can be added to an iterative DO statement.

6.4.2. Terms and Phrases

Write out definitions and/or usage descriptions of these terms. Check yourself against the text.

absolute value |X|
built-in function
exponential notation
factorial N!
floating-point constants
prime number
sine curve

PROBLEMS

Problem 6.1. *True or false?*

a. ____ Exponential notation is most commonly used to represent character-string values.

b. ____ FLOAT variables can store much larger numbers than FIXED variables can.

c. ____ A built-in function is invoked with the CALL statement.

d. ____ The following is a valid statement, assuming that variable X is declared as FLOAT:

```
X = ABS (TRUNC(SQRT(SIN(0.3))));
```

Use the problem-solving process to develop a solution for each of the following problems.

Problem 6.2. The rounding problem.

The input consists of an unknown number of numeric data values. Round each value to the nearest integer, but do not use the ROUND function.

Sample input: 25.8 19.2 −6.9 14.89

Sample output:

ROUNDING PROBLEM

INPUT VALUE	ROUNDED VALUE
25.8	26
19.2	19
−6.9	−7
14.89	15

Problem 6.3. The perfect-square problem.

The input consists of an unknown number of numeric data values. If a data value is a positive integer, determine whether or not it is a perfect square. Otherwise, display an appropriate message.

Sample input: 17.5 4 −4 9 18 25

Sample output:

PERFECT-SQUARE PROBLEM

INPUT VALUE	PERFECT SQUARE?
17.5	INVALID
4	YES
−4	INVALID
9	YES
18	NO
25	YES

Problem 6.4. Digit-sum check.

Financial institutions often use the last digit of a customer account number as a validity check. This last digit is computed by performing some operation on the digits in the account number. In this problem, compute the check digit by finding the sum of the squares of the digits and then taking the last digit of that sum as the check digit. For example, the six-digit account number 762083 is really a five-digit account number with a validity check. The check digit 3 is found from:

$$7^2 + 6^2 + 2^2 + 0^2 + 8^2 = 153$$

where 3 is the last digit. The input consists of an arbitrary number of six-digit positive integers. Find out which of them are valid account numbers, and display an appropriate message.

Sample input: 762083 421765

Sample output:

DIGIT-SUM CHECK

ACCOUNT NUMBER	VALID?
762083	YES
421765	NO

Problem 6.5. Square-root approximation.

The square root of 2 can be approximated by repeatedly applying the statement

$$X = X - \frac{X^2 - 2}{2 * X}$$

after assuming an initial value for X. After several iterations, X will approximate the square root of 2. Use an initial value of 0.5 for X, and repeatedly apply the statement until the absolute value of the difference between two successive computations of X is less than 0.00005.

Sample input: None

Sample output: SQUARE-ROOT APPROXIMATION

NUMBER	X
1	0.5
2	.
3	.
.	.
.	.
.	.
.	.

Problem 6.6. Economic Order Quantity.

The Economic Order Quantity (EOQ) is used to calculate the optimal number of items to purchase for a particular product, based on several known costs. The formula to compute the EOQ is:

$$EOQ = \sqrt{\frac{2 * N * P}{S}}$$

where

N is the number of items needed per month,
P is the cost of preparing the purchase order (assume $5), and
S is the monthly storage cost per item.

The input consists of data for an arbitrary number of items. Each item is represented by the following:

Identification Number
N (number of items needed per month)
S (monthly storage cost per item)

Sample input:

9835	1000	0.10
3416	80	0.25
5094	10	1000.00

Sample output:

ECONOMIC ORDER QUANTITY

ID#	N	S	EOQ
9835	10000	0.10	1000.00
3416	80	0.25	56.56
5094	10	1000.00	0.31

Problem 6.7. Area computation.

Suppose that a parcel of land has X, Y-coordinates established at each corner, as shown in Figure 6.2. The X-coordinate is the first coordinate in each X, Y-coordinate pair. The input consists of a series of X, Y-coordinate pairs, where the first and last coordinate pairs are identical. In other words, the first coordinate pair represents the upper left corner of the map, and succeeding coordinate pairs are arrived at by clockwise traversal of the corners, so that the last coordinate pair is also the point of beginning.

The area of this parcel of land is computed as follows: To calculate the area of a parcel of land when the coordinates of its corners are known, multiply the Y-coordinate of each corner by the difference between the X-coordinates of the following and the preceding corners, always algebraically subtracting the following from the preceding. One half the final sum is the area of the parcel of land. The final sum might be a negative value; so use the absolute value of the computed final sum for the area.

Sample input:

```
100 100
215 110
240  80
220  50
130  25
100 100
```

Sample output:

AREA COMPUTATION

X	Y
100	100
215	110
240	80
220	50
130	25
100	100

THE COMPUTED AREA IS XXXXX

Problem 6.8. Number systems.

Display a number-conversion table by converting the decimal numbers from 1 to 20 to binary and octal.

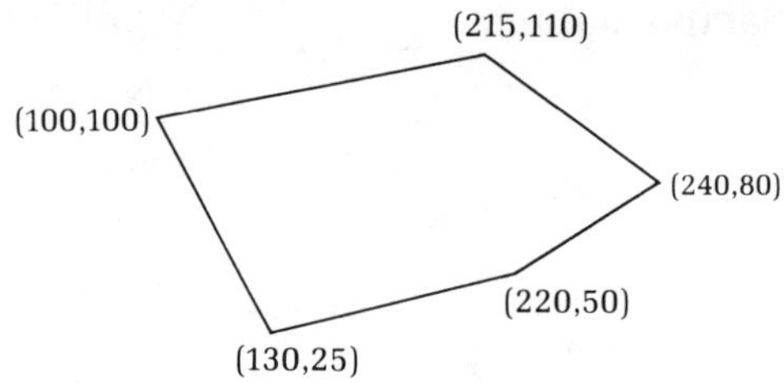

Figure 6.2. *A parcel of land (not drawn to scale).*

Sample input: None

Sample output:

NUMBER SYSTEMS

DECIMAL	BINARY	OCTAL
1	1	1
2	10	2
3	11	3
4	100	4
.	.	.
.	.	.
.	.	.
20	10100	24

A decimal number D is converted to a number with base B (where B is 2 or 8) as follows:

```
DO WHILE D > 0
    R = MOD(D,B)
      (R is the next least significant digit
       of the converted number)
    D = D/B
END
```

Assume that D, B, and R are all integer values.

Problem 6.9. Date conversion.

The input consists of a series of dates in the form

YYYYMMDD

where

YYYY represents the year
MM represents the month
DD represents the day

Each of these dates is to be converted to American-style and European-style dates, i.e., dates of the form

MM/DD/YYYY
DD/MM/YYYY

Sample input: 20011125 19841214 19601019

Sample output:

DATE CONVERSION

DATE	AMERICAN	EUROPEAN
20011125	11/25/2001	25/11/2001
19841214	12/14/1984	14/12/1984
19601019	10/19/1960	19/10/1960

Problem 6.10. Series computation.

The infinite series for e^x is:

$$e^x = 1 + x + \frac{x^2}{2!} + \frac{x^3}{3!} + \ldots + \frac{x^n}{n!} + \ldots$$

For $x = 0.7$, compute the first 30 terms of the series, and compare the computed value of e^x with the value returned by the built-in function EXP.

Sample input: None

Sample output: SERIES COMPUTATION
X = 0.7
E**X (COMPUTED) = XX.XXXX
E**X (FUNCTION) = XX.XXXX

Problem 6.11. Area computation.

Compute the shaded area under the curve in Figure 6.3 by using the "trapezoidal" technique. The area under this curve is approximated by dividing the area into trapezoids, as in Figure 6.4, and by computing the sum of the

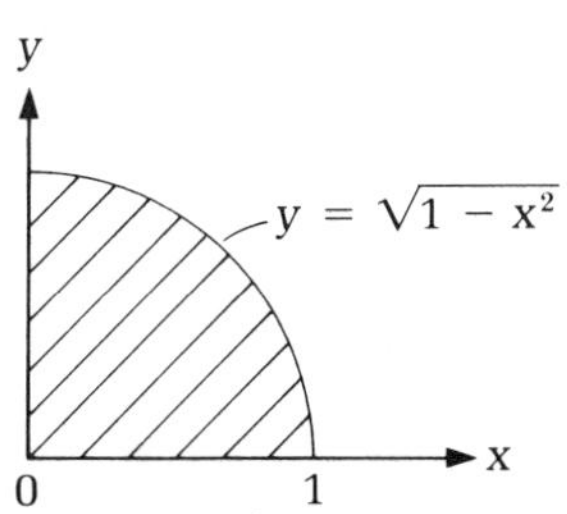

Figure 6.3.

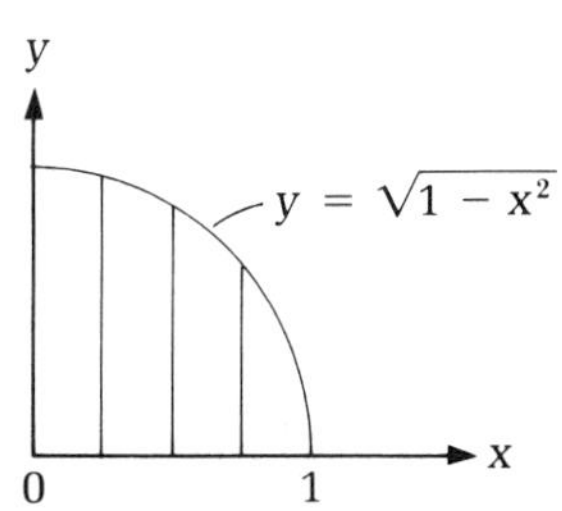

Figure 6.4.

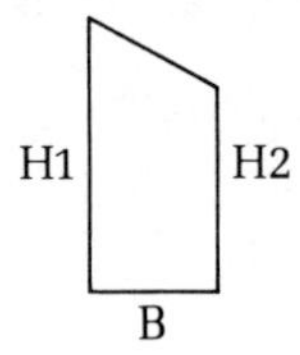

Figure 6.5.

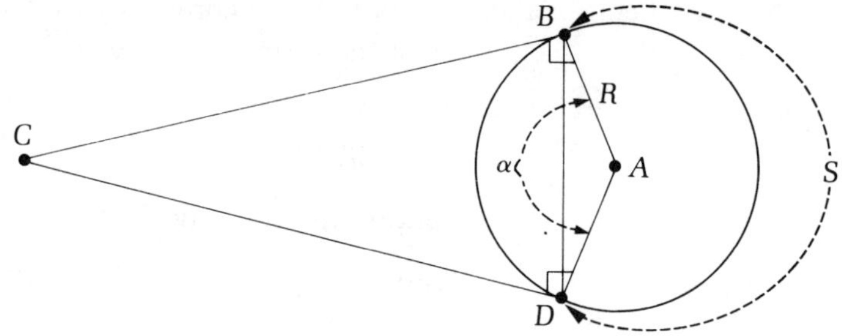

Figure 6.6.

areas of the trapezoids. The area of a typical trapezoid is B * (H1 + H2)/2, where B is the base of the trapezoid and the heights are H1 and H2, as in Figure 6.5.

All the trapezoids under the curve have the same base B, i.e., B = 1/N, where N is the number of trapezoids. The larger N is, the more accurate is the computation of the area.

Sample input: None

Sample output: COMPUTED AREA OF A QUARTER CIRCLE

N = 5	AREA = XX.XX
N = 10	AREA = XX.XX
N = 20	AREA = XX.XX

Problem 6.12. Ice-cream-cone problem.

In Figure 6.6, the arc distance S from point B to point D is 1. The tangent distance from point B to point C ($\overline{BC}$) is 1, and the tangent distance from point D to point C ($\overline{DC}$) is also 1. Compute the radius R of the circle, accurate to three decimal places. (Figure 6.6 is not drawn to scale.) Some useful observations:

$$R = \overline{DA} = \overline{BA}$$

$$\overline{DC} = \overline{BC} = R * \tan\left(\frac{\alpha}{2}\right) = 1$$

$$\overline{DB} = 2 * R * \sin\left(\frac{\alpha}{2}\right)$$

$$S = R * (2\pi - \alpha) = 1$$

angle α is measured in radians

Hint: iterate on the value of α several times,

$$0.1 \leqslant R \leqslant 0.4,$$
$$2 \leqslant \alpha \leqslant 3$$

Sample input: None

Sample output:

ICE-CREAM-CONE PROBLEM

ALPHA	R * TAN(ALPHA/2)	R * (2 * PI – ALPHA)	R
2.	.	.	.
2.05	.	.	.
2.10	.	.	.
.	.	.	.
.	.	.	.

7 Character Manipulation

7.1. CHARACTER-STRING CONCEPTS AND OPERATIONS

The operations performed on character strings (or simply strings) generally involve the creation or building up of strings, extracting or removing portions of strings, and the searching of strings to find occurrences of other strings. Several character-string concepts and operations have been discussed in previous chapters; these include declaration of variable-length strings, assignment of character strings to character variables, replication of strings, and concatenation of character strings. Each of these concepts and operations is briefly reviewed in the following examples.

1. DCL C CHAR(5);
   Character variable C is declared as a character string of length 5. The length of C is fixed and does not vary.
2. DCL T CHAR(20) VAR INIT('ABC');
   Character variable T is declared as a character string of length 20. The length of T can vary from zero (the null string) to 20. T is initialized to string 'ABC', which has length 3.
3. T = '';
   Given that variable T is declared according to example 2, the string of length zero (the null string) is assigned to T.
4. C = '';
   Given that variable C is declared according to example 1, the string 'b̸b̸b̸b̸b̸' (five blanks) is assigned to C. Even though the null string is apparently assigned to C, the string actually assigned to C is padded with enough blanks to equal the length of C, because C is a fixed-length character variable. Data stored in character variables is left-justified; i.e., data is placed in the left-most portion of the string, and blanks are padded on the right. For example, the string 'ABb̸b̸b̸' is stored in C by executing this assignment statement:

   C = 'AB';
5. T = (3)'ABC';
   Given that variable T is declared according to example 2, the string 'ABCABCABC' is assigned to T, because a replication factor of 3 is used. The replication factor can also be used in the INITIAL attribute of the DECLARE statement.
6. T = 'GOOD' || 'b̸' || 'GRIEF';
   Given that variable T is declared according to example 2, the string 'GOOD GRIEF' is assigned to T because of the two concatenation operations.

There are also several built-in functions that provide more extensive manipulations on character strings. These functions and several examples are discussed in the next two sections.

7.2. BUILT-IN CHARACTER-STRING FUNCTIONS

PL/I provides many built-in function procedures that are quite useful for problem solving. Several built-in numeric functions were presented in Chapter 6; here we discuss four character-string functions. Both types of functions are invoked in the same manner, and only one value is returned by a function invocation. However, numeric functions return only numeric values, whereas character-string functions return either character strings or numeric values that pertain to character strings.

The four built-in character-string functions used in this section are listed in Table 7.1, which gives a short description of the arguments and the values returned. There is at least one argument that is a string expression in each of the functions (recall that constants and variables are also considered expressions). However, only the SUBSTR function returns a string; the other functions return integer values.

The first function described in Table 7.1 is the LENGTH function, which counts the number of characters in the string expression that is the argument for this function. Function LENGTH then returns this character count. The following examples illustrate how the LENGTH function is used.

1. I = LENGTH ('ABC');	The value 3 is stored in variable I.
2. I = LENGTH ('');	The value 0 is stored in variable I.
3. I = LENGTH ('ABC' || 'DE');	The value 5 is stored in variable I.
4. I = LENGTH ('ABC') + LENGTH ('DE');	The value 5 is stored in variable I.

In example 2, the null string is an argument to the LENGTH function. The null string contains no characters (not even blanks) and has length zero. The concatenation operator is used in example 3 to show that an argument can be any string expression. The value returned by the LENGTH function is an integer value, and example 4 shows how these values can be used in a numeric expression.

Table 7.1 contains two variations of the SUBSTR function, which is used to specify a portion of a given character string. The only difference in the two variations is the length of the specified substring. (The name SUBSTR is quite appropriate, because it is an acronym for substring.) The first argument to this function is the string from which a substring is specified. The second argument is the position in the string of the first character of the substring being specified. The optional third argument to this function specifies the number of characters in the substring. If this argument is missing, the substring consists of all remaining characters in the string, starting from the position indicated by the second argument.

TABLE 7.1. Built-in character-string functions.

Typical function invocation	*Meaning of arguments*	*Value returned*
LENGTH (SE)	SE, string expression	Integer value equal to the number of characters in SE
SUBSTR (SE,I,N)	SE, string expression I, integer expression N, integer expression	The substring of SE beginning with the Ith character and consisting of N consecutive characters
SUBSTR (SE,I)	same	The substring of SE beginning with the Ith character and continuing to the end of SE
INDEX (SE,P)	SE, string expression P, string expression	If P is a substring in SE, the starting position of the first character of P in SE is returned. If P is not a substring in SE, zero is returned.
VERIFY (SE,C)	SE, string expression C, string expression	If every character in SE appears somewhere in C, zero is returned. Otherwise, the position of the first character in SE which does not appear in C is returned.

For each of the following examples, assume that character variables SE and C are declared with this statement:

```
DCL  SE  CHAR(20)  VAR  INIT('THE QUICK BROWN FOX'),
     C   CHAR(10)  VAR;
```

1. C = SUBSTR (SE,7,7);	The value 'ICK BRO' is stored in variable C.
2. C = SUBSTR (SE,13);	The value 'OWN FOX' is stored in variable C.
3. C = SUBSTR(SE,12,3) || SUBSTR(SE,4,6);	The value 'ROW QUICK' is stored in the variable C.
4. C = SUBSTR (SUBSTR(SE,11),1,5);	The value 'BROWN' is stored in variable C.

5. SUBSTR (SE,11,5) = 'GREEN'; The substring 'BROWN' is replaced with the string 'GREEN'. Variable SE then contains the string 'THE QUICK GREEN FOX'.

Examples 1 and 2 illustrate common uses of the SUBSTR function. In example 1, the function returns a substring that begins at position 5 of the string contained in variable SE and consists of seven characters. In example 2, the function returns the substring that begins with the 13th character of the string contained in variable SE and ends with the last character in that string. The substrings returned by the SUBSTR function in example 3 are joined together by the concatenation operator. In example 4, a substring returned by the SUBSTR function is used as an argument in another invocation of that function.

Example 5 shows the use of the SUBSTR function as a *pseudovariable*. A function is called a pseudovariable when it appears on the left side of an equals sign in an assignment statement or when it appears as a data item in a GET statement. When the SUBSTR function is used as a pseudovariable, only a specified substring is replaced, rather than the entire string. In example 5, the substring that begins at position 11 in variable SE and consists of five characters is replaced by another string. The remainder of the string in SE is left intact. When used as a pseudovariable, the SUBSTR function can change the characters within a substring, but the length of the original string cannot be changed. Consider the following statements, where SE is declared as before:

```
SUBSTR (SE,11,5) = 'ORANGE';
SUBSTR (SE,11,5) = '';
```

According to the first statement, a substring of length 5 is replaced with a string of length 6. Replacement of the substring is done character by character; so the string 'THE QUICK ORANG FOX' is stored in variable SE after this statement is executed. Similarly, in the second statement, the length of SE cannot be altered; so the string 'THE QUICK b̸b̸b̸b̸b̸ FOX' is stored in variable SE after that statement is executed.

Table 7.1 contains a summary of the INDEX function, which is used to search a string for the first occurrence of a particular substring. If the substring is located, then the starting position within the string is returned; otherwise the value zero is returned.

For each of the following examples, assume that variables SE and I are declared with this statement:

```
DCL  SE  CHAR(25)  VAR  INIT ('TO BE OR NOT TO BE'),
     I   FIXED;
```

1. I = INDEX (SE,'B');	The value 4 is stored in variable I.
2. I = INDEX (SE,'BET');	The value 0 is stored in variable I.
3. I = INDEX (SE,'OR NOT TO');	The value 7 is stored in variable I.

Although the character B occurs twice in the string contained by variable SE, only the position of the first occurrence is returned in example 1. In example 2, the substring 'BET' cannot be found; so the value zero is returned. Finally, in example 3 the substring 'OR NOT TO' is found, and the position of the first character of that substring within the string being searched is returned.

The last built-in character-string function summarized in Table 7.1 is the VERIFY function, which is used to find out whether the string in the first argument is composed solely of characters that appear somewhere in the string in the second argument. The value zero is returned if this condition is true. If this condition is not true, the position of the first nonmatching character in the first argument is returned.

For each of the following examples, assume that variables SE and I are declared with this statement:

```
DCL  SE  CHAR(20)  VAR  INIT ('AN APPLE A DAY'),
     I   FIXED;
```

1. I = VERIFY (SE,'ABC');	The value 2 is stored in variable I.
2. I = VERIFY ('$456.83','0123456789.$');	The value 0 is stored in variable I.
3. I = VERIFY ('X=X+X+X','X=+');	The value 0 is stored in variable I.

In example 1, the character N does not appear anywhere in the string 'ABC', so the position of character N within the string contained in variable SE is returned. There are other characters in this string that do not appear in 'ABC', but only the position of the first mismatch is returned. In examples 2 and 3, all the characters in the first argument are found somewhere in the second argument; so the value zero is returned.

These four functions are very useful for performing many character-string manipulations, and they play an important role in the solutions to the problems in the next section. Of all the functions discussed so far, only the SUBSTR function can be used as a pseudovariable. All the functions can be used in numeric or character expressions, as long as there is no conflict of data type; e.g., one cannot add a numeric value to a string of alphabetic characters.

7.3. EXAMPLES

Solutions to two complete problems are presented in this section. The problems involve character manipulation, and the functions discussed in section 7.2 are used extensively.

7.3.1. Vowel Counting

The problem here is to count the number of each of the vowels (A,E,I,O, and U) that appear in several lines of text. The character functions used in this problem are the VERIFY function and the SUBSTR function. This problem also reinforces the concepts of stream input and nested IF statements.

The SUBSTR function is used in Program 7.1 to generate the lines of the histogram; in this case, the substring returned is a specified number of asterisks of character variable SPLATS. The VERIFY function decides whether the input character is a vowel. If the character is a vowel, the nested IF statements are executed to decide which vowel it is. If the input character is not a vowel, no further checking is done, and the next input character is obtained. The character variable SPLATS is initialized to 100 asterisks, with a replication factor in the INITIAL clause. Note also that in the last PUT EDIT statement there are several sets of data elements, but only one set of specifications. This is perfectly valid, and the specifications are used repeatedly as necessary.

7.3.2. The Censor Problem

A small newspaper has decided to censor all incoming text from its wire services by replacing all four-letter words with asterisks. This is an ideal character-string handling problem; it makes good use of concatenation and of most of the character-string functions. In particular, the SUBSTR function is used both as a pseudovariable and as a value-returning function.

An arbitrary number of input lines are processed with the help of the ON ENDFILE statement. This statement works equally well with either punched-card input or computer-terminal input. The end-of-file condition for terminals is generally raised by depressing the "return" key one extra time.

The IF statement is really the heart of the preceding program, because it decides which words consist of four letters. The THEN portion of the IF statement contains an invocation of the SUBSTR function (or pseudovariable, in this case), which replaces four-letter words with asterisks.

Concatenation is used to build an output line with the help of the SUBSTR function, which returns a substring consisting of the current word and the next adjacent blank (if any). Character variable TEXT shrinks with the aid of another SUBSTR function, which has two arguments. Ultimately, the string in variable TEXT will become empty; the output line is then displayed, another line of input text is obtained, and the entire process is repeated as long as input data is available.

PROGRAM 7.1.

PROBLEM DEFINITION

The input consists of an arbitrary number of lines of text. Each character in this text is checked to find out whether it is a vowel. If the character is a vowel, then the counter for that vowel is incremented. The output consists of the input text, followed by the number of occurrences of each of the vowels and a histogram representing these occurrences.

Sample input:

```
THIS IS THE FIRST LINE OF TEXT
AND THIS IS THE FINAL LINE
```

Sample output:

```
**TEXT TO BE PROCESSED**
THIS IS THE FIRST LINE OF TEXT
AND THIS IS THE FINAL LINE
```

VOWEL OCCURRENCES	HISTOGRAM
#A'S = 2	* *
#E'S = 5	* * * * *
#I'S = 8	* * * * * * * *
#O'S = 1	*
#U'S = 0	

Each line of the histogram is limited to 100 characters. If the actual count for a vowel exceeds 100, then only MOD(101,X) asterisks appear on that line, where X is the desired number of asterisks.

ALGORITHM DESIGN

Variables to be used:

C	each individual character (input)
A,E,I,O,U	counters for the vowels
FLAG	set to 1 when end-of-file encountered
SPLATS	100 asterisks
OTHERS	blank plus the consonants

PSEUDOCODE

```
Initialize counters A,E,I,O,U to zero
GET a character C
DO while input data is available
    IF C is a vowel
        THEN add 1 to A,E,I,O,U as appropriate
    GET next character C
END
PUT A,E,I,O,U and corresponding histogram
END
```

ALGORITHM IMPLEMENTATION

```
/* PROGRAM TO COUNT THE NUMBER OF VOWELS */
VOWELS: PROC OPTIONS(MAIN);
          DCL C CHAR(1),
              (A,E,I,O,U,FLAG) FIXED INIT(0),
              SPLATS CHAR(100) INIT((10)‘**********’);
          ON ENDFILE (SYSIN) FLAG = 1;
          PUT LIST(‘**TEXT TO BE PROCESSED**’);
          PUT SKIP;
          GET EDIT (C) (A(1));
          DO WHILE (FLAG = 0);
             PUT EDIT (C) (A(1));
             IF VERIFY(C,‘AEIOU’) = 0
               THEN IF C = ‘A’
                      THEN A = A + 1;
                      ELSE IF C = ‘E’
                             THEN E = E + 1;
                             ELSE IF C = ‘I’
                                    THEN I = I + 1;
                                    ELSE IF C = ‘O’
                                           THEN O = O + 1;
                                           ELSE U = U + 1;
          GET EDIT (C) (A(1));
          END;
          PUT EDIT(‘VOWEL’,‘OCCURRENCES’,‘HISTOGRAM’)
                (SKIP(2),COL(4),A,COL(1),A,COL(20),A);
          PUT EDIT(‘#A’‘S=’,A,SUBSTR(SPLATS,1,MOD(A,101)),
                ‘#E’‘S=’,E,SUBSTR(SPLATS,1,MOD(E,101)),
                ‘#I’‘S=’,I,SUBSTR(SPLATS,1,MOD(I,101)),
                ‘#O’‘S=’,O,SUBSTR(SPLATS,1,MOD(O,101)),
                ‘#U’‘S=’,U,SUBSTR(SPLATS,1,MOD(U,101)))
                (COL(1),A,F(3),COL(20),A);
       END VOWELS;
```

PROGRAM 7.2.

PROBLEM DEFINITION

The input consists of an arbitrary number of lines of text. Each line of text contains words that are separated by one or more blanks; i.e., every word has one or more blanks to its right (including the last word in a line). No punctuation is used, and a word may not span two lines of text. Each four-letter word is replaced with four asterisks. The output consists of the input lines of text, which have been properly censored.

Sample input: ALL FOUR-LETTER WORDS MUST BE
REPLACED WITH FOUR ASTERISKS

Sample output: CENSORED OUTPUT
ALL FOUR-LETTER WORDS **** BE
REPLACED **** **** ASTERISKS

ALGORITHM DESIGN

Variables to be used:

TEXT	Input line of text
OUT	Output line of text
FLAG	Set to 1 when end of file encountered
I	Position of next blank in TEXT

PSEUDOCODE

```
GET TEXT
DO while input is available
    place null string in OUT
    DO while TEXT is not empty (null)
        find next word
        IF word length = 4
           then replace word with 4 asterisks
        concatenate OUT with word
        remove word from TEXT
    END
    PUT OUT
    GET TEXT
END
END
```

ALGORITHM IMPLEMENTATION

Most of the pseudocode can be translated to PL/I in a straightforward manner. However, finding the next word requires locating the blanks that separate words. The INDEX function is well-suited for this task, as is the LENGTH function for counting the length of character strings.

```
/* CENSOR PROGRAM                         */
/* REPLACE FOUR-LETTER WORDS WITH **** */
CENSOR: PROC OPTIONS(MAIN);
          DCL (TEXT,OUT) CHAR(80) VAR,
               (FLAG,I) INIT(0);
          ON ENDFILE(SYSIN) FLAG=1;
          PUT SKIP LIST('CENSORED OUTPUT');
          PUT SKIP(2);
          GET EDIT(TEXT) (A(80));
          DO WHILE(FLAG = 0);
              OUT = '';
              DO WHILE (LENGTH(TEXT) > 0);
                  I = INDEX(TEXT,' ');
                  IF I - 1 = 4
                     THEN SUBSTR(TEXT,1,4)='****';
                  OUT = OUT || SUBSTR(TEXT,1,I);
                  TEXT = SUBSTR(TEXT,I+1);
              END;
              PUT EDIT (OUT) (COL(1),A);
              GET EDIT (TEXT) (A(80));
          END;
     END CENSOR;
```

7.4. SUMMARY

The purpose of this chapter is twofold:

a. to introduce several built-in character-string functions
b. to present techniques for solving problems that involve character strings

Four built-in character-string functions are discussed in this chapter. Character-string expressions are used as one or more arguments for each of these functions.

7.4.1. Key Concepts

1. A character-string variable must be declared with a specific length; however, the VARYING (VAR) and INITIAL (INIT) attributes are optional.
2. The LENGTH function counts the numbers of characters in a string.
3. The SUBSTR function deals with substrings and can be used as a pseudovariable.
4. The INDEX function locates a substring within another string.
5. The VERIFY function decides whether every character in one string appears in another string.
6. The built-in character-string functions can be used in any statement where character-string expressions are allowed.

7.4.2. Terms and Phrases

Write out definitions and/or usage descriptions of these terms. Check yourself against the text.

built-in character-string function	pseudovariable
concatenation	replication
INDEX	SUBSTR
LENGTH	variable-length string
null string	VERIFY

PROBLEMS

Problem 7.1. Assume that this declaration statement holds for each of the following:

```
DCL (A,B) CHAR(15) VAR INIT('BILLDAVEMISS'),
    N FIXED;
```

a. B = SUBSTR(A,6,3) || SUBSTR(A,2,4) || 'BON';
   The value stored in variable B is ______________________

b. N = LENGTH(A) − 4;
   SUBSTR(B,N,2) = A;
   The value stored in variable B is ______________________

c. N = INDEX (A,'DAVE');
   B = SUBSTR(A,1,N−1) || SUBSTR(A,N+4);
   The value stored in variable B is ______________________

Problem 7.2. Use the problem-solving process to develop a solution for this problem. The input consists of one character string that contains an unknown number of integers, where the integers are separated by one or more blanks. Find and display the sum of those integers.

Sample input: '6 85 −13 612 38 101'

Sample output:

```
SUMMATION PROBLEM
-----------------
    INTEGERS
-----------------
          6
         85
        -13
        612
         38
        101
  THE SUM IS 829
-----------------
```

Problem 7.3. Detection of IF statements.

The input consists of a syntactically correct PL/I program. Count the number of IF statements in that program, but ignore anything contained in the comments. Don't forget to count the IF statements which are part of a THEN or ELSE clause.

Sample input:

```
/* COUNT THE IF STATEMENTS */
SAMPLE:
  PROC OPTIONS(MAIN);
    DCL(A,B,C) FIXED;
    GET LIST(A,B,C);
    IF A > B
      THEN IF B > C
        THEN A = 2;
/*    ELSE IF A < C
        THEN B = 6;
    IF C = 4
      THEN A = 16;              */
    PUT LIST(A,B,C);
  END SAMPLE;
```

Sample output: Display the input program and note the IF statements detected:

THE NUMBER OF IFS IS 2

Problem 7.4. Checking the syntax of assignment statements.

The input consists of an arbitrary number of PL/I-like assignment statements. The problem is to decide whether each of these statements is syntactically correct. If such a statement is correct, the message "ERROR FREE" is displayed; otherwise a list of all detected errors is displayed, as illustrated in the sample output.

The syntax for this special type of assignment statement is

variable = *expression;*

where *variable* is a single letter A–Z, and
expression is any one of:

a. *variable*
b. *constant* (single digit 0–9)
c. *variable* or *constant operator expression*, with operator being one of +, −, *, /
(i.e., exponentiation and unary operators are not permitted)

Additional restrictions:

a. blanks are not permitted
b. only one statement per line
c. parentheses are not permitted

The possible error messages are:

1. MISSING SEMICOLON
2. IMPROPERLY FORMED EXPRESSION
3. OTHER THAN ONE VARIABLE PRECEDES THE EQUALS SIGN
4. MISSING EQUALS SIGN
5. MORE THAN ONE EQUALS SIGN
6. TWO OPERATORS APPEAR CONSECUTIVELY

Sample input:

```
Z=AB+-;
X=6;
AB
A=B=5;
```

Sample output:

SYNTAX CHECKER

STATEMENT	COMMENTS
Z=AB+−;	2. IMPROPERLY FORMED EXPRESSION
X=6;	** ERROR FREE **
AB	1. MISSING SEMICOLON
	2. IMPROPERLY FORMED EXPRESSION
	4. MISSING EQUALS SIGN
A=B=5;	5. MORE THAN ONE EQUALS SIGN

Problem 7.5. Justification of type lines.

The input consists of an arbitrary number of lines of text, each containing no more than 80 characters. For each of these lines, an output line is created that contains exactly 80 characters and is both left- and right-justified. Extra blanks may be needed to achieve this, and they should be distributed between the various words of that line as evenly as possible.

Sample input: (For convenience only 20-character lines are used)

```
THIS IS A SAMPLE OF
JUSTIFICATION FOR
THREE TYPE LINES.
```

Sample output:

```
THIS IS A SAMPLE OF
JUSTIFICATION    FOR
THREE   TYPE  LINES.
```

Problem 7.6. Counting word occurrences.

The input consists of any arbitrary number of lines of text. The problem is to count the number of occurrences of the words 'THESE', 'THEM', and 'THOSE'.

Sample input: lines of text

Sample output:

COUNTING WORD OCCURRENCES

WORD	# OCCURRENCES
THESE	___
THEM	___
THOSE	___

Problem 7.7. Encoding and decoding.

Encoding is the process of transforming a message into a coded form by means of some coding scheme. Decoding is the process of transforming the coded form back to the original message. Encoding and decoding are both done character by character, and blanks are ignored. The coding scheme is as follows:

```
Alphabet: A B C D E F G H I J K L M N O P Q R S T U V W X Y Z , .
Code:     F O K P R G W N V A L U D Q E Z T J K Y , M I S . B H C
```

The input consists of an arbitrary number of lines of text. If the first character of a line is a '1', then that line should be encoded by means of the coding scheme. If the first character of a line is a '0', then that line should be decoded into the English message using the coding scheme. The input may consist of both text to be encoded and text to be decoded.

Sample input: '1THIS IS A TOP SECRET MESSAGE.'
'0YNVX VEELX DRXX.C'

Sample output: THIS IS A TOP SECRET MESSAGE.
YNVX VX F YEZ KRKJRY DRXXFWRC

YNVX VEELX DRXX.C
THIS LOOKS MESSY.

Problem 7.8. Palindromes.

A palindrome is a character string or a number that is the same whether read from right to left or from left to right. The input consists of an arbitrary number of character strings and numbers to be checked.

Sample input: 'CAT', 'TOOT', 'MOM', '123', '5143415',
'ABLE WAS I ERE I SAW ELBA'

Sample output:

INPUT	REVERSED	PALINDROME?
CAT	TAC	NO
TOOT	TOOT	YES
MOM	MOM	YES
123	321	NO
5143415	5143415	YES
ABLE WAS I ERE I SAW ELBA	ABLE WAS I ERE I SAW ELBA	YES

Problem 7.9. Underlining.

Underline all the input words which begin with the letter T. The input consists of an arbitrary number of lines of text. Each line contains one or more words separated by blanks, but does not contain any punctuation. Note: underlining may not be possible for many interactive terminals.

Sample input: 'THIS IS THE INPUT TEXT'
'THROW THE BALL TO TOM'

Sample output: <u>THIS</u> IS <u>THE</u> INPUT <u>TEXT</u>
<u>THROW</u> <u>THE</u> BALL <u>TO</u> <u>TOM</u>

Problem 7.10. Eliminating excess blanks.

The input consists of an arbitrary number of lines of text, where there may be excess blanks between the words. The output must have only one blank between each word and two blanks between each sentence.

Sample input:

```
'THIS IS A SAMPLE. THE TASK'
'IS TO ELIMINATE      EXCESS'
'BLANKS. THE              END.'
```

Sample output:

```
THIS IS A SAMPLE. THE TASK
IS TO ELIMINATE EXCESS
BLANKS. THE END.
```

8 Arrays

Suppose that the solution to a problem requires the storing of 100 data items for subsequent use. To do so, we could create 100 variable names and store the values with a long series of GET statements or assignment statements. This process would be lengthy, time-consuming, and highly error-prone.

Fortunately, this task can be greatly simplified by the use of an array. An array is simply a construct which permits storing and referring to many data values (or data elements) with only one variable name. The rules for creating names for arrays are the same as those for creating variable names, because an array is simply a variable that has more than one data value associated with it. An array can be FIXED, FLOAT, or CHARACTER, and all data elements in the array have exactly the same characteristics; e.g., if the array is FIXED, then every data element in the array is FIXED.

8.1. ONE-DIMENSIONAL ARRAYS

The simplest form of an array is the one-dimensional array, which can be visualized as a column of values. For example, array A, which contains five data elements, would appear as in Figure 8.1.

If array A were FIXED, then each data element in A could be used anywhere that any other FIXED variable could be used, e.g., in assignment statements or in GET statements. However, we will need to uniquely identify each element in the array in order to use it. For example, how would the third element of array A be labeled? Note that in Figure 8.1 the elements of A are numbered 1, 2, 3, 4, and 5. These numbers uniquely label each element in the array and are called *subscripts*. A subscript is enclosed in parentheses and immediately follows the array name when a particular data element is referred to. For example, A(3) (pronounced "A sub 3") refers to the third element of array A. Similarly, A(5) refers to the fifth element of array A. We can also refer to A(3) and A(5) as *subscripted variables*, meaning data elements in an array.

Subscripted variables can be used wherever other variables can be used. Consider the following assignment statements and their effect on array A, which is FIXED:

```
A(1) = 0;
A(2) = 25;
A(3) = 0;
A(4) = A(2) - 6;
A(5) = 0;
```

After these statements are executed, array A would appear as in Figure 8.2.

Note that in the fourth statement of the preceding assignment statements, the subscripted variable A(2) is used in an expression to compute a value for A(4). Recall that a subscripted variable can be used wherever a nonsubscripted variable can be used.

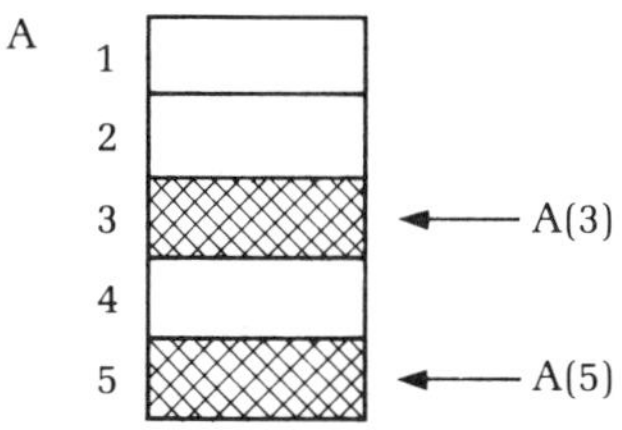

Figure 8.1.

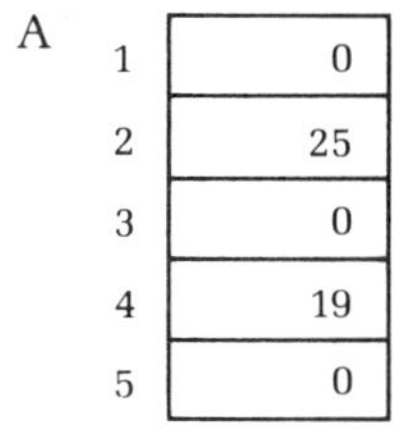

Figure 8.2.

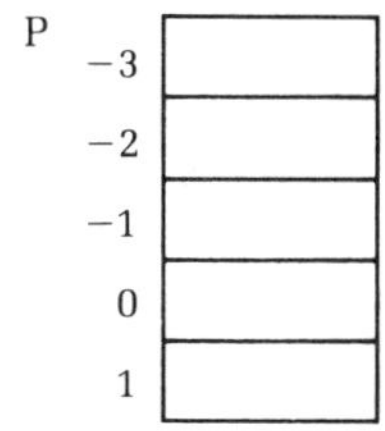

Figure 8.3.

The compiler must be given information about an array with a DECLARE statement. For example, array A in the previous example is declared as:

```
DCL        A(5)        FIXED;
```

This declaration statement specifies the name of the array, the size of the array, and the data type of each element in the array. All arrays must be declared; if array A were not declared, a reference to a subscripted variable such as A(3) would result in a fatal error. The general forms of the DECLARE statement for one-dimensional arrays are:

1. DCL *array name (upper subscript bound) attribute(s);*
2. DCL *array name (lower subscript bound: upper subscript bound) attribute(s);*

The "upper subscript bound" is the maximum subscript value permitted for that array. Similarly, the "lower subscript bound" (general form 2) is the minimum subscript value permitted. If the lower subscript bound is omitted, as in general form 1, then the lower bound is assumed to be 1. Subscripts are always integer values, but they can be negative, zero, or positive. Consider the following declaration and the depiction of its corresponding array in Figure 8.3. The first element of array P is the subscripted variable P(−3) and the last element is P(1). Subscripted variable P(0) is permitted, but P(2) is not, because the subscript 2 exceeds the upper subscript bound, which here is 1.

Subscripts have been represented as integer constants in the preceding examples, but are not restricted to constants. Subscripts can be numeric expressions, preferably integer expressions.* However, if the value of an expression is not an integer number, all digits to the right of the decimal point are truncated. Consider the following statements, where A is an array and X is a FLOAT variable.

```
X = 5.8;
A(X+2) = 19;
```

*All subscripts must be integer values for Subset G.

The expression X+2 results in the value of 7.8, but the actual subscript is truncated to 7.

Some situations arise in which subscripts are not used at all to refer to arrays. In general, when an array name is referred to in a statement, but a subscript is not included, the entire array is referred to, not just one data element. The following examples illustrate this point. (Assume that A is declared as: DCL A(10) FIXED;)

```
1. GET LIST (A);
2. PUT LIST (A);
3. A = 0;
4. A = A+1;
```

Example 1 is logically equivalent to the statements

```
DO I = 1 TO 10;
   GET LIST (A(I));
END;
```

In other words, ten data values are taken from the input stream and placed into A(1), A(2), . . . A(10), respectively. Similarly, example 2 is logically equivalent to the statements

```
DO I = 1 TO 10;
   PUT LIST (A(I));
END;
```

Examples 1 and 2 provide a convenient notation for the input and output of entire arrays. Example 3 illustrates how every element in an array can be assigned a value by only one statement. This statement is logically equivalent to the statements

```
DO I = 1 TO 10;
   A(I) = 0;
END;
```

Finally, example 4 demonstrates how a value can be added to each element in an array. The statement in this example is logically equivalent to the statements

```
DO I = 1 TO 10;
   A(I) = A(I) + 1;
END;
```

All four of these examples involved a numeric array. However, similar operations can be performed with CHARACTER arrays. Suppose that C is a varying CHARACTER array in which each of ten elements can contain up to 15 charac-

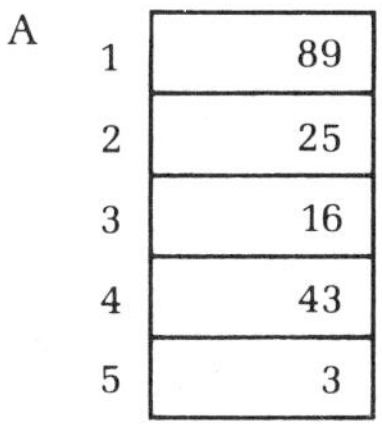

Figure 8.4.

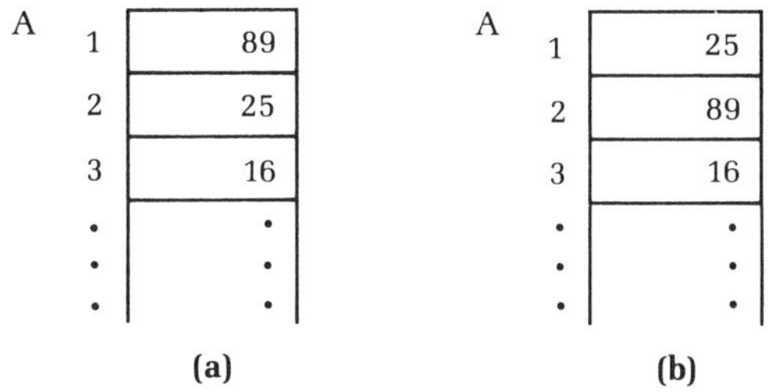

Figure 8.5. *(a) Before exchange, the first pair of values is out of order. (b) After exchange, the second pair of values is out of order.*

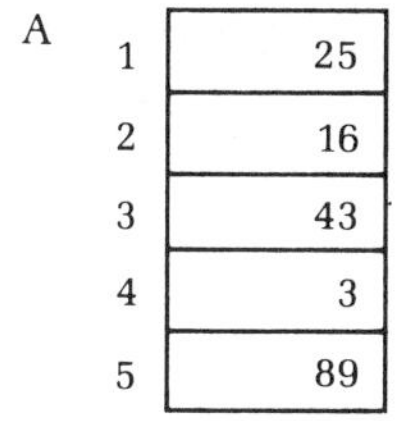

Figure 8.6. *Array A after the first pass.*

ters. The following character-string examples are analogous to the preceding numeric examples:

1. GET LIST (C);
2. PUT LIST (C);
3. C = 'ABC';
4. C = C||'MORE';

The only significant difference between these sets of examples is that in example 4 here, a concatenation operation is performed, rather than addition, as in the numeric example.

Following are three completely solved problems that use arrays. The sort problem uses a FIXED array; the mean and standard-deviation problem uses a FLOAT array; and the French-verb problem uses a CHARACTER array.

8.1.1. The Bubble-Sort Problem

The primary purpose of this problem is to sort the elements of FIXED array A in ascending order; i.e., to place the smallest value in A(1), the next smallest value in A(2), and so on.

For simplicity, assume that array A has 5 elements and contains the values shown in Figure 8.4.

One way to sort the array is to test the values in adjacent pairs of elements to determine whether the values in that pair are in the proper order. If the two values are not in the proper order, they are exchanged. In this example, the pairs of elements are A(1) – A(2), A(2) – A(3), A(3) – A(4), and A(4) – A(5). The values in the first pair are out of order and need to be exchanged, as shown in Figure 8.5. This process of comparing and exchanging, if necessary, continues for the A(2) – A(3) pair, the A(3) – A(4) pair, and the A(4) – A(5) pair. After this first "pass" through the array, A has the values shown in Figure 8.6. The array is still not sorted, so the entire process must be repeated, starting with the A(1) – A(2) pair. In fact, a total of four sorting passes is required to sort

PROGRAM 8.1.

PROBLEM DEFINITION

Array A is FIXED and contains ten elements. The input consists of ten arbitrary integer values, which are stored in array A. The array is sorted in ascending order (smallest first) by the bubble-sort technique. The output consists of the sorted values of array A. Although this problem is defined for a specific array size, the solution must be general. That is, only minor modifications should be necessary to sort arrays of any size.

Sample input: 62 103 96 13 89 26 18 72 41 2

Sample output:

```
THE SORTED DATA VALUES ARE
 2  13  18  26   41
62  72  89  96  103
```

ALGORITHM DESIGN

A subroutine is used to perform the sorting, and the main procedure handles the input and the output.

Variables to be used:

A	array of FIXED data elements
I	subscript
N	number of elements in array A
TEMP	temporary variable (for exchanging)
J	counter

PSEUDOCODE

Main Procedure:

```
GET A
assign 10 to N
CALL SORT
PUT A
END
```

Subroutine SORT:

```
Do the following N−1 times (or DO J = 1 to N − 1)
  DO I = 1 TO N − J
    IF A(I) < A(I + 1)
      THEN exchange A(I) and A(I + 1)
  END
END
RETURN
```

ALGORITHM IMPLEMENTATION

```
/* SORT VALUES IN ARRAY USING THE BUBBLE SORT
   TECHNIQUE */
BUBBLE: PROC OPTIONS (MAIN);
          DCL (A(10),I,J,N,TEMP) FIXED;
          GET LIST (A);
          N=10;
          CALL SORT;
          PUT SKIP LIST('THE SORTED DATA VALUES ARE');
          PUT SKIP LIST (A);
SORT: PROC;                              /* SUBROUTINE SORT */
        DO J = 1 TO N - 1;               /* N - 1 PASSES    */
          DO I = 1 TO N - J;             /* BEGIN A PASS    */
            IF A(I) > A(I + 1)
              THEN DO;                   /* EXCHANGE        */
                     TEMP = A(I);
                     A(I) = A(I + 1);
                     A(I + 1) = TEMP;
                   END;
          END;
        END;
        RETURN;
      END SORT;
      END BUBBLE;
```

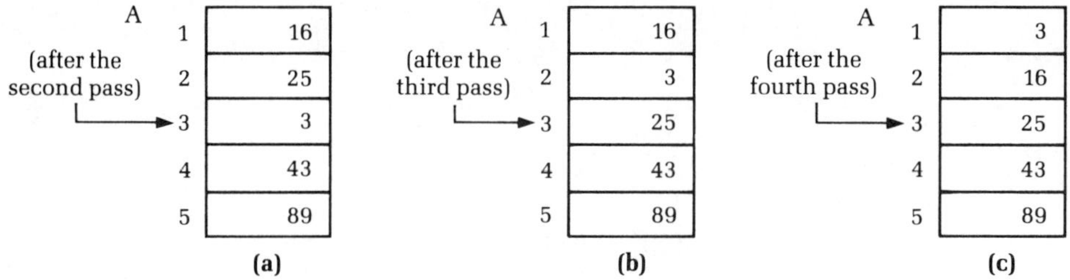

Figure 8.7.

this array. The results of the remaining passes are displayed in Figure 8.7.

This sorting technique is called the bubble sort, because the smallest values in the array bubble up with each successive sorting pass. Note that the larger values drop down in the array. After the first pass, the largest value in the array is guaranteed to be placed in the last position of the array. Similarly, after the second pass, the next largest value is in the next to last position in the array. With each successive pass, one less pair of values needs to be compared.

The second DO statement in subroutine SORT is

```
DO I = 1 TO N - J;
```

The final value of variable I is specified as N − J rather than N − 1, because one less pair of values needs to be compared with each successive pass through the array, since the larger values drop to the bottom of the array in a predictable manner.

The temporary variable TEMP is necessary to preserve the values of A(I) and A(I + 1) while their values are being exchanged. Consider the following statements, which do not use a temporary variable:

```
A(I) = A(I + 1);
A(I + 1) = A(I);
```

The original value of A(I) is lost, and the value of A(I+1) is placed in both of these variables. If a temporary variable is used, both values are saved, and the values of the variables are exchanged as follows:

```
TEMP = A(I);
A(I) = A(I + 1);
A(I + 1) = TEMP;
```

Here the original value of variable A(I) is saved, in TEMP, and can then be placed in variable A(I + 1), after A(I) acquires the original value of A(I + 1). This same principle of using a temporary variable for exchanging the contents of two variables is used in the sorting examples of Chapter 5.

8.1.2. The Mean and Standard-Deviation Problem

The purpose of this problem is to compute the mean and standard deviation for a group of floating-point numbers. The mean (M) and standard deviation (SDEV) are defined as

$$M = \sum_{i=1}^{N} X_i/N$$

$$\text{SDEV} = \sqrt{\frac{\sum_{i=1}^{N} (X_i - M)^2}{N - 1}}.$$

There are N data values ($N > 1$), and the notation X_i represents an individual data element. The mean is computed by summing all the data elements and dividing by N. The mean is then used in the computation of the standard deviation, which also uses a summation operation.

The following computation shows how these formulas are applied in a relatively simple case. Suppose that there are only three data values, 2, 3, 4:

$$N = 3$$
$$\Sigma X = 2 + 3 + 4 = 9$$
$$M = 9/3 = 3$$
$$\Sigma(X - M)^2 = (2 - 3)^2 + (3 - 3)^2 + (4 - 3)^2 = 2$$
$$\text{SDEV} = \sqrt{\frac{2}{3 - 1}} = \sqrt{1} = 1$$

Two special cases must be considered in order to design a solution to this problem. (1) If there are less than two input data values, i.e., $N < 2$, division by zero would occur. (2) There may be too many input data values to be stored in the array. An array is declared to be a certain size, i.e., it contains a specific number of elements, say 50 for this problem. Consequently, if there are more than 50 input data values, only the first 50 are used.

The use of an array is essential to the solution of this problem, because each data value must be referred to twice. The first reference occurs during the input and summation of data values in preparation for the computation of the mean. The second reference occurs during the summation needed to compute the standard deviation.

There are several other noteworthy features of this program. The variable X is not really necessary in this program, because data can be stored in an array directly and retrieved directly. All the references to variable X can be replaced with an appropriate reference to the array A; e.g., the statement "SX = SX + A(I);" could be used in place of the statement "SX = SX + X;" that appears in the program. In fact, the program could be shortened by one statement if variable X were not used. Despite this, the variable X is used, because its appear-

PROGRAM 8.2.

PROBLEM DEFINITION

The input consists of an arbitrary number of floating-point data values. The mean and standard deviation of these numbers are computed using the formulas given above. The output consists of all input values, the computed mean, and the computed standard deviation. An error message is displayed if less than two input data values are available. If more than 50 input data values are available, only the first 50 are processed.

Sample input: 75.6 89.3 73.4 66.2

Sample output: DATA VALUES ARE:
75.6 89.3 73.4 66.2
THE MEAN IS 76.125
THE STANDARD DEVIATION IS 9.6573

ALGORITHM DESIGN

Assume that A is a FLOAT array which contains 50 elements. The pseudocode is developed in two steps; the first step illustrates the general solution, and the second step is a refinement of the first step.

Variables to be used:

A	array of FLOAT data elements
N	number of elements in array A
X	an individual input data value
SX	ΣX
M	Mean
SD2	$\Sigma(X - M)^2$
SDEV	standard deviation
I	subscript
FLAG	signals end-of-file condition

PSEUDOCODE

```
Initialize variables
GET and PUT input data values
  store data values in array A
  check the number of data values to determine whether to pro-
    ceed
  compute the mean
Compute the standard deviation using the mean and values stored
    in A
PUT mean and standard deviation
```

PSEUDOCODE REFINEMENT

```
Initialize variables N, SX, SD2 to zero
GET X
PUT heading
DO I = 1 TO 50 while input data is available
    PUT X
    A(I) = X
    SX = SX + X
    GET X
END
N = I − 1
IF N is greater than or equal to 2
  THEN M = SX/N
         DO I = 1 TO N
              SD2 = SD2 + (A(I) − M)²
         END
         SDEV = SQRT (SD2/(N − 1))
         PUT M, SDEV
  ELSE PUT error message
END
```

ALGORITHM IMPLEMENTATION

```
/* COMPUTE THE MEAN AND STANDARD DEVIATION                    */
/* OF AN ARBITRARY NUMBER OF INPUT DATA VALUES                */
STATS: PROC OPTIONS (MAIN);
          DCL (SX,SD2) FLOAT INIT(0),
              (X, M, SDEV, A(50)) FLOAT,
              (N, I, FLAG) FIXED INIT(0);
          ON ENDFILE (SYSIN) FLAG = 1;
          GET LIST (X);
          PUT SKIP LIST('DATA VALUES ARE:');
          PUT SKIP;
          DO I = 1 TO 50 WHILE (FLAG = 0);
             PUT LIST(X);
             A(I) = X;
             SX = SX + X;
             GET LIST (X);
          END;
          N = I - 1;
          IF N >= 2
            THEN DO;
                     M = SX/N;
                     DO I = 1 TO N;
                        SD2 = SD2 + (A(I) - M)**2;
                     END;
                     SDEV = SQRT (SD2/(N-1));
                     PUT SKIP LIST('THE MEAN IS', M);
                     PUT SKIP LIST('THE STANDARD DEVIATION IS',
                       SDEV);
                 END;
            ELSE PUT SKIP LIST
              ('ERROR — INSUFFICIENT INPUT DATA');
       END STATS;
```

ance helps make the program more readable and allows the program to more closely resemble the formula for the computation of the mean. Hopefully, persons other than the programmer would find the program to be more understandable because of the presence of the variable X.

Another interesting feature of this program is the statement "N = I − 1;" which immediately follows the first DO loop. This statement is an adjustment of the value of variable I and is necessary because of the manner in which the DO loop is performed. Even though the DO statement has a WHILE clause, when the END statement of the DO loop is encountered, the variable I is incremented before the WHILE condition is checked. Consequently, the variable I contains a number which is larger (by one) than the actual number of input data values.

Finally, some liberties are taken with the appearance of the sample output. The output values are all in exponential form, because variable X, M, and SDEV are all declared as FLOAT.

8.1.3. Initialization of One-Dimensional Arrays

The INITIAL attribute has been used in many of the preceding examples to initialize variables that can contain only one value (these variables are also called *scalars*). Arrays can also be initialized with the INITIAL attribute, but a slightly different approach is needed, because many elements can be associated with one array name. For example, consider the following DECLARE statement, where variables A, B, and C are scalars:

```
DCL (A,B,C) FIXED INIT(0);
```

Here variables A, B, and C are each initialized to zero. However, suppose that variables D, E, and F are arrays and are declared with one of the statements

```
DCL (D(10), E(10), F(10)) FLOAT INIT(0);
DCL (D,E,F) (10) FLOAT INIT(0);
```

These two statements are logically equivalent. Note that the array size can be factored, but it must appear before all other attributes. Arrays D, E, and F each contain ten elements and are FLOAT. However, only one value appears in the INITIAL attribute, and only D(1), E(1), and F(1) are initialized to zero. The remaining elements in those arrays are not initialized. The following statements, which are logically equivalent, initialize every element of each array to zero:

```
DCL (D,E,F) (10) FLOAT INIT((10)0);
DCL (D,E,F) (10) FLOAT INIT(0,0,0,0,0,0,0,0,0,0);
```

The INITIAL attribute in the first DECLARE statement contains a repetition factor that creates ten occurrences of the value zero. However, in the second statement, the ten values are explicitly stated; so no repetition factor is needed. The INITIAL attribute can be used in a flexible manner, as the following examples indicate.

1. DCL A(5) FIXED INIT(0);
2. DCL A(5) FIXED INIT((5)0);
3. DCL A(5) FIXED INIT(0,0,0,0,0);
4. DCL A(5) FIXED INIT(2,3,4,(2)0);
5. DCL A(5) FIXED INIT(1,2,3,4,5);
6. DCL A(5) FIXED INIT((3)0);

```
7. DCL A(5) FIXED INIT(0,0,0);
8. DCL A(5) FIXED INIT((8)0);
```

Examples 1, 2, and 3 have already been discussed and are repeated here for comparison purposes. Example 4 shows that the INITIAL attribute can contain both repetition factors and explicit values. Example 5 demonstrates that every element in an array can be initialized to a different value. Examples 6 and 7 show that a portion of an array can be initialized, i.e., the first three elements. Example 8 shows that if the INITIAL attribute contains more values than elements of the array, then the excess values are ignored; here the first five values are used, and the last three are ignored.

Character-string arrays can also be initialized with the INITIAL attribute. However, a combination of repetition and replication factors is sometimes necessary to achieve the desired effect, as the following examples show.

```
1. DCL C(5) CHAR(10) VAR INIT((5)'A');
2. DCL C(5) CHAR(10) VAR INIT('A','A','A','A','A');
3. DCL C(5) CHAR(10) VAR INIT((5)(1)'A');
4. DCL C(5) CHAR(10) VAR INIT((6)(5)'A');
```

In example 1, the string 'AAAAA' is placed into C(1), and the remaining elements of C are not initialized. The value (5) is regarded as a replication factor, and the string 'A' is replicated five times, producing 'AAAAA'. Examples 2 and 3 are logically equivalent, because each causes the value 'A' to be placed in every element of the array. In example 3, the value (1) is a replication factor, and the value (5) is a repetition factor. In example 4, the value 'AAAAA' is placed into every element of the array. The value (5) is the replication factor, and the value (6) is the repetition factor. The sixth occurrence of the string 'AAAAA' is ignored because it is not needed.

8.1.4. The French-Verb Problem

The completely solved problem in this section uses character arrays and the INITIAL attribute.

There are three major groups of regular French verbs, distinguished by the endings of the verbs in the infinitive form. One of these groups, the "er" group, always has the characters "er" at the end of the infinitive form. Consider the French verbs and their English counterparts in Table 8.1.

The problem is to compute and display the six forms of the present tense for a given er-type verb. For example, the six forms of the verb *chanter* and their English equivalents are listed in Table 8.2.

No knowledge of French grammar is required to solve this problem. The characters "er" are removed from the end of the verb, and the endings "e," "es," "e," "ons," "ez," and "ent" are appended to create the six verb forms. This is all that needs to be done for any er-type French verb.

TABLE 8.1.

French verb (infinitive form)	*English verb (infinitive form)*
chanter	to sing
depenser	to spend
employer	to employ
inviter	to invite
porter	to carry
voyager	to travel

TABLE 8.2.

Forms of "chanter"	*English*
chante	I sing
chantes	you sing
chante	he sings
chantons	we sing
chantez	you sing
chantent	they sing

Arrays are used for this problem to store the various verb endings and the pronouns "je," "tu," "il," "nous," "vous," and "ils," which mean I, you, he, we, you, and they, respectively. An appropriate pronoun precedes each verb form, so that the output is a bit more realistic.

The two character-string arrays used in Program 8.3 are initialized with strings of varying length. For example, one element of the ENDING array is initialized with a string of length one (e.g., 'E'), and another element is initialized with a string of length three (e.g., 'ONS'). The importance of arrays is dramatized in this problem, for which they provide a relatively simple solution. Without the use of arrays, the solution to this problem would be cumbersome and much more complex.

The built-in string functions LENGTH and SUBSTR also play an important role in the solution. In particular, they are very useful for deciding whether a verb is an er-type and for extracting the "root" portion of a verb.

8.2. MULTIDIMENSIONAL ARRAYS

Section 8.1 deals with one-dimensional arrays, i.e., arrays whose elements can be identified with only one subscript. This section is concerned with arrays that require more than one subscript to label an element. A one-dimensional array can be visualized as a single column of values, a two-dimensional array as a grid or a matrix of values, and a three-dimensional array as a cube-like structure of values. Visualizing more than three dimensions is a difficult task, but 15 to 32 dimensions can be manipulated by many PL/I compilers.

Two-dimensional arrays are emphasized here because, for most problems of an introductory nature, arrays of higher dimensions are not appropriate.

PROGRAM 8.3.

PROBLEM DEFINITION

The input consists of one character string, which is assumed to be a French verb in the infinitive form. The verb is checked, and if it is an er-type, then the six forms of the present tense of that verb are found and placed in the output stream. Otherwise, an appropriate message is placed in the output stream.

Sample input: CHANTER

Sample output:

```
FORMS OF THE VERB CHANTER

     JE CHANTE
     TU CHANTES
     IL CHANTE
     NOUS CHANTONS
     VOUS CHANTEZ
     ILS CHANTENT
```

ALGORITHM DESIGN

Two character-string arrays are required for this problem, as well as concatenation and several of the built-in string functions, especially LENGTH and SUBSTR.

Variables to be used:

VERB	infinitive verb form (input)
ROOT	verb without er ending
ENDING	array of verb endings
PRONOUN	array of pronouns
I	subscript
L	verb length

PSEUDOCODE

```
GET VERB
IF VERB has ER-ending
   THEN find and display the 6 forms
   ELSE display an appropriate message
END
```

ALGORITHM IMPLEMENTATION

```
/* FIND THE SIX FORMS OF PRESENT TENSE */
/* FOR ER-TYPE FRENCH VERBS            */

FRENCH: PROC OPTIONS (MAIN);

          DCL (VERB, ROOT) CHAR(20) VAR,
               ENDING(6) CHAR(3) VAR INIT
                 ('E','ES','E','ONS','EZ','ENT'),
               PRONOUN(6) CHAR(4) VAR INIT
                 ('JE','TU','IL','NOUS','VOUS','ILS'),
               (I,L) FIXED;

          GET LIST (VERB);
          L = LENGTH(VERB);

          IF SUBSTR(VERB, L - 1,2) = 'ER'
            THEN DO;
                      ROOT = SUBSTR(VERB, 1, L - 2);
                      PUT SKIP LIST('FORMS OF THE VERB'
                        || VERB);
                      DO I = 1 TO 6;
                        PUT SKIP LIST('     ' || PRONOUN(I)
                          || '  ' || ROOT || ENDING(I));
                      END;
                 END;
            ELSE PUT SKIP LIST (VERB || ' IS NOT ER-TYPE');

          END FRENCH;
```

Consider the two-dimensional array T in Figure 8.8. Array T has four rows and three columns and could be declared as

```
DCL  T  (4,3)  FIXED;
```

Two dimensions are specified in this statement, the first (i.e., 4) specifies the number of rows, and the second (i.e., 3) specifies the number of columns. There are a total of 12 elements in array T, which is said to be a "4 by 3" array. Two subscripts are used to label elements in a two-dimensional array; the first subscript refers to the row number, and the second subscript refers to the column number. For example, consider the references to elements in array T shown in Figure 8.9. Most of the features pertaining to one-dimensional arrays are also applicable to two-dimensional arrays. In other words, two-dimensional subscripted variables can appear in any statement where scalar variables are permitted, and numeric expressions can be used as subscripts. Elements can be assigned values with GET statements, assignment statements, and INITIAL attributes of DECLARE statements. Nested DO loops, such as the following, are commonly used with two-dimensional arrays:

```
DO I = 1 TO 4;
   DO J = 1 TO 3;
      T(I,J) = (I - 1)*3 + J;
   END;
END;
```

After these statements are executed, array T contains the values shown in Figure 8.10.

The compiler must be given information about two-dimensional arrays with a DECLARE statement. The two general forms of the DECLARE statement for two-dimensional arrays are:

1. DCL *array name* (*upper subscript bound (rows)* , *upper subscript bound (columns)*) *attribute(s);*

2. DCL *array name* (*lower subscript bound (rows)* : *upper subscript bound (rows)* , *lower subscript bound (columns)* : *upper subscript bound (columns)*) *attribute(s);*

The array name can be any valid variable name. The lower subscript bound is assumed to be 1 if it is missing, as in general form 1. The attributes apply to every element in the array; i.e., all elements in the array have the same data-type characteristics. Of course, various elements in an array can be initialized to different values. Following are two typical declaration statements; the corresponding arrays are shown in Figure 8.11.

```
DCL  B (-2:1, 2:7)  FIXED;
DCL  A (6,2)  FLOAT;
```

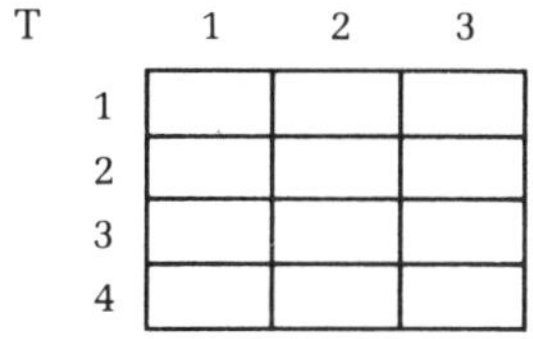

Figure 8.8.

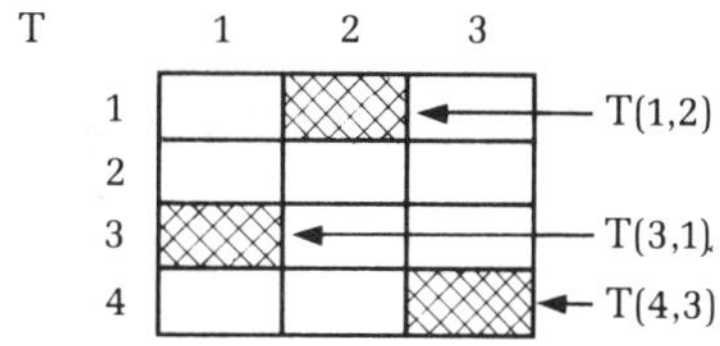

Figure 8.9.

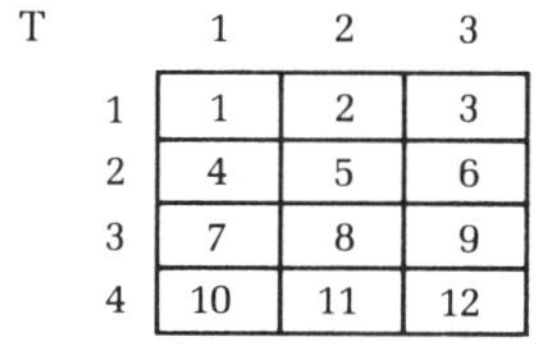

Figure 8.10.

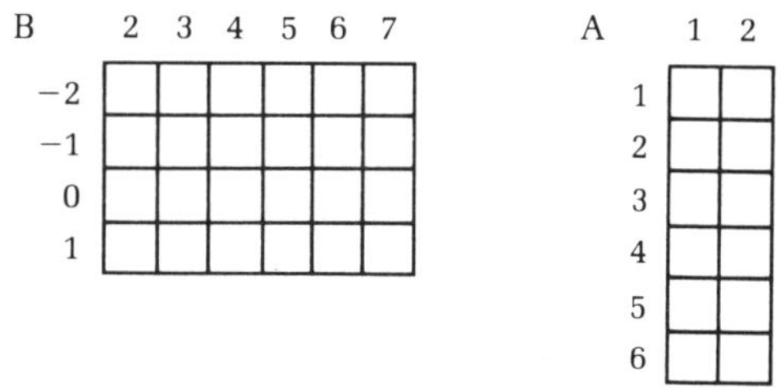

Figure 8.11.

8.2.1. Array Operations*

Whenever an array name is referred to, but subscripts are not included, then the reference is to the entire array, rather than to one element in that array. The following examples refer to array A, which has just been declared.

1. A = 0;
2. A = A + 1;
3. GET LIST (A);
4. PUT LIST (A);
5. A = A*A;

Every element in array A is assigned the value zero as a result of example 1. The value 1 is added to every element in array A because of example 2. In example 3, data is taken from the input stream and placed into every element of array A row by row. Suppose the input stream consists of these values:

6.5 8.3 9.2 1.3 6.4 3.8 9.2 7.2 1.3 6.4 9.1 8.4

Then array A would have the values shown in Figure 8.12 after the statement in example 3 is executed. Similarly, the entire contents of array A would be copied into the output stream row by row as a result of example 4. Finally, in example 5, every element in array A is squared. Array A is multiplied by itself; i.e., when arithmetic operators are applied to arrays, the computation is done for each element. Arithmetic operators may be applied to different arrays if the arrays

*Expressions containing array operations are not permitted with Subset G.

A

1	6.5	8.3
2	9.2	1.3
3	6.4	3.8
4	9.2	7.2
5	1.3	6.4
6	9.1	8.4

Figure 8.12.

have the same dimensions and are compatible. For example, adding a FIXED array to a CHARACTER array might cause serious errors.

Two-dimensional arrays can be initialized with the INITIAL attribute, but initialization is done row by row, as is indicated by the following examples.

1. DCL A(4,3) FIXED INIT (0,0,0);
2. DCL A(4,3) FIXED INIT ((12)0);
3. DCL (A,B,C) (4,3) FIXED INIT ((12)0);
4. DCL A(6,6) FLOAT INIT (1.5);
5. DCL A(3,5) CHAR(1) INIT ((15)(1)'X');

The elements of the first row of array A are initialized to zero in example 1, and every element is initialized to zero in example 2. Example 3 shows that the dimension attribute can be factored, but it must appear before any other attribute. For example, the following DECLARE statement is invalid because it violates this rule:

```
DCL (A FIXED, B FLOAT) (4,3) INIT ((12)0);
```

Also in example 3, every element of arrays A, B, and C is initialized to zero. In example 4, only A(1,1) is initialized and in example 5, every element of array A is initialized to the character string 'X'.

8.2.2. Cross Sections

The cross-section notation permits references to entire rows or columns of a two-dimensional array, rather than to individual elements or the entire array. Consider the statements

```
DCL T(6,4) FLOAT,
    R(4) FLOAT,
    C(6) FLOAT;
R = T(3,*);
C = T(*,2);
```

The notation "T(3,*)" refers to the third row of array T, and the notation "T(*,2)" refers to the second column of array T. The action performed by these assignment statements is illustrated in Figure 8.13.

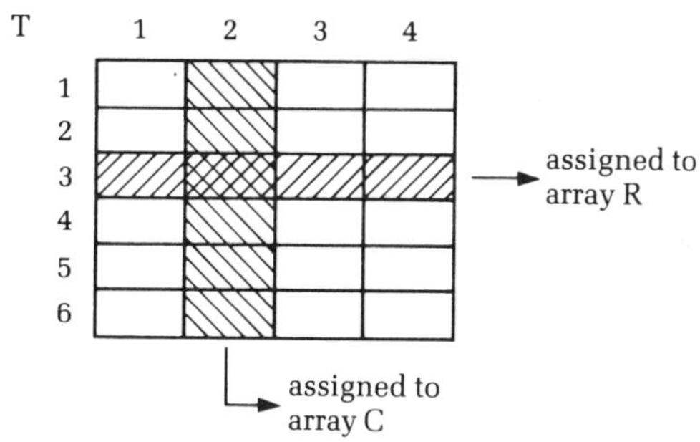

Figure 8.13.

Consider the bubble-sort problem that was solved for one-dimensional arrays in section 8.1.1. Suppose that a two-dimensional array A is to be sorted in ascending order according to the values appearing in the first column. The major difference here is that when two values in column 1 need to be exchanged, two entire rows need to be exchanged. Exchanging rows is ideally suited for cross sections, as the following statements show:

```
DCL A(20,10) FIXED,            /* ARRAY TO BE SORTED */
    TEMP(10) FIXED;            /* TEMPORARY ARRAY    */
    .
    .
    .    assume that row I and
    .    row I + 1 need to be
    .    exchanged
    .
    .
    TEMP = A(I,*);
    A(I,*) = A(I + 1,*);
    A(I + 1,*) = TEMP;
    .
    .
    .
```

Other operations on rows and columns are permitted with cross sections. For example, every element in row 10 of array A is multiplied by 20 by the statement

```
A(10,*) = A(10,*) * 20;
```

8.3. INPUT/OUTPUT

A reference to an array name without a subscript refers to the entire array. Sections 8.1 and 8.2 contain several examples of GET and PUT statements that refer to entire arrays. These examples use only list-directed input, but array I/O can also be performed with data- and edit-directed I/O statements, as the following statements show:

```
DCL (A(5),B(10),C(4,5)) FIXED;
 .
 .
 .
 .
 .
GET DATA (A);
PUT DATA (A);
 .
 .
 .
 .
 .
GET LIST (B);
PUT LIST (B);
 .
 .
 .
 .
 .
GET EDIT (C) ((4)(COL(1),(5)F(3)));
PUT EDIT (C) (COL(1),(5)F(3));
```

The I/O of entire one-dimensional arrays begins with the element that has the smallest subscript and continues with all subsequent elements in the array. In previous examples that refer to arrays A and B, the GET or PUT operation is performed on elements A(1) through A(5) or from B(1) to B(10). However, I/O of entire two-dimensional arrays is performed by rows; i.e., all of the first row, followed by all the second row, etc. Note that in the specification for the GET EDIT statement, a repetition factor of four is used to specify the form for all four rows of the array. However, the specification for the PUT EDIT specifies the form for only one row of the array, and this specification is automatically repeated as many times as is necessary (here, four times).

If I/O of two-dimensional arrays by rows is not sufficient, other approaches, such as I/O by columns can be performed with DO loops. Suppose array A contains the values shown in Figure 8.14, and that these are to be displayed both by rows and by columns. The statement

```
PUT LIST (A);
```

A	1	2	3	4
1	12	10	14	2
2	9	5	21	4
3	8	6	3	11

Figure 8.14.

will give

12 10 14 2 9 5 21 4 8 6 3 11

as the output by rows, and the statements

```
DO J = 1 TO 4;
    PUT LIST ((A(I,J) DO I = 1 TO 3));
END;
```

will give

12 9 8 10 5 6 14 21 3 2 4 11

as the output by columns.

Two DO loops are used in the preceding example, one of which is nested in the PUT statement. Note that if a nested DO loop is used in a GET or PUT statement, an extra set of parentheses is required. The following PUT statement uses a deeper level of nested DO loops to produce output of array A by columns:

```
PUT LIST (((A(I,J) DO I = 1 TO 3) DO J = 1 TO 4));
```

The subscript I varies faster than subscript J, because subscript I is in the inner DO loop. Note that yet another extra set of parentheses is required because of the deeper level of nested DO loops. This one PUT LIST statement is equivalent to the following group of statements:

```
DO J = 1 TO 4;
    DO I = 1 TO 3;
        PUT LIST (A(I,J));
    END;
END;
```

Most of the examples here use PUT LIST statements. However, all array I/O and nested DO loops apply to GET statements as well as data- and edit-directed

C	1	2	3	4	5	6
1	T	H	I	S		I
2	S		A		S	E
3	C	R	E	T		M
4	E	S	S	A	G	E

Figure 8.15.

A	
1	106
2	49
3	35
4	421
5	301

Figure 8.16.

I/O. For example, consider the following input line, which begins in column 1, and the corresponding I/O statements:

```
TSCEHb̸RSIAESSb̸TAb̸Sb̸GIEME
  DCL C(4,6) CHAR(1);
     .
     .
     .
     .
  GET EDIT (((C(I,J) DO I = 1 TO 4) DO J = 1 TO 6));
           (A(1));
  PUT EDIT (C) (COL(1),(24)A(1));
```

After the GET statement is executed, array C contains the values shown in Figure 8.15. The PUT statement produces the output

```
THIS IS A SECRET MESSAGE
```

Nested DO loops are not restricted to two-dimensional arrays and can be used with one-dimensional arrays. For example, suppose that the one-dimensional array A contains the five elements shown in Figure 8.16 and that the output is to consist of the values of these elements in reverse order, i.e., A(5), A(4), A(3), A(2), and then A(1). This is accomplished by the PUT statement

```
PUT LIST ((A(I) DO I = 5 TO 1 BY −1));
```

which produces the output

```
301  421  35  49  106
```

Nested DO loops can be used with arrays of any dimension, as the following statements show:

```
DCL T(4,8,6) FLOAT;
   .
   .
   .
   .
GET LIST((((T(I,J,K) DO I = 1 TO 4) DO J = 1 TO 8)
  DO K = 1 TO 6));
```

The subscript I varies most rapidly, because it is in the innermost DO loop, and the subscript K varies the least, because it is in the outermost DO loop. Note the extra sets of parentheses required by the nested DO loops.

8.4. SUMMARY

One- and two-dimensional arrays are emphasized in this chapter, and several problems are solved that require use of such arrays. Arithmetic operations with arrays are discussed, and the concept of cross sections is introduced. Various array I/O features are discussed, including the use of nested DO loops in GET and PUT statements.

8.4.1. Key Concepts

1. An array is a collection of data elements, which can be referred to by one variable name.
2. Every element in an array has the same data type, i.e., FIXED, FLOAT, or CHARACTER.
3. Elements in an array are referred to by subscripts.
4. A one-dimensional array can be visualized as a column of values, and its elements are referred to by means of one subscript.
5. A two-dimensional array can be visualized as a matrix or a grid of values, and its elements are referred to by means of two subscripts.
6. A subscripted variable can be used wherever a scalar variable can be used.
7. An array declaration can include upper and lower subscript bounds. If the lower subscript bound is omitted, it is assumed to be the value 1.
8. Subscripts are integer values and can be positive, negative, or zero, depending on the declared subscript bounds.
9. Subscripts are numeric expressions, preferably integer expressions.
10. An entire array can be referred to by citing the array name with no subscripts.
11. Sorting is the arrangement of data in some predefined order, such as ascending or descending order.
12. Arrays are particularly useful for problems that require several references to the same data values.
13. The INITIAL attribute can be used to initialize one, several, or all elements in an array.
14. If several elements of a character-string array are to be initialized to the same value, then a repetition factor and a replication factor are both required.
15. Two-dimensional arrays are initialized row by row.
16. An entire row or an entire column of a two-dimensional array can be referred to by means of cross sections.
17. Input/output of entire two-dimensional arrays is performed by rows; i.e., when a GET or PUT statement refers to an array name only (no subscripts).

18. Nested DO loops can be used in GET or PUT statements, but an extra set of parentheses is required.

8.4.2. Terms and Phrases

Write out definitions and/or usage descriptions of these terms. Check yourself against the text.

array
array initialization
ascending order
bubble sort
cross section
dimension
French verbs
lower subscript bound
mean
nested DO loop
standard deviation
subscript
subscripted variable
upper subscript bound

PROBLEMS

Use the problem-solving process to develop a solution for each of the following problems.

Problem 8.1. Sum of two prime numbers.

Many people believe that any positive, even integer can be expressed as the sum of two prime numbers. The input for this problem consists of an arbitrary number of integers. The output consists of these integers, together with the two corresponding prime numbers, or a message indicating that the integer is not even, is not positive, or is larger than 1,500. HINT: Create an array of prime numbers.

Sample input: 30 45 2696 12

Sample output: SUM OF TWO PRIME NUMBERS

INPUT VALUE	ERROR MESSAGE OR PRIME NUMBERS	
30	7	23
45	** NOT EVEN **	
2696	** TOO LARGE **	
12	5	7

Problem 8.2. Key Word In Context (KWIC) index.

The input consists of an unknown number of titles of books or articles. The output consists of index entries for each keyword in the title. The words in the title are shifted, so that the first word in each index entry is a different keyword.

An "ordinary-word" table is created, so that those words which convey very little information (ordinary words) can be distinguished from keywords.

Suppose that the ordinary-word table contains the following words: A, AN, THE, TO, FOR, AND, INTRODUCTION, and OF. For convenience, each title will end with an asterisk (*), so that the end of a title can be detected. The KWIC index for a title consists of as many entries as there are keywords in the title.

Sample input: AN INTRODUCTION TO SNAKES AND LIZARDS*
THE FLORA AND FAUNA OF MARTINIQUE*

Sample output: TITLE: AN INTRODUCTION TO SNAKES AND LIZARDS*
KWIC INDEX ENTRIES:
SNAKES AND LIZARDS*AN INTRODUCTION TO
LIZARDS*AN INTRODUCTION TO SNAKES AND
TITLE: THE FLORA AND FAUNA OF MARTINIQUE*
KWIC INDEX ENTRIES:
FLORA AND FAUNA OF MARTINIQUE*THE
FAUNA OF MARTINIQUE*THE FLORA AND
MARTINIQUE*THE FLORA AND FAUNA OF

Problem 8.3. Roman-number conversion.

The input consists of arbitrarily many Roman numbers, and the output consists of each Roman number with its decimal equivalent, or an error message for an invalid Roman number.

TABLE P8.3. The Roman numerals and their decimal equivalents.

Roman	*Decimal*
M	1000
C	100
L	50
X	10
V	5
I	1

Roman numbers are converted to decimal numbers by scanning the Roman number from left to right and comparing each pair of adjacent Roman numerals. Suppose A and B represent a pair of Roman numerals where A is to the left of B.

If A >B
  then add A to the sum
  else subtract A from the sum

Assume that no Roman number contains more than ten numerals. Use an array to store the Roman number.

Sample input: CCXXIX MCMLXXX MQL

Sample output:

ROMAN-NUMBER CONVERSION	
ROMAN NUMBER	DECIMAL EQUIVALENT
CCXXIX	229
MCMLXXXII	1982
MQL	** INVALID **

Problem 8.4. Tag sort.

The bubble-sort technique in section 8.1.1 provides a method of sorting data in an array by physically exchanging adjacent pairs of data. However, the elements of some arrays might be so large that exchanging them becomes cumbersome and time-consuming. The "tag-sort" technique provides a way to sort such an array—but not exchange any of the elements—by manipulating a second array which consists only of subscripts. For example, consider the arrays in Figure 8.17. Tag sorting is similar to the bubble sort in that elements of array A are compared, but only elements of array T are exchanged. The statement

IF A(T(I)) > A(T(I+1))
  THEN exchange T(I) and T(I+1)

is the essence of sorting in ascending order—for appropriate values of I of course. After being sorted, the arrays appear as in Figure 8.18.

Sample input: 20 integer values

Sample output: The unsorted values and the values sorted in ascending order using the tag-sort technique.

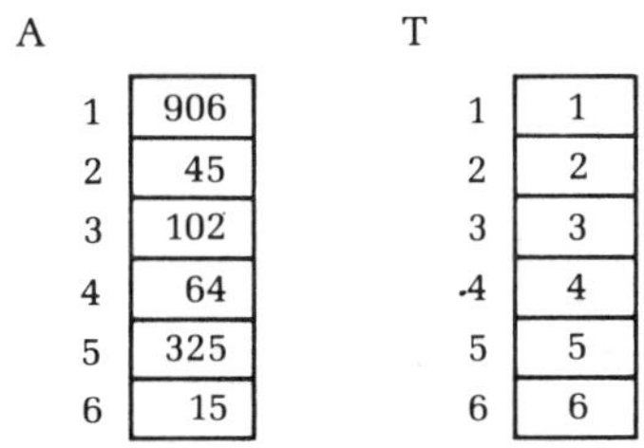

Figure 8.17. *Before sorting.*

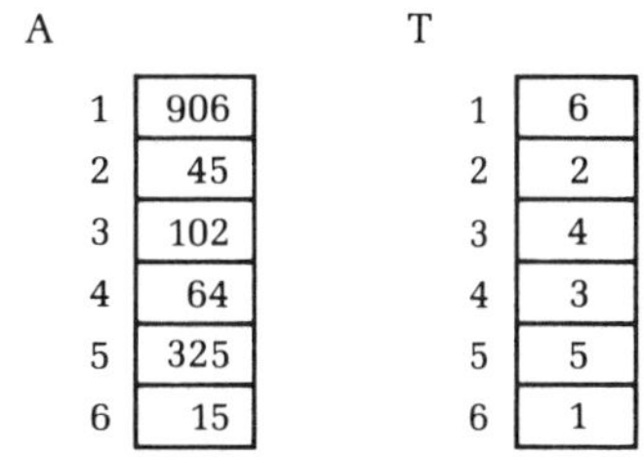

Figure 8.18. *After sorting.*

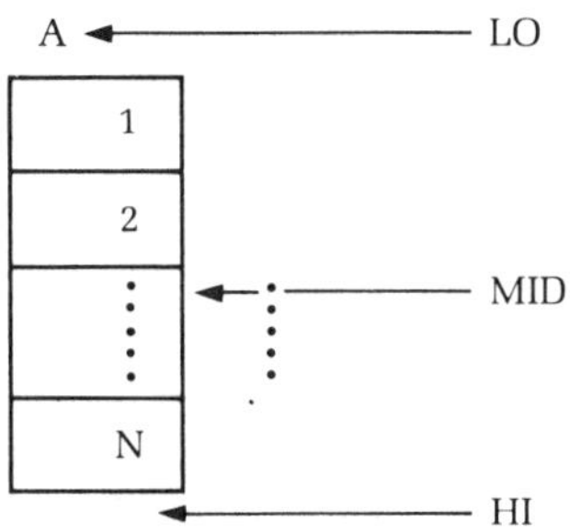

Figure 8.19.

Problem 8.5. Binary Search.

Suppose an array A consists of N elements which are sorted in ascending order. If the position for a particular data element is sought, the array can be searched sequentially by starting with the first element of the array and comparing it with the desired value. If the desired value is not found, this process is repeated for each successive element of the array. This is a simple search technique, and it is easy to implement. However, for large arrays, it may take too long to be practical.

The *binary search* technique is more efficient than sequential search, but does require that the elements in the array to be searched are sorted in ascending order. The key concept of binary search is that with each comparison of the desired value with an array element, half the remaining array is removed from consideration. Several additional subscript variables are needed, as shown in Figure 8.19.

Initially, variable LO is assigned the value 0, and variable HI is assigned N + 1. The variable MID is used as a subscript to compare an array element with a desired value. Suppose the desired value is X. The pseudocode to locate that value in array A is as follows.

```
LO = 0
HI = N+1
FOUND = 0
DO WHILE FOUND = 0
    IF HI = LO+1
       THEN X IS NOT IN A
              FOUND = −999
       ELSE MID = TRUNC((LO+HI)/2)
    IF A(MID) = X
       THEN FOUND = MID
       ELSE IF A(MID) < X
              THEN LO = MID
              ELSE HI = MID
END
PUT FOUND
```

For example, find the position of value 527 in array A, Figure 8.20. Table P8.5 is a trace table showing the binary search process for the value 527. The value 527 is located on the third comparison of elements in array A. Although the array in this example is quite small, binary search is quite effective for searching large arrays.

The problem is to implement the binary search technique to locate several values in a sorted array. Subroutines are very useful in solving this problem.

Sample input: Data values for the array
Several values to be located in the array

Sample output:

BINARY SEARCH PROBLEM

DESIRED VALUE	POSITION IN ARRAY
___	___
___	___
___	___

Problem 8.6. The change-maker problem.

The input consists of several monetary values less than one dollar. The output consists of the minimum number of coins needed to equal each input value.

Sample input: .98 .27 .86 .54

A

1	203
2	248
3	317
4	346
5	428
6	509
7	527
8	604

Figure 8.20.

TABLE P8.5

X	N	FOUND	LO	HI	MID
527	8	0	0	9	4
		7	4		6
			6		7

Sample output:

MAKE CHANGE FOR .98	
COIN VALUE	NO. OF COINS NEEDED
.50	1
.25	1
.10	2
.05	0
.01	3
MAKE CHANGE FOR .27	
___	___
___	___
___	___

Problem 8.7. Character counting.

The input consists of a page of this book (selected by the instructor). Count the number of occurrences of each letter of the alphabet (A–Z), of the digits (0–9), and of the special characters ( ) , ; / * + _ .

Sample input: page XXX

Sample output:

CHARACTER COUNTING	
A	___
B	___
C	___
.	
.	
.	

Problem 8.8. Matrix Multiplication.

The input consists of data for two FIXED 4 × 4 arrays A and B. The matrix product of these arrays is placed in 4 × 4 FIXED array C. Matrix multiplication is defined as

$$c_{ij} = \sum_{k=1}^{4} a_{ik} \, b_{kj},$$

where c_{ij}, a_{ik}, and b_{kj} are elements of arrays C, A, and B, respectively.

Sample input:

```
 3  4   8   6
 8  7   4   2
12  0   8   7
 3  2  15   6

 6  8  12   4
 7  2   5   0
 2  9   8  11
 4  3  15   2
```

Sample output:

```
ARRAY A
3  4  8  6
.
.
.

ARRAY B
6  8  12  4
.
.
.

ARRAY C
86  __  __  __
.
.
.
```

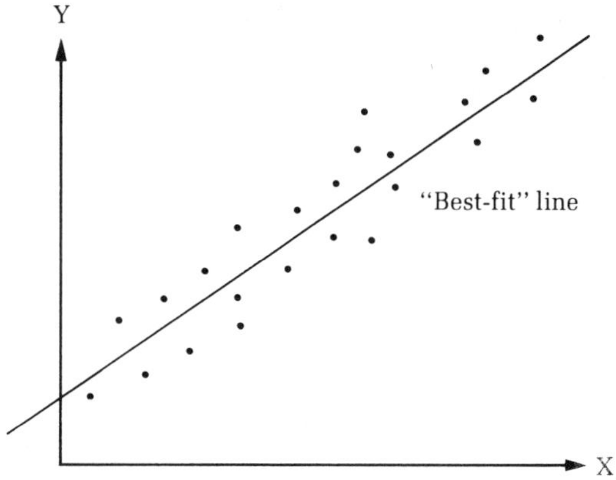

Figure 8.21.

Problem 8.9. Best-fit line equation.

Given N pairs of X, Y-coordinates, one can compute a "best-fit" line equation as shown in Figure 8.21.

The equation for the best-fit line is:

$$Y = SLOPE * X + INTERCEPT$$

For N pairs of X, Y-coordinates, SLOPE and INTERCEPT are computed as follows:

$$SLOPE = \frac{\Sigma(X - M_x)*(Y - M_y)}{\Sigma(X - M_x)^2},$$

$$INTERCEPT = M_y - SLOPE * M_x,$$

where

$$M_x = \frac{\Sigma X}{N},$$

$$M_y = \frac{\Sigma Y}{N}.$$

The input consists of N pairs of X, Y-coordinates, where the X-coordinate represents years, and the Y-coordinate represents sales in millions of dollars. The output consists of the computed SLOPE and INTERCEPT and the predicted sales for the next three years based on the best-fit line equation.

Sample input: 1978 .77 1979 .82 1980 .93
1981 .87 1982 1.23

Sample output:

BEST-FIT LINE EQUATION FOR N = 5

YEAR	SALES
1978	0.77
.	
.	
.	
.	
.	
1982	1.23

SLOPE = ____
INTERCEPT = ____

PREDICTED SALES FOR THE NEXT 3 YEARS

YEAR	PREDICTED SALES
1983	____
1984	____
1985	____

Problem 8.10. Sign maker.

Each input line consists of up to 11 letters and blanks. Each of these input characters is transformed into an output image five columns wide and five lines high. Each output image is separated by two blanks.

Sample input:

```
THE
SIGN
MAKER
```

Sample output:

```
       *****  *   *  *****
         *    *   *  *
         *    *****  *****
         *    *   *  *
         *    *   *  *****

*****  *****  *****  *   *
*        *    *      **  *
*****    *    *  **  * * *
    *    *    *   *  *  **
*****  *****  *****  *   *

*   *    *    *   *  *****  *****
** **   * *   *  *   *      *   *
* * *  *****  ***    *****  *****
*   *  *   *  *  *   *      *  *
*   *  *   *  *   *  *****  *   *
```

Problem 8.11. Monetary transformation.

The input consists of a series of monetary quantities in the form

XXX.XX

Each numeric quantity is transformed into its corresponding narrative form; e.g., 27.63 is "TWENTY-SEVEN AND 63/100 DOLLARS."

Sample input: 4.19 108.75 999.00

Sample output:

MONETARY TRANSFORMATION

NUMERIC FORM	NARRATIVE FORM
4.19	FOUR AND 19/100 DOLLARS
108.75	ONE HUNDRED EIGHT AND 75/100 DOLLARS
999.00	NINE HUNDRED NINETY-NINE AND NO/100 DOLLARS

Problem 8.12. Monthly calendar.

The input consists of a month and the day on which that month begins. Display the calendar for that month, but ignore leap years.

Sample input: MAY SAT

Sample output:

MAY

SUN	MON	TUE	WED	THUR	FRI	SAT
						1
2	3	4	5	6	7	8
9	10	11	12	13	14	15
16	17	18	19	20	21	22
23	24	25	26	27	28	29
30	31					

9 Complex Control Structures

9.1. THE COMPLETE DO STATEMENT

Several variations of the DO statement have been used in the preceding chapters for problems that require DO groups or DO loops. Following are several examples of DO statements that were discussed in earlier chapters.

```
 1. DO;
 2. DO I = 1 TO 10;
 3. DO I = 2 TO 20 BY 2;
 4. DO I = 10 TO 1 BY −1;
 5. DO WHILE (X > Y);
 6. DO WHILE (X > Y & A = B | C < D);
 7. DO I = 1 TO 10 WHILE (A < B);
 8. DO I = 1 TO 10 BY 3 WHILE (D = E);
 9. DO I = 1 BY 1 WHILE (A > 0);
10. DO I = 10 TO 1 BY −1 WHILE (A = B | C = D);
```

The DO statement in example 1 is used to begin a DO group. Iterative DO statements are illustrated in examples 2 through 4, and DO WHILE statements are displayed in examples 5 and 6. Combinations of iterative DO statements and DO WHILE statements appear in examples 7 through 10. Note that iterative DO statements may contain a negative increment, but the final value must be less than the starting value.

Although the preceding examples represent a rich variety of DO statements, additional variations are possible, particularly with iterative DO statements. Consider the following examples.

```
11. DO I = 3, 7, 5;
12. DO I = 1, 3, 5 TO 10;
13. DO I = 1 TO 3, 7 TO 10;
14. DO I = 2 TO 4, 6, 8 TO 10;
15. DO K = 'A', 'B', 'C';
16. DO X = 1.57 TO 3.14 BY 0.3;
```

The preceding statements are also used in the following program segments.

```
11. DCL (I,A(10)) FIXED;
    A=0;
     .
     .
    DO I = 3, 7, 5;
       A(I) = 9;
    END;
```

Contents of array A, after the preceding statements have been executed, are shown in Figure 9.1.

A	1	2	3	4	5	6	7	8	9	10
	0	0	9	0	9	0	9	0	0	0

Figure 9.1.

A	1	2	3	4	5	6	7	8	9	10
	9	0	9	0	9	9	9	9	9	9

Figure 9.2.

A	1	2	3	4	5	6	7	8	9	10
	9	9	9	0	0	0	9	9	9	9

Figure 9.3.

A	1	2	3	4	5	6	7	8	9	10
	0	9	9	9	0	9	0	9	9	9

Figure 9.4.

12.
```
DCL (I,A(10)) FIXED;
A=0;
  .
  .
DO I = 1, 3, 5 TO 10;
   A(I) = 9;
END;
```

Contents of array A, after the preceding statements have been executed, are shown in Figure 9.2.

13.
```
DCL (I,A(10)) FIXED;
A=0;
  .
  .
DO I = 1 TO 3, 7 TO 10;
   A(I) = 9;
END;
```

Contents of array A, after the preceding statements have been executed, are shown in Figure 9.3.

14.
```
DCL (I,A(10)) FIXED;
A=0;
  .
  .
DO I = 2 TO 4, 6, 8 TO 10;
   A(I) = 9;
END;
```

Contents of array A, after executing the preceding statements have been executed, are shown in Figure 9.4.

```
15. DCL (K,L) CHAR(3) VAR INIT('');
    DO K = 'A','B','C';
        L = L||K;
        PUT LIST (L);
    END;
```

Output produced by execution of the preceding statements:

```
A  AB  ABC
```

```
16. DCL X FLOAT;
        .
        .
        .
    DO X = 1.57 TO 3.14 BY 0.3;
        PUT EDIT(X)(F(6,2));
    END;
```

Output produced by execution of the preceding statements:

```
1.57  1.87  2.17  2.47  2.77  3.07
```

Most examples of the iterative DO statement use an index or control variable that has the attribute FIXED. However, examples 15 and 16 provide valid illustrations of index variables that are CHARACTER and FLOAT, respectively. All six of the preceding DO statements can also be combined with WHILE clauses.

9.2. THE BEGIN BLOCK

Suppose the solution to a problem required the use of a variable-size array, e.g., an array that could contain, say, 6, 10, 8, or 20 elements at various times during the execution of a program. Unfortunately, variable-size arrays are not permitted in a DECLARE statement for a main procedure. Arrays defined in such declaration statements are given exact bounds for each of the array dimensions.

The BEGIN block provides a solution to this problem, because variable-size arrays are easily defined. A BEGIN block is simply a collection of statements

```
BEGIN;                                        DO;
  DECLARE ...... (optional)                     __________
  __________                                    __________  statement(s)
  __________                                    __________
  __________  statement(s)                      __________
  __________                                    __________
  __________                                  END;
END;
```

Figure 9.5.

(possibly including a DECLARE statement) that are executed whenever the block is encountered. In this respect, a BEGIN block closely resembles a DO group. For comparison, the general forms for the BEGIN block and the DO group are shown in Figure 9.5.

If a BEGIN block does not contain a DECLARE statement, then it behaves as though it were a DO group, as in the following example.

```
IF A >= B
  THEN BEGIN;
            T = A;
            A = B;
            B = T;
       END;
```

However, if a BEGIN block contains a DECLARE statement, then the variables declared in that statement are known only to that BEGIN block. Furthermore, storage for these variables is allocated when the BEGIN block is entered, and storage is released when the block is exited (this is called AUTOMATIC storage allocation). Consequently, subscript bounds for arrays can be specified with variables, so that variable-size arrays become possible, as the following example shows.

```
DCL N FIXED;
  .
  .
  .
DO N = 5, 8, 20, 10;
     BEGIN;
          DCL A(N) FLOAT;
          ________
          ________
          ________
          ________
          ________
     END;
END;
```

In the preceding example, array A exists only while the BEGIN block is activated. The first time the block is activated, array A contains five elements; the next time the block is activated, array A contains eight elements, etc. However, the variable N is known to the BEGIN block and to the procedure that contains this block. In other words, variable N exists as long as the procedure exists, but array A exists only during the time that statements within the BEGIN block are executed. Program 9.1 will clarify these points.

PROGRAM 9.1.

```
DCL (N,I) FIXED,
  A(20) CHAR(5);
DO I = 1 TO 3;
    GET LIST (N);
    IF N > 0
       THEN BEGIN;
                  DCL (K,SUM,A(N)) FIXED;
                  SUM = 0;
                  GET LIST(A);
                  DO K = 1 TO N;
                      SUM = SUM + A(K);
                  END;
                  PUT SKIP LIST ('THE SUM IS',SUM);
             END;
END;
```

There are two arrays in Program 9.1, one in the procedure, the other in the BEGIN block. Both arrays have the name A but are completely different. The array in the BEGIN block is "local" to that block and can only be referred to by statements within that block. The character array can be referred to by statements in the procedure that are outside of the BEGIN block.

9.3. THE GO TO STATEMENT

Structured programming involves the proper use of the following control structures:

Sequence
Alternation
Repetition
Subroutines

However, there are some circumstances in which the unconditional branch, or GO TO statement, can be effectively used. The purpose of the GO TO statement is to transfer control to another statement in the program. Unrestricted use of the GO TO statement causes problems in debugging and maintenance activities, because the program logic is more difficult to understand. However, some complex situations arise in which a well-placed GO TO statement is the best solution to the problem. No problems in this book are sufficiently complex to warrant use of this statement. If used at all, GO TO statements should refer only to other statements further down in the program (e.g., terminate a loop), as in Figure 9.6.

The general form of the GO TO statement is

GO TO *statement label;*

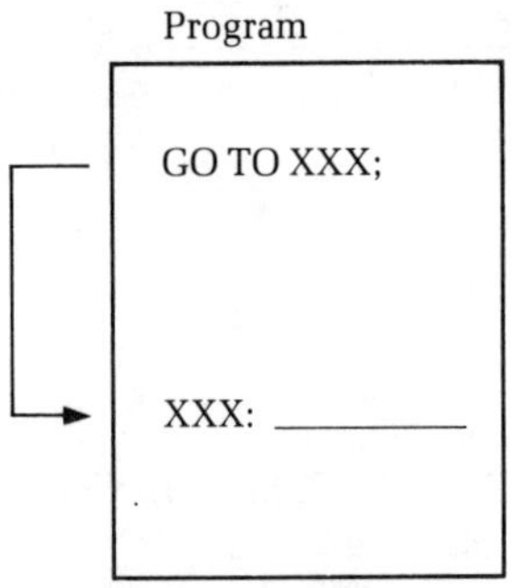

Figure 9.6. *The GO TO statement should make only "downward" references in the program.*

Any executable statement can have a statement label, in the form

statement label : *statement;*

The rules for creating statement labels are identical to those for creating variable names (see Chapter 2). However, variable names and statement labels cannot be identical.

One possible use for a GO TO statement is to terminate a loop when the ENDFILE condition is raised. For comparison, the structured loop termination is placed beside the "GO TO" loop termination in Program 9.2.

PROGRAM 9.2.

STRUCTURED LOOP TERMINATION

```
DCL (X,FLAG) FIXED INIT(0);
ON ENDFILE (SYSIN) FLAG = 1;
.
.
.
GET LIST (X);
DO WHILE (FLAG = 0);
.
.
.
.
    GET LIST (X);
END;
```

GO TO LOOP TERMINATION

```
DCL (X,FLAG) FIXED INIT(0);
ON ENDFILE(SYSIN)
  GO TO DONE;
.
.
.
.
.
DO WHILE (FLAG = FLAG);
    GET LIST(X);
    .
    .
    .
    .
END;
```

TABLE 9.1. Some condition built-in functions.

Function name	*Explanation*
ONCHAR*	Returns the character in function ONSOURCE that caused the condition to be raised.
ONCODE	Returns an error number that indicates why the condition was raised. Each compiler has its set of diagnostic messages; see the appropriate systems manual for the meanings of the error numbers.
ONLOC*	Returns the name of the procedure that contains the statement that caused the condition to be raised.
ONSOURCE*	Returns the character string that caused the CONVERSION condition to be raised.

*Not available with Subset G.

Note that the structured loop termination requires two GET statements, but the GO TO loop termination requires only one, because the loop is terminated immediately when the end-of-file condition is raised. By contrast, in the structured approach, the loop is terminated only when the END statement is encountered.

9.4. ON STATEMENTS*

The ENDFILE condition has been used in many of the preceding chapters as a convenient way to detect the end-of-file condition. However, the ON statement is particularly useful for program debugging, because erroneous situations can be handled by programmer-defined actions, rather than by system actions. The various forms of the ON statement used in this book are:

ON *condition* SNAP *on-unit;*
ON *condition* SNAP SYSTEM;
ON *condition on-unit;*
ON *condition* SYSTEM;

The SNAP option is sometimes called a *snap dump,* because diagnostic information is displayed when the specified condition is raised. The SNAP output consists of an error message, the name of the condition raised, the statement number of the erroneous statement, the names of the procedures leading to that statement, and the relevant values of condition built-in functions. Condition built-in functions provide information about a condition that has arisen. These functions can be referred to in an on-unit to help discover the location and cause of the condition. Some of the available condition built-in functions are shown in Table 9.1. Condition built-in functions can be used to display information about a condition which has arisen. For example:

ON ENDFILE(SYSIN) PUT SKIP LIST (ONCODE, ONLOC);

*See the appendixes for ON statement restrictions for PL/C and Subset G.

The various statements which can be used in programmed on-units are:

ALLOCATE statement
assignment statement
BEGIN statement
CALL statement
CLOSE statement
FREE statement
GET statement
GO TO statement
null statement
OPEN statement
PUT statement
RETURN statement
SIGNAL statement
STOP statement (terminate execution)

The first or only statement of an on-unit cannot have a statement label. The SYSTEM option provides for standard system action rather than programmer-defined action.

The conditions which can be detected are:

CONDITION	COND
CONVERSION	CONV
ENDFILE	
ENDPAGE	
ERROR	
FIXEDOVERFLOW	FOFL
OVERFLOW	OFL
SIZE	
STRINGRANGE	STRG
SUBSCRIPTRANGE	SUBRG
UNDERFLOW	UFL
ZERODIVIDE	ZDIV

One. The CONDITION Condition* (abbreviation COND). The CONDITION condition is a programmer-defined condition; all other conditions are standard system conditions. Any condition can be raised by the SIGNAL statement, but the CONDITION condition can be raised only by the SIGNAL statement. Each programmer-defined condition must be given a name (or identifier), which is enclosed in parentheses and follows the word CONDITION; for example,

*Not available with Subset G.

```
ON CONDITION (MYCOND) FLAG = 1;
        .
        .
        .
        .
SIGNAL CONDITION (MYCOND);
```

Two. The CONVERSION Condition* (abbreviation CONV). The CONVERSION condition is raised when an invalid attempt is made to convert a character string to FIXED, FLOAT, PICTURE, or BIT data types. PICTURE and BIT data types are discussed in Chapter 12. The following statements raise the CONVERSION condition:

```
ON CONVERSION PUT SKIP LIST ('CONVERSION');
DCL X FLOAT;
.
.
.
.
X = 'ABCD';
```

Three. The ENDFILE Condition. The ENDFILE condition is raised when an input statement attempts to read past the end of a file.

Four. The ENDPAGE Condition. The ENDPAGE condition is raised when an output statement attempts to begin a line beyond the end of the page. This condition can be raised only for files with the attributes

```
STREAM OUTPUT PRINT
```

For example,

```
ON ENDPAGE (SYSPRINT);
.
.
.
.
/* NO PAGE EJECTION BECAUSE OF NULL ON-UNIT */
```

Five. The ERROR Condition. The ERROR condition is raised as a standard action for most system on-units and for certain programming errors, such as improper arguments for built-in functions or exponentiation errors during the evaluation of an expression; for example,

*Not available with Subset G.

```
ON ERROR FLAG = 1;
.
.
.
.
A = SQRT (-25);          /* ERROR CONDITION RAISED */
```

Six. The FIXEDOVERFLOW Condition (abbreviation FOFL). The FIXEDOVERFLOW condition is raised when a FIXED computation exceeds the maximum precision for FIXED values; for example,

```
ON FIXEDOVERFLOW FLAG = 1;
DCL A FIXED INIT (99999);
.
.
.
.
A = A * A * A * A;          /* FOFL CONDITION RAISED */
```

Seven. The OVERFLOW Condition (abbreviation OFL). The OVERFLOW condition arises when the computation of FLOAT data values results in an exponent that exceeds the maximum precision.

Eight. The SIZE Condition*. The SIZE condition is raised when the conversion of a value to a FIXED or PICTURE data type is too large and loss of significant digits would occur; for example,

```
DCL A FIXED DECIMAL (4);
.
.
.
.
A = 999 * 99;          /* SIZE CONDITION RAISED */
```

See section 12.1 for a discussion on FIXED DECIMAL.

Nine. The STRINGRANGE Condition* (abbreviation STRG). The STRINGRANGE condition is raised when the indicated substring is not contained within the specified string during the evaluation of the SUBSTR function; for example,

*Not available with Subset G.

```
ON STRINGRANGE PUT LIST ('SUBSTR ERROR');
DCL (A, B) CHAR(10) INIT ((5)'AB');
.
.
.
.
A = SUBSTR (B, 6, 5);       /* STRG RAISED */
A = SUBSTR (B, 11, 1);      /* STRG RAISED */
A = SUBSTR (B, 11, 0);      /* STRG RAISED */
A = SUBSTR (B, 8, 3);       /* STRG RAISED */
```

Ten. The SUBSCRIPTRANGE Condition (abbreviation SUBRG). The SUBSCRIPTRANGE condition is raised during the evaluation of an array subscript that is outside the bounds declared for that array; for example,

```
ON SUBSCRIPTRANGE PUT LIST ('SUBSCRIPT ERROR');
DCL A(10) FIXED;
.
.
.
.
A(12) = 9;      /* SUBRG RAISED */
A(−1) = 0;      /* SUBRG RAISED */
```

Eleven. The UNDERFLOW Condition (abbreviation UFL). The UNDERFLOW condition is raised when the computation of FLOAT data values results in an exponent that is smaller than the allowable minimum.

Twelve. The ZERODIVIDE Condition (abbreviation ZDIV). The ZERODIVIDE condition is raised when an attempt is made to divide a value by zero; for example,

```
DCL A FIXED;
.
.
.
.
A = A / 0;      /* ZDIV RAISED */
```

Most of the conditions discussed in this section are normally *enabled;* that is, they are automatically activated by the system. However, the SIZE, STRINGRANGE, and SUBSCRIPTRANGE conditions are normally *disabled,* and a *condition prefix* must be used to activate these conditions; for example,

```
(SIZE):                          /* ACTIVATE SIZE
                                    CONDITION */
  TEST: PROC OPTIONS(MAIN);
(SIZE, SUBSCRIPTRANGE):          /* ACTIVATE SIZE AND
                                    SUBSCRIPTRANGE */
  BEGIN;
```

Condition prefixes are usually attached to PROCEDURE or BEGIN statements, and are active for the duration of those PROCEDURE or BEGIN blocks.

9.5. SUMMARY

Several variations of the DO statement are discussed, with an emphasis on the iterative DO statement. The BEGIN block is introduced, along with variable-size arrays and local variables. A possible application of the GO TO statement is presented, followed by a brief discussion of ON statements.

9.5.1. Key Concepts

1. The index variable of an iterative DO statement can be FIXED, FLOAT, or CHARACTER. If it is CHARACTER, the "TO" and "BY" options cannot be used.
2. If a BEGIN block does not contain a DECLARE statement, then it behaves as though it were a DO group.
3. Storage for variables declared in a BEGIN block is automatically allocated when the BEGIN block is activated (or entered).
4. Variable-size arrays can be declared in a BEGIN block by specifying subscript bounds with variables.
5. The GO TO statement is an unconditional branch, or jump, to another part of the program.
6. GO TO statements should be used sparingly and, when used, should make only downward or forward references in the program.
7. The ON statement is used to detect the end-of-file condition, various other system conditions, and programmer-defined conditions.
8. The ON statement is executable and may be placed anywhere in the program. However, the intended condition cannot be detected until the corresponding ON statement is executed.

9.5.2. Terms and Phrases

Write out definitions and/or usage descriptions of these terms. Check yourself against the text.

AUTOMATIC
BEGIN block
condition prefix
GO TO
index variable
local variable
on-unit
ON statement
SNAP dump
variable-size array

PROBLEMS

Problem 9.1. Under what circumstances is the use of the BY option in an iterative DO statement forbidden?

Problem 9.2. What is the principal difference between DO groups and BEGIN blocks?

Problem 9.3. Can a BEGIN block be used in place of any DO group? Is the converse true?

Problem 9.4. Are there any circumstances where a GO TO statement can be used effectively?

Problem 9.5. Give several different reasons why ON statements are useful.

10 Procedures

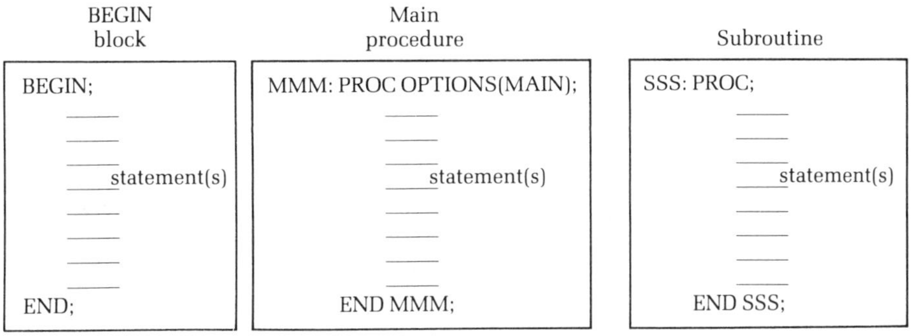

Figure 10.1.

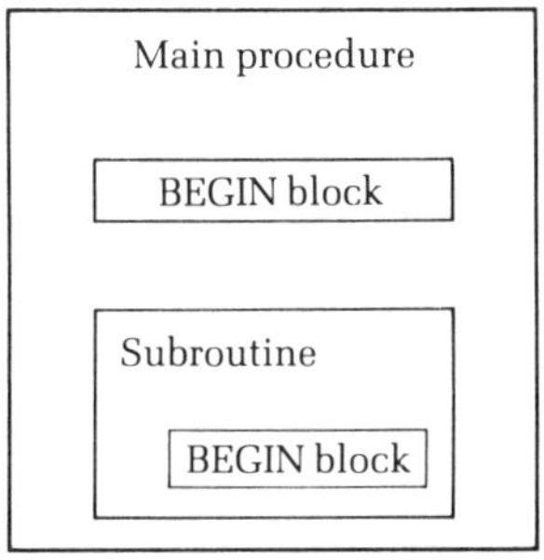

Figure 10.2.

10.1. BLOCKS

The terms "program" and "procedure" have been used interchangeably up to this point, because every program has consisted of a main procedure that sometimes contains a subroutine. However, a program actually consists of one or more *blocks*, where a procedure is a type of block.

A block is a section of a program or a collection of statements within which declared variables are known. Variables can be declared within a block, and storage for certain variables can be allocated and freed within a block. Processing and input/output operations can be contained within other blocks. Blocks can be contained within other blocks, e.g., a subroutine contained within a main procedure.

The two types of blocks are BEGIN blocks and procedure blocks. Procedure blocks include the main procedure, subroutines, and functions, which are discussed later in this chapter. The blocks used in previous chapters are diagrammed in Figure 10.1.

A main procedure can contain other blocks, such as subroutines and BEGIN blocks, as shown in Figure 10.2.

Within each block, variables can be declared and are known only in that block. Unless specified otherwise, storage for such declared variables is al-

Subroutine invocation:	Function invocation:
CALL *name* *(argument(s))*;	*name* *(argument(s))*
Subroutine name → *name*; argument list → *(argument(s))*	Function name → *name*; argument list → *(argument(s))*
A subroutine is invoked with a CALL statement, for example,	A function is invoked by referring to the function name and argument list in some statement, for example,
CALL ADD(X,Y,Z); CALL HEAD;	X = SUM(A,B); PUT LIST (SQRT(X));

Figure 10.3.

```
(a)  name: PROC (parameter(s));
        _____
        _____
        _____
        _____
        _____
        _____
        RETURN; (RETURN is an optional statement)
     END; or END name;

(b)  name: PROC (parameter(s)) RETURNS (attribute(s));
        _____
        _____
        _____
        _____
        _____
        RETURN (expression); (RETURN is required)
     END; or END name;
```

Figure 10.4. *General forms for (a) subroutines and (b) functions.*

located when the block is activated, because AUTOMATIC is the default storage-allocation attribute.

10.2. SUBROUTINES AND FUNCTIONS

Subroutines were introduced in Chapter 5, and built-in functions in Chapters 6 and 7. Both subroutines and functions are blocks, but the method of invoking them is different, as shown in Figure 10.3.

Subroutines and functions differ in the way in which they are invoked and the way in which they return values. Several values can be returned by subroutines, but only one value can be returned by a function. Furthermore, subroutines use parameter variables to return values, and functions use a RETURN statement to return a value. This difference appears in the general forms for subroutines and functions shown in Figure 10.4.

Arguments appear in the invocation of a subroutine or a function, but parameters appear in the subroutines and functions. An argument can be an expression, but a parameter must be a variable. Values are returned by subroutines when desired values are assigned to one or more of the parameters. However, the value returned by a function may appear as an expression in the RETURN statement, and the attribute(s) of the return value must appear in the RETURNS option. This distinction is highlighted in Program 10.1, in which a subroutine and a function each perform an identical task, i.e., add three integer numbers.

PROGRAM 10.1.

```
EXAMPLE: PROC OPTIONS (MAIN);                      /* MAIN
                                                      PROCEDURE */
              DCL (SUM1,SUM2) FIXED;
                .
                .
                .
              CALL ADDSUBR (40,20,30,SUM1);         /* SUBROUTINE
                                                       INVOCATION */
              SUM2 = ADDFUNC (40,20,30);            /* FUNCTION
                                                       INVOCATION */
              PUT LIST (SUM1,SUM2);
                .
                .
                .
ADDSUBR: PROC (A,B,C,RESULT);                      /* SUBROUTINE */
              DCL (A,B,C,RESULT) FIXED;
              RESULT = A + B + C;
              RETURN;
           END ADDSUBR;
                .
                .
                .
ADDFUNC: PROC (X,Y,Z) RETURNS(FIXED);               /* FUNCTION */
              DCL (X,Y,Z) FIXED;
              RETURN (X + Y + Z);
           END ADDFUNC;
                .
                .
                .
           END EXAMPLE;
```

The parameter variables A, B, and C in subroutine ADDSUBR are called *input parameters,* because they provide data to be manipulated. RESULT is called an *output parameter,* because it is used to return a value to the invoking block. No such distinction is made with parameters in a function, because the parameters usually provide information to the function. The value returned by the function is the expression in the RETURN statement. Note that the function is invoked from an assignment statement, and the subroutine is invoked with a CALL statement. A function reference can appear in any statement where a variable or a subscripted variable may appear. The rules for creating function and subroutine names are the same as the rules for creating variable names.

10.3. INTERNAL AND EXTERNAL BLOCKS

The three principal types of procedures are:

main procedures
subroutine procedures (or simply, subroutines)
function procedures (or simply, functions)

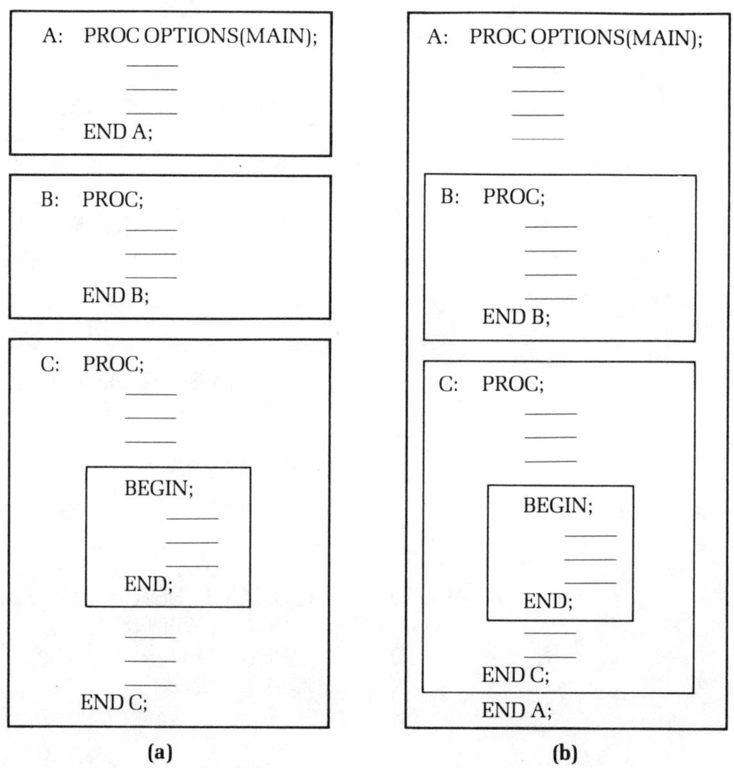

Figure 10.5. *In (a) the external blocks are A, B, and C; and the internal block is the BEGIN block contained in C. In (b), the external block is A; and the internal blocks are B, C, and the BEGIN block in C.*

Each of these procedures is a block and is further classified as "internal" or "external," depending on its relationship with other blocks.

An internal block is one that is completely embedded or contained in another block. BEGIN blocks are always internal blocks, because they must be contained in a procedure or another BEGIN block. Subroutine ADDSUBR and function ADDFUNC, which appear in the previous section, are examples of internal blocks, because they are both completely contained in a main procedure.

By contrast, external blocks* are not contained in other blocks and are physically separate from other blocks. For example, a main procedure is always an external block, as are the built-in functions. Figure 10.5 depicts the difference between internal and external blocks.

However, any block that invokes an external procedure should declare that external procedure name as an "ENTRY" point and should also specify the attributes of the arguments passed to that external procedure. Assume that procedures EXAMPLE, ADDSUBR, and ADDFUNC, which appear in section 10.2, are external procedures. Each of these procedures would appear as shown in Program 10.2.

PROGRAM 10.2.

```
EXAMPLE: PROC OPTIONS (MAIN);              /* MAIN PROCEDURE */
           DCL (SUM1, SUM2) FIXED,
               ADDSUBR ENTRY (FIXED, FIXED, FIXED, FIXED),
               ADDFUNC ENTRY (FIXED, FIXED, FIXED) RETURNS
                 (FIXED);
           .
           .
           .
           CALL ADDSUBR (40,20,30,SUM1);
           SUM2 = ADDFUNC(40,20,30);
           PUT LIST (SUM1,SUM2);
           .
           .
           .
       END EXAMPLE;
ADDSUBR: PROC (A,B,C,RESULT);              /* SUBROUTINE */
           DCL (A,B,C,RESULT) FIXED;
           RESULT = A + B + C;
           RETURN;
       END ADDSUBR;
ADDFUNC: PROC (X,Y,Z) RETURNS (FIXED);     /* FUNCTION */
           DCL (X,Y,Z) FIXED;
           RETURN (X + Y + Z);
       END ADDFUNC;
```

*Some systems require additional JCL in order to handle external procedures.

Note that there are two uses of the RETURNS phrase in Program 10.2. When used in a DECLARE statement, it is called the *RETURNS attribute,* and when used in a PROCEDURE statement, it is called the *RETURNS option.* Using the ENTRY attribute and the RETURNS attribute/option is not always required, because compiler defaults can be used. However, not all compilers have the same defaults; so, in the interest of creating PL/I programs that are machine-independent, ENTRY and RETURNS are used with all external procedures.

PROGRAM 10.3.

```
A:  PROC;
        DCL X FLOAT:
           .
           .
           .
           .
           .
      BEGIN;
          DCL X FIXED;
             .
             .
             .
             .
             .
      END;
         .
         .
         .
         .
         .
    B:  PROC;
          DCL Y CHAR(20);
             .
             .
             .
        END B;
    C:  PROC;
          DCL X CHAR(10) VAR;
             .
             .
             .
             .
             .
        END C;
        END A;
```

```
                                  ┌──────────────argument list
                                  ↓
CALL SUB    (A+B,   20,   E)  ;
              .      .    .
              .      .    .
              .      .    .
SUB: PROC   ( X,     Y,   Z)  ;
                     ↑
                     └──────────── parameter list
```

Figure 10.6.

10.4. SCOPE OF VARIABLES

The *scope* of a variable refers to the extent to which that variable is known throughout a program. When a variable is declared in a block, it is known to that block and to all contained blocks, unless that variable name is declared in a contained block. Program 10.3 shows the scope of several variables.

The scope of the variable X declared in procedure A includes procedure A and procedure B but not the BEGIN block and procedure C. The scope of the variable X declared in the BEGIN block is limited to the BEGIN block. Similarly, the scope of the variable X declared in procedure C is limited to that procedure. There are three declarations of variable X in this example; despite the similarity in name, each is a completely different variable, and each is stored in a different location in memory.

The terms *global variable* and *local variable* are often used to describe the scope of a variable. A global variable is one used in a block but not declared in that block. A local variable is one declared and used in a particular block. In Program 10.3, the variable X declared in procedure A is a global variable in procedure B.

10.5. ARGUMENTS AND PARAMETERS

Arguments are expressions that appear in the invocation of a procedure, and parameters are variables in the procedure that match the corresponding arguments. Arguments and parameters should agree in number and in data type. For example, consider the argument list and parameter list in Figure 10.6.

When a procedure is invoked, the actual value of an argument is not passed; instead, the *address* or memory location of that argument is passed. However, some arguments are not variables, such as "A+B" in the preceding example; so an argument address cannot be passed directly. In these situations, *dummy arguments* are used to pass information to the invoked procedure. A dummy argument is a compiler-generated internal address that is created for

1. Arguments that are not variables
2. Arguments whose data attributes do not match their corresponding parameters
3. Arguments passed by value

PROGRAM 10.4.

```
/* COMPARE VARIABLES PASSED BY REFERENCE AND BY VALUE */
COMPARE: PROC OPTIONS (MAIN);
            DCL (A,B,C) FIXED INIT(999);
            CALL SUB1((A),(B),C);
            CALL SUB2(A,(B),(C));
            PUT LIST (A,B,C);
SUB1:       PROC (X,Y,Z);
            DCL (X,Y,Z) FIXED;
            X = 10;
            Y = 25;
            Z = 50;
            RETURN;
         END SUB1;
SUB2:    PROC (C,A,B);
            DCL (A,B,C) FIXED;
            A = 98;
            B = 46;
            C = 103;
            RETURN;
         END SUB2;
         END COMPARE;
```

Normally, arguments that are variables are passed *by name* or *by reference*, i.e., the address of the variable is passed to the invoked procedure. However, arguments that are variables (and other expressions) can be passed *by value* by enclosing that argument in parentheses. The following subroutine call contains both forms of argument passing:

CALL SUB (A, (B), C, 25);

Variables A and C are passed by reference, while variable B is passed by value. The compiler creates two dummy arguments, one for variable B and the other for the constant 25. Only the compiler has access to these dummy arguments. An invoked procedure can change the value of variables passed by reference but not of any variable (or expression) passed by value, as Program 10.4 shows.

Variables A and B are passed by value in the call to procedure SUB1, and variable C is passed by reference; hence, SUB1 cannot change the values of A and B but can (and does) change the value of variable C to 50. Similarly, variables B and C are passed by value in the call to procedure SUB2, and the variable A is passed by reference. SUB2 changes the value of A (in the main procedure) to 103. Consequently, the values that appear in the output list generated by the PUT statement are 103, 999, and 50.

PROGRAM 10.5.

```
          DCL ARRAY (25) FLOAT;
           .
           .
           .
          CALL SUB (ARRAY);
           .
           .
           .
SUB: PROC (MATRIX);
            DCL MATRIX (25) FLOAT;
             .
             .
             .
```

PROGRAM 10.6.

```
/* PASS VARIABLE-SIZE ARRAYS TO A SUBROUTINE */
PASS:
    PROC OPTIONS (MAIN);
        DCL (A(50), B(20)) FIXED;
        GET LIST (A,B);
        CALL SUM (50,A);
        CALL SUM (20,B);
SUM:
    PROC (N,ARRAY);
        DCL (ARRAY(*),N,I,S) FIXED;
        S = 0;
        DO I = 1 TO N;
            S = S + ARRAY(I);
        END;
        PUT SKIP LIST ('SUM OF ALL ELEMENTS =',S);
        RETURN;
    END SUM;
    END PASS;
```

Arrays can also be passed to procedures as Program (segment) 10.5 indicates.

However, subroutines and functions can accept arrays of various sizes by specifying the dimension(s) with asterisk(s) in the array declaration of the invoked procedure. Program 10.6 contains an example of passing variable-size arrays to subroutines.

The asterisk notation in the declare statement can only be used to specify array dimension, not upper and lower subscript bounds. For example, the following statement

```
DCL A(*:*) FIXED;
```

is invalid. The asterisk notation can also be used to specify variable-size character strings, as in

```
DCL CH CHAR(*);
```

10.6. THE EXTERNAL ATTRIBUTE

One way for external blocks to communicate is by argument passing. Another method is to declare variables with the EXTERNAL attribute. The EXTERNAL attribute expands the scope of a variable to any other procedure for which that variable is declared as EXTERNAL. Program 10.7 consists of three external procedures that have EXTERNAL variable declarations.

In order for a variable to be known in various external procedures, each procedure must declare that variable with the EXTERNAL attribute and must use the same name and the same data attributes.

When a variable is declared as EXTERNAL, the storage allocation is STATIC; i.e., storage for that variable is allocated at compile time and remains allocated for the life of the program. In other words, variables with the EXTERNAL attribute are always available while the program is being executed. By contrast, the default storage allocation is AUTOMATIC, which means that storage is allocated for a declared variable in a block only when that block is invoked or activated.

10.7. THE RECURSIVE ATTRIBUTE

A *recursive* procedure is one which can invoke itself. This may seem a strange action for a procedure to perform, but several types of problems are easily handled by recursive procedures. For example, consider the problem of computing $n!$, the factorial for a given integer, which is defined as

$$N! = N*(N-1)*(N-2)* \ldots *1,$$

where if $n < 2$, then $n! = 1$. We can also define $n!$ as

$$n! = n*(n-1)!$$

or as

$$n! = n*(n-1)*(n-2)!.$$

This last definition of $n!$ should suggest a way to compute the factorial with a self-invoked function. The first time such a function was invoked, variable N would be checked to find out whether it was less than the value two and,

PROGRAM 10.7.

```
/* PROCEDURE INVOCATION WITHOUT ARGUMENT PASSING */
NOARGS: PROC OPTIONS (MAIN);
                DCL (A,B,C) EXTERNAL FLOAT;
                  .
                  .
                  .
                CALL SUB1;
                CALL SUB2;
                  .
                  .
                  .
            END NOARGS;
SUB1:       PROC;
                DCL (A,B,C) EXTERNAL FLOAT;
                  .
                  .
                  .
            END SUB1;
SUB2:       PROC;
                DCL (A,B,C) EXTERNAL FLOAT:
                  .
                  .
                  .
            END SUB2;
```

if so, to return the value one. Otherwise, the function (say, FACT) would multiply N by the value returned by self-invoking FACT with a value of N−1. This process would continue as

$$\begin{aligned} \text{FACT(N)} &= \text{N*FACT(N}-1) \\ &= \text{N*(N}-1)\text{*FACT(N}-2) \\ &\quad \text{etc.} \end{aligned}$$

The RECURSIVE attribute is necessary for a procedure to be able to invoke itself. The recursive function FACT that computes n! is shown in Program 10.8.

Variables N and V have the default storage-allocation attribute of AUTOMATIC. Each time FACT is invoked, storage is again allocated for these variables, and only the "newest" variables are used. Consequently, FACT can invoke itself with the argument N−1 but can use the parameter N to correspond with that argument. The RECURSIVE attribute also enables the compiler to set up the additional mechanisms necessary to handle recursive procedures.

PROGRAM 10.8.

```
/* RECURSIVE FUNCTION TO COMPUTE N! */
FACT:
   PROC(N) RECURSIVE RETURNS(FIXED);
      DCL (N,V) FIXED;
      IF N < 2
         THEN V = 1;
         ELSE V = N*FACT(N-1);
      RETURN(V);
   END FACT;
```

10.8. EXAMPLES

Here we will solve two complete problems that use function and subroutine procedures. The first problem is a simulation of a dice-throwing experiment. This problem uses a random-number generator to simulate the throwing of each die. The second problem processes transactions in an inventory system and automatically reorders an item when the amount in stock drops to a certain number. The first problem uses a function, and the second problem uses several subroutines.

10.8.1. Dice-Throwing Simulation

The objective of this problem is to simulate the throwing of a pair of dice 1,000 times and to keep a record of the results. However, in order to perform this simulation, a random-number generator is required to simulate the unpredictability of the dice. Random numbers are simply numbers that do not follow any sequence and cannot be accurately predicted from one number to the next. However, the function described in this section is a *pseudo*-random-number generator, because a *seed* or starting value is specified, and a sequence of values is calculated. If the same seed is always used, the same sequence of values is always produced. The values computed by a random-number generator are not truly random, but they appear to be random and are adequate for many simulation problems.

RND is the name of the function that generates FLOAT random numbers from 0.0 up to, but not including, 1.0. This may seem a strange range of values, but it reflects the general case and can be easily used in various situations. For example, to simulate the throwing of a die, multiply such a random value by 6, add 1, then truncate digits to the right of the decimal point. Thus an integer from 1 through 6 is randomly produced.

The random-number generator used in the dice-throwing simulation is shown in Program 10.9.

PROGRAM 10.9.

```
/* FUNCTION TO PRODUCE A RANDOM NUMBER */
/* IN THIS RANGE:                      */
/* 0.0 <= RND(SEED) < 1.0              */
RND:
  PROC(SEED) RETURNS(FLOAT);
    DCL SEED FIXED,                         /* STARTING VALUE */
      MAXIMUM FLOAT INIT(2147483647), /* 2**31-1       */
      MULTIPLIER FLOAT INIT(20707);      /* ARBITRARY
                                                MULTIPLIER     */
    SEED = MOD(SEED*MULTIPLIER,MAXIMUM);
    RETURN (SEED/MAXIMUM);
  END RND;
```

RND is an external function which has one parameter, SEED. Before RND is invoked for the first time, SEED must be assigned a positive integer greater than zero. For example, RND can be invoked by

```
DCL SEED FIXED INIT(190134),
  I FIXED,
  X FLOAT;
  .
  .
  .
  .
DO I = 1 TO 5;
   X = RND (SEED);
   PUT EDIT(X) (COL(15), F(8,6));
```

The output produced by this program segment is

```
0.833357
0.328812
0.713093
0.017741
0.370635
```

Many computers have built-in random-number generators, and some provide several different ranges for the returned random numbers. For example, some random-number generators can produce integers in the range of 1 to 6 inclusive. However, the function RND works quite satisfactorily for the dice-throwing simulation in Program 10.10.

PROGRAM 10.10.

PROBLEM DEFINITION

Simulate the throwing of a pair of dice 1,000 times. There is no input for this problem, and the output consists of a tabulation of the total number of each of the possible sums; i.e., the number of 2s, the number of 3s, . . . , the number of 12s.

Sample input: None

Sample output:

DICE-THROWING SIMULATION

SUM	# OCCURRENCES
2	
3	
4	
.	
.	
.	
.	
.	
12	

ALGORITHM DESIGN

The function RND is invoked to simulate the throwing of each die. Assume that RND exists as an external function.

Variables to be used:

SEED	starting value
A	array of totals
DIE1	first die
DIE2	second die
I	counter

Array A contains the total for each possible sum and is initialized to zero.

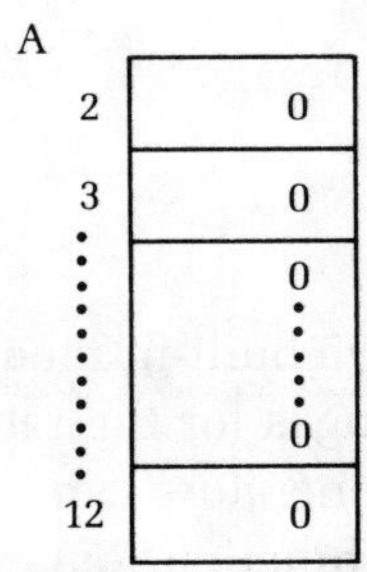

If a simulated dice throw produced a sum of 8, then 1 is added to A(8).

PSEUDOCODE

```
Initialize A, SEED
Do the following 1,000 times:
    DIE1 = random value between 1 and 6 inclusive
    DIE2 = random value between 1 and 6 inclusive
    Add 1 to A(DIE1 + DIE2)
END
PUT A
END
```

ALGORITHM IMPLEMENTATION

```
/* DICE THROWING SIMULATION USING */
/* FUNCTION RND                   */

DICE:
    PROC OPTIONS(MAIN);

        DCL A(2:12) FIXED INIT((11)0),    /* ARRAY OF TOTALS */
          SEED FIXED INIT(64389),         /* STARTING VALUE  */
          DIE1 FIXED,                     /* FIRST DIE       */
          DIE2 FIXED,                     /* SECOND DIE      */
          I FIXED,                        /* COUNTER         */
          RND ENTRY(FIXED)                /* FUNCTION RND    */
            RETURNS(FLOAT);

        DO I = 1 TO 1000;
            DIE1 = TRUNC(RND(SEED)*6+1);
            DIE2 = TRUNC(RND(SEED)*6+1);
            A(DIE1+DIE2) = A(DIE1+DIE2)+1;
        END;

        PUT SKIP LIST('DICE THROWING SIMULATION');
        PUT EDIT('SUM','#OCCURRENCES')(COL(4),A,COL(10),A);
        PUT EDIT((I,A(I) DO I = 2 TO 12))
                (COL(4),F(3),COL(15),F(3));

    END DICE;
```

TABLE 10.1.

SUM	*Expected number of occurrences for 1,000 throws*
2	28
3	56
4	83
5	111
6	139
7	166
8	139
9	111
10	83
11	56
12	28

TABLE 10.2. Inventory

Item	*Identification*	*Quantity on hand*	*Reorder point*	*Amount to order*
1	4395	75	15	20
2	6217	4	10	5
3	7028	1962	1256	900
.				
.				
.				
.				
.				
.				
.				
50				

The advantage of an external function is illustrated by Program 10.10. Function RND can be used by many different programs for different types of problems. The built-in function TRUNC, which is also an external function, is useful in this program.

Array A plays an important role in the solution to this problem, because it is used to keep track of the number of occurrences for each sum. The subscripts represent the individual sums. There is no subscript value of 1, because a sum of 1 is impossible when two dice are thrown.

Execute the preceding program and compare the output with the expected values, which are shown in Table 10.1.

10.8.2. The Inventory Problem

A small business maintains its inventory of 50 items with a two-dimensional array as shown in Table 10.2. Each item has a unique identification number in column 2, and the quantity on hand, reorder point, and amount to order for each item are represented in columns 3 through 5. Various transactions are received, and the array must be updated to reflect the processing of these transactions. Each transaction has the form

TYPE, IDENTIFICATION, QUANTITY

TYPE can only be one of two values: "REQUEST" or "ARRIVAL." If TYPE has the value "REQUEST," then the transaction is a request for inventory items. The number of items is specified by QUANTITY. IDENTIFICATION is used to specify which item in the inventory. If TYPE has the VALUE "ARRIVAL," then the transaction represents the arrival of a number of items to be added to the inventory.

The purpose of this problem is to maintain the array that represents the inventory by processing a series of transactions. For example, consider the following transactions, assuming the values shown in Table 10.2.

```
'REQUEST', 6217, 5
'REQUEST', 4395, 60
'ARRIVAL', 6217, 5
```

The first request cannot be honored, because there are not enough items in the inventory. The second request can be honored, but doing so causes the quantity on hand to fall below the reorder point; so an order for five items must be placed. The third transaction represents an arrival of items, and the quantity on hand must be updated.

The solution to this problem uses several subroutines and is a good example of how a relatively complex problem can be broken down into several smaller pieces or modules. Each of these modules can be developed separately, and each represents only one aspect of the problem. Consequently, each of these modules is relatively easy to develop, and the final solution to the problem should be easier to understand, because it is composed of several small modules.

Program 10.11 shows how subroutines are used to break a larger problem into several smaller problems. This problem could be solved by developing and testing the subroutines one at a time. For example, the main procedure and subroutine ERROR would be developed first, because they are the simplest. While one is testing subroutine ERROR, the subroutines REQUEST and ARRIVAL could exist as *stubs*, i.e., subroutines that contain a minimal number of statements to show that the subroutines are properly entered. These stubs could appear as shown in Program 10.12.

Subroutine ARRIVAL would be developed next, and the most complex subroutine saved for last. When subroutine ARRIVAL is being developed and tested, the stub for subroutine REQUEST remains. In general, the simplest module should be developed first, and stubs should be established for the remaining modules. The stubs should be replaced with developed subroutines or functions for modules of increasing complexity. One advantage of using this

PROGRAM 10.11.

PROBLEM DEFINITION

Given the array INVEN described in Table 10.2, which lists the current status of an inventory, update this array by processing an arbitrary number of transactions of this form:

TYPE, IDENTIFICATION, QUANTITY

TYPE is a character-string value, and the other items are integer values. The input consists of data to fill array INVEN, followed by a series of inventory transactions. The two types of transactions are inventory items, as previously described. The output consists of responses to the transactions, including actions taken, or error messages for an illegal transaction; i.e., invalid type or nonexistent identification number.

Sample input:

```
4395    75    15   20
6217     4    10    5
7028  1962  1256  900
  .
  .
  .
  .   data to fill
  .   array INVEN
  .
  .
  .
'REQUEST'  6217    5
'REQUEST'  4395   60
'ARRIVAL'  6217    5
'REKUEST'  7028  400
```

Sample output: RECORD OF INVENTORY TRANSACTIONS

```
REQUEST FOR 5 ITEMS OF #6217
INSUFFICIENT NUMBER OF ITEMS
IN INVENTORY, PLEASE ORDER AGAIN.

REQUEST FOR 60 ITEMS OF #4395
  REQUEST HONORED
  REORDER 20 ITEMS

ARRIVAL OF 5 ITEMS OF #6217

INVALID TRANSACTION:
  REKUEST 7028 400
```

ALGORITHM DESIGN

There are four major aspects or modules to the solution to this problem, as this diagram shows.

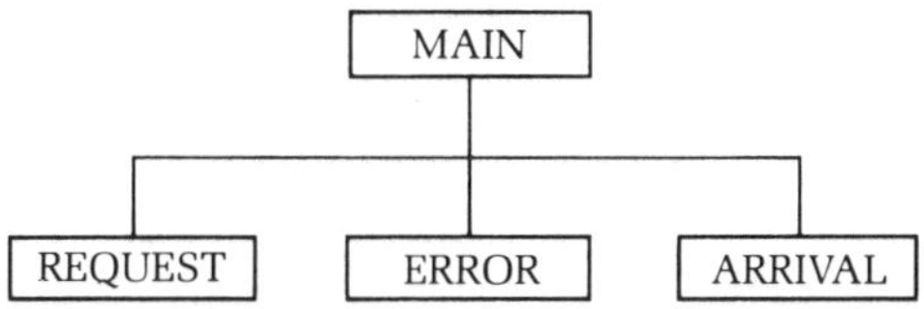

The MAIN module controls the entire process and passes control to the other modules as appropriate. The REQUEST module processes transactions that are identified as requests. The ARRIVAL module processes transactions identified as arrivals, and the ERROR module displays error messages for invalid transactions. The pseudocode is developed for each of these four modules.

Variables to be used:

INVEN	inventory array
TYPE	transaction type
IDENTIFICATION	inventory ID#
QUANTITY	number of items specified
EOF	end-of-file flag
SEARCH_FLAG	search flag
ERROR_FLAG	error flag
I, J	subscripts

PSEUDOCODE

MAIN module:

```
        GET INVEN
        GET a transaction
        PUT Heading
        DO while transactions remain
        IF transaction type is REQUEST
           THEN CALL REQUEST
           ELSE IF transaction type is ARRIVAL
                   THEN CALL ARRIVAL
                   ELSE ERROR_FLAG = 1
        IF ERROR_FLAG = 1
           THEN CALL ERROR
        GET the next transaction
        END
      END
```

REQUEST module:

```
        PUT heading message
        IF QUANTITY > 0 and transaction IDENTIFICATION is
          found in INVEN
          THEN IF transaction QUANTITY ≤ Quantity on hand
                  THEN subtract QUANTITY from Quantity on hand
                       PUT 'REQUEST HONORED'
                       IF Quantity on hand ≤ Reorder point
                          THEN PUT Reorder message
                  ELSE PUT insufficient inventory message
          ELSE ERROR_FLAG = 1
        RETURN
        END
```

ARRIVAL module:

```
        PUT heading message
        IF QUANTITY > 0 and transaction IDENTIFICATION is
          found in INVEN
          THEN add QUANTITY to Quantity on hand
          ELSE ERROR_FLAG = 1
        RETURN
        END
```

ERROR module:

PUT error message
RETURN
END

ALGORITHM IMPLEMENTATION

The MAIN module is implemented as the main procedure, and the other modules are implemented as internal subroutines. Global variables are used, so that no arguments are passed to the subroutines.

```
/* INVENTORY MAINTENANCE PROGRAM                   */
/* ARRAY INVEN IS UPDATED BY                       */
/* PROCESSING REQUEST AND ARRIVAL TRANSACTIONS */
XACTS:                              /* *** MAIN PROCEDURE *** */
   PROC OPTIONS (MAIN);
      DCL INVEN (50,4) FIXED,       /* INVENTORY ARRAY        */
          TYPE CHAR(7),             /* TRANSACTION TYPE       */
          IDENTIFICATION FIXED,     /* INVENTORY ID #         */
          QUANTITY FIXED,           /* # ITEMS SPECIFIED      */
          EOF FIXED INIT(0),        /* END-OF-FILE FLAG       */
          SEARCH_FLAG FIXED,        /* SEARCH FLAG            */
          ERROR_FLAG FIXED,         /* ERROR FLAG             */
          I FIXED;                  /* SUBSCRIPT              */
      ON ENDFILE(SYSIN) EOF = 1;
      GET LIST(INVEN);
      GET LIST(TYPE, IDENTIFICATION, QUANTITY);
      PUT SKIP(5) LIST('RECORD OF INVENTORY TRANSACTIONS');
      DO WHILE (EOF = 0);
         ERROR_FLAG = 0;
         IF TYPE = 'REQUEST'
            THEN CALL REQUEST;
            ELSE IF TYPE = 'ARRIVAL'
                    THEN CALL ARRIVAL;
                    ELSE ERROR_FLAG = 1;
         IF ERROR_FLAG = 1
            THEN CALL ERROR;
         GET LIST (TYPE, IDENTIFICATION, QUANTITY);
      END;
```

```
REQUEST:
   PROC;                                /* *** SUBROUTINE REQUEST *** */
      PUT EDIT('REQUEST FOR', QUANTITY, 'ITEMS OF #',
               IDENTIFICATION)(SKIP(2),A,F(6),A,F(6));
      SEARCH_FLAG = 0;
      DO I = 1 TO 50 WHILE (SEARCH_FLAG = 0);
         IF IDENTIFICATION = INVEN(I,1)
           THEN SEARCH_FLAG = 1;
      END;
      I = I - 1;
      IF QUANTITY > 0 & SEARCH_FLAG = 1
        THEN IF QUANTITY <= INVEN(I,2)
               THEN DO;
                       INVEN(I,2) = INVEN(I,2) - QUANTITY;
                       PUT SKIP LIST('REQUEST HONORED');
                       IF QUANTITY >= INVEN(I,3)
                          THEN PUT SKIP LIST('REORDER',
                            INVEN(I,4),'ITEMS');
                          ELSE:
                       END;
               ELSE PUT EDIT('INSUFFICIENT NUMBER OF ITEMS',
                             'IN INVENTORY, PLEASE ORDER AGAIN')
                             (SKIP,COL(3),A,COL(3),A);
        ELSE ERROR_FLAG = 1;
      RETURN;
      END REQUEST;
```

PROGRAM 10.12.

```
REQUEST:
  PROC;                                /* *** SUBROUTINE REQUEST *** */
     PUT SKIP(2) LIST('SUBROUTINE REQUEST ENTERED');
     RETURN;
  END REQUEST;
ARRIVAL:
  PROC;                                /* *** SUBROUTINE ARRIVAL *** */
     PUT SKIP(2) LIST('SUBROUTINE ARRIVAL ENTERED');
     RETURN;
  END ARRIVAL;
```

```
ARRIVAL:
    PROC;                              /* *** SUBROUTINE ARRIVAL *** */
        PUT EDIT ('ARRIVAL OF', QUANTITY, 'ITEMS OF #',
                  IDENTIFICATION)(SKIP(2),A,F(6),A,F(6));
        SEARCH_FLAG = 0;
        DO I = 1 TO 50 WHILE (SEARCH_FLAG = 0);
           IF IDENTIFICATION = INVEN(I,1)
              THEN SEARCH_FLAG = 1;
        END;
        I = I - 1;
        IF QUANTITY > 0 & SEARCH_FLAG = 1
          THEN INVEN(I,2) = INVEN(I,2) + QUANTITY;
          ELSE ERROR_FLAG = 1;
        RETURN;
    END ARRIVAL;
ERROR:
    PROC;                              /* *** SUBROUTINE ERROR *** */
        PUT EDIT('INVALID TRANSACTION:', TYPE, QUANTITY,
                 IDENTIFICATION)(SKIP(2),A,COL(3),A,F(6),X(5),F(6));
        RETURN;
    END ERROR;
    END XACTS;
```

modular approach is that simpler (and presumably easier) modules can be developed independently, so that one need not try to solve the entire problem with only one main procedure.

Several other features in Program 10.11 are worth comment.

1. Notice the error flag used to communicate between the main procedure and the three subroutines.
2. The search flag in both the REQUEST and the ARRIVAL subroutines is used to signal the location of a particular identification number. Following each search loop is an assignment statement that decrements variable I by one, compensating for the action of the DO loop.
3. The null ELSE statement in the REQUEST subroutine is not required, but its presence improves the readability of that procedure.

Several other approaches to solving this problem can be employed, such as using external rather than internal subroutines and/or passing arguments to the various subroutines instead of using global variables. Global variables and internal procedures are useful for relatively small problems, such as the inventory problem. However, for large, complex problems, external procedures and argument passing are preferred, because several people can be assigned simultaneously to the development of different procedures. Argument passing rather than use of EXTERNAL variables is often preferred, so that communication between procedures can be simplified.

10.9. SUMMARY

Subroutines and functions introduced in previous chapters are discussed in much more detail in this chapter. Internal and external blocks are compared, and the scope of variables is presented. The methods of argument passing are discussed, including the correspondence between arguments and parameters. Recursive procedures are also briefly introduced.

10.9.1. Key Concepts

1. A block is a group of statements within which variables can be declared.
2. There are two types of blocks: BEGIN blocks and procedure blocks.
3. A procedure block can be a main procedure, a subroutine, or a function.
4. A subroutine is invoked with a CALL statement. A function is invoked by referring to the function name and argument list.
5. A subroutine can return many values, but a function returns only one value.
6. Arguments appear in the invocation of a subroutine or a function, but parameters appear in the subroutines or functions.
7. An internal block is one that is completely contained within another block. BEGIN blocks are always internal blocks.
8. External blocks are not contained in other blocks and are physically separate from other blocks.
9. Any block that invokes an external procedure should declare that external procedure name as an ENTRY point, and it should also specify the attributes of the arguments passed to that external procedure.
10. The RETURNS attribute is used in a DECLARE statement, but the RETURNS option is used in a PROCEDURE statement.
11. The RETURNS attribute is used with the ENTRY attribute for functions only. The RETURNS option is used in the function, but both specify the attributes of the value returned by the function.
12. The scope of a variable refers to the extent to which that variable is known throughout a program.
13. A global variable is one used in a block but not declared in that block. A local variable is one that is both declared and used in a particular block.

14. Arguments can be passed by name or by value.
15. Asterisk notation is used to specify variable-size arrays or variable-size character strings in a subroutine or function.
16. The EXTERNAL attribute expands the scope of a variable to any other procedure for which that variable is declared as EXTERNAL.
17. A recursive procedure is one that can invoke itself.
18. A pseudo-random-number generator produces a sequence of numbers based on a seed or starting value. These numbers appear to be random, but are not, because they can be calculated from the seed.
19. Pseudo-random-number generators are adequate for many simulation problems.

10.9.2. Terms and Phrases

Write out definitions and/or usage descriptions of these terms. Check yourself against the text.

argument
asterisk notation
AUTOMATIC
BEGIN block
block
CALL
dummy argument
ENTRY
EXTERNAL
external block
factorial
function
global variable
internal block
invocation
local variable
module
parameter
pass by name
pass by value
procedure block
program
random number
RECURSIVE
RETURN
RETURNS
scope of a variable
simulation
STATIC
stub
subroutine

PROBLEMS

Problem 10.1. Which of the following always returns a single value?

a. external procedure
b. internal procedure
c. main procedure
d. function
e. subroutine

Problem 10.2. Which of the following is contained entirely within another procedure?

a. external procedure

b. internal procedure

c. main procedure

d. function

e. subroutine

Problem 10.3. Declare A as a variable-size array in a function or subroutine, but not a BEGIN block.

a. DCL A(*) FIXED;

b. DCL A(N) FIXED;

c. DCL A(N:M) FIXED;

d. DCL A(*:*) FIXED;

e. DCL A(*–*) FIXED;

Problem 10.4. Which describes how the value of C is passed in the statement:

CALL SUB (A, B, (C));

a. by reference

b. by dummy argument

c. by value

d. by name

e. by parentheses

Problem 10.5. A recursive procedure

a. is usually a BEGIN block

b. is a procedure that can invoke itself

c. must be an internal procedure

d. is also called a reentrant procedure

e. is a procedure that can only be invoked by other procedures

Problem 10.6. ______________ are passed to a subroutine, but in the subroutine, the corresponding items are called ______________.

a. expressions, variables

b. internal values, external values

c. main values, sub values

d. parameters, arguments

e. arguments, parameters

Use the problem-solving process, functions, and/or subroutines to solve the following problems.

Problem 10.7. Revise the Roman-number problem (8.6.3), so that a subroutine is used that has two parameters: the Roman number to be converted, and the result of the conversion.

Sample invocation: CALL ROMAN ('XIV', RESULT);

Problem 10.8. Revise Problem 10.7 so that a function is used instead of a subroutine. The function has one parameter, the Roman number to be converted.

Sample invocation: RESULT = ROMAN ('XIV');

Problem 10.9. Addition of large integers.

The input consists of two 60-digit integers, and the output consists of the sum of those two integers. *Hint:* Use arrays to represent each integer; let each array element contain one digit of an integer.

Problem 10.10. Multiplication of large integers.

The input consists of two 30-digit integers, and the output consists of the product of these two integers. Use the hint in Problem 10.9.

Problem 10.11. Morse-code translation.

The input consists of one English sentence, and the output consists of the individual words in that sentence, together with the Morse code equivalent. Only the letters A through Z and the blank can be used.

TABLE P10.11. Morse code equivalents for the letters A through Z.

A	.-	J	.---	S	...
B	-...	K	-.-	T	-
C	-.-.	L	.-..	U	..-
D	-..	M	--	V	...-
E	.	N	-.	W	.--
F	..-.	O	---	X	-..-
G	--.	P	.--.	Y	-.--
H	....	Q	--.-	Z	--..
I	..	R	.-.		

Sample input: 'THIS IS AN EXAMPLE'

Sample output:

MORSE-CODE TRANSLATION

WORD	MORSE CODE
THIS	- ....
IS	.. ...
AN	.- -.
EXAMPLE	. -..- .- -- .--. .-.. .

Problem 10.12. Poker-hand simulation.

Simulate the dealing of a poker hand, and display that hand. Assume that many decks of cards are being used, so that the probability of getting a particular card never changes; i.e., if an ace of hearts has already been dealt, the probability of getting another ace of hearts is unchanged. Use the RND function in section 10.8.1 to generate the card values and suits.

Sample output:

POKER-HAND SIMULATION

CARD NO.	SUIT	VALUE
1	HEART	9
2	CLUB	ACE
3	HEART	2
4	SPADE	KING
5	DIAMOND	7

Problem 10.13. Mean, median, and mode.

The input consists of an arbitrary number of unsorted integers. The output consists of the mean, median, and mode for that collection of numbers. Use one subroutine to sort the integers and another subroutine to perform the computations. The mean, or average, of a group of numbers is found by dividing the sum of those numbers by the number of occurrences of those numbers. The median is found by sorting the numbers and selecting the number that is in the "middle" of the sorted numbers. For example, if there are n numbers, where n is odd, the median is the number in the $n + 1/2$ position. However, if n is even, the median is the mean of the number in the $n/2$ position and the number in the $n/2 + 1$ position. The mode is the number that occurs most frequently. If the mode is not unique, display all modes.

Sample input: 46 89 23 46 19 23 95

Sample output:

MEAN, MEDIAN, AND MODE

SORTED DATA: 19 23 23 46 46 89 95
MEAN: 48.7
MEDIAN: 46
MODE: 23 46

Problem 10.14. Dart throwing.

Simulate the throwing of ten darts, and decide whether each dart lands inside a circle with radius 5, whose center is at X, Y-coordinates (6,6). The position of each thrown dart is represented by simulating an X-coordinate and a Y-coordinate. The X- and the Y-coordinate must be within the range from 0 to 12, inclusive, as shown in Figure 10.7. The equation for the circle in Figure 10.7 is $(X - 6)^2 + (Y - 6)^2 = 25$.

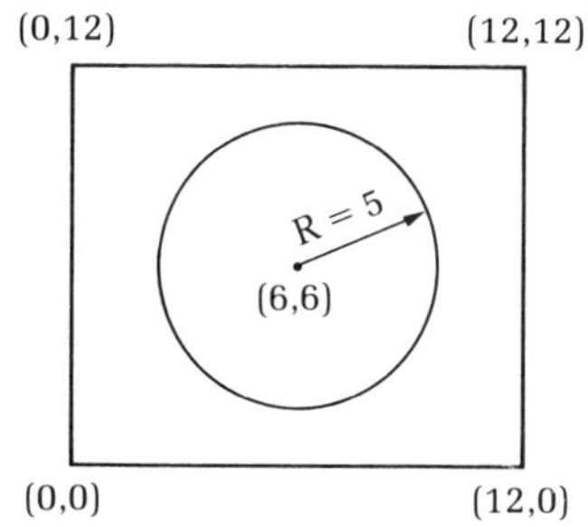

Figure 10.7.

Sample output:

DART THROWING

DART NO.	X	Y	INSIDE THE CIRCLE?
1	2	8	YES
2	1	0	NO
3	9	10	ON THE BORDER
.	.		.
.	.		.

THE NUMBER OF DARTS LANDING
INSIDE THE CIRCLE: ___

11 Structures

A *data aggregate* is a collection of data elements that can be referred to by one name. There are two types of data aggregates in PL/I: *arrays* and *structures*. Arrays were introduced in Chapter 8, and structures are emphasized in this chapter.

The primary difference between arrays and structures is that an array is a collection of homogeneous data elements, but a structure can be a collection of heterogeneous data elements. For example, consider the following declaration statement:

```
DCL A(10) FIXED;
```

Array A is a FIXED array of ten elements. Each and every element of this array has the same data attributes, whether the array is one-dimensional or multidimensional. However, structures permit collections of data in which each element could have a different data attribute.

Structures are especially useful in handling many commercial and business problems. For example, a personnel problem might require storage of such information about people as

Name	(character)
Social security number	(integer)
Street address	(character)
City and state	(character)
Zip code	(integer)

Consequently, the information for each person consists of both CHARACTER and FIXED data types. This information can be represented as a series of separate variables, but this becomes awkward or cumbersome when many variables are involved. The chief advantage of structures is that they provide a convenient method of representing very many dissimilar data elements.

11.1. COMPONENTS OF STRUCTURES

A structure is organized as a hierarchy, and the terms

major structure
minor structure
elements

are used to describe the three components of a structure.

The term *major structure* refers to the entire structure, and the term *minor structure* refers to a substructure of the major structure. There can be arbitrarily many minor structures, and each minor structure consists of one or more minor structures and/or *elements*. The relationship between these terms is shown in Figure 11.1.

Level numbers are used to specify relationships between the various components, and each component is assigned a name. The level numbers are posi-

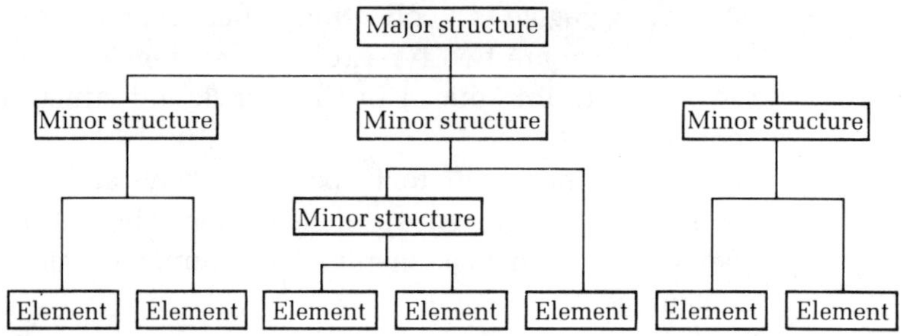

Figure 11.1.

tive integers starting with level 1, which is assigned to the major structure name. The level numbers specify containment or ownership between the various components. The level numbers and placement of components within the DECLARE statement reflect containment or ownership, as indicated in the following DECLARE statement (which is incomplete, because data attributes are missing):

```
DCL 1 PERSON,
      2 NAME,
         3 LAST,
         3 FIRST,
      2 SSN,
      2 ADDRESS,
         3 STREET,
         3 CITY,
         3 STATE,
         3 ZIP;
```

The name of this major structure is PERSON, and the names of the minor structures are NAME and ADDRESS. The names of the elements are LAST, FIRST, SSN, STREET, CITY, STATE, and ZIP. Note that NAME and SSN are each assigned level 2, but NAME is a minor structure and SSN is an element. The structure is shown in Figure 11.2.

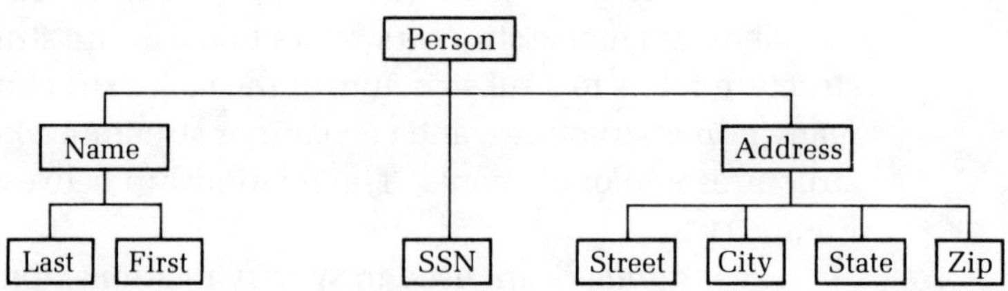

Figure 11.2.

The placement of components in a DECLARE statement is important. In the preceding DECLARE statement, SSN and ADDRESS have the same level number. If these two names were exchanged, then ADDRESS would be an element and SSN would be a minor structure. Consequently, some rules are necessary to declare structures properly. The more important rules are as follows:

1. Level 1 is assigned only to the major-structure name. All other level numbers are larger than 1.
2. The major-structure name must precede all other component names.
3. A minor-structure name must precede names of all components contained in that minor structure. Level numbers of component names contained in a minor structure must be larger than the level number of the minor-structure name.
4. Level numbers need not be assigned as consecutive integers (2, 3, 4, . . .) as long as the correct relationship of lower to higher level numbers is used for minor structures and elements.
5. Only elements have data attributes.
6. A minor structure is terminated by a component name that has a level number smaller than or equal to the minor-structure number.
7. Commas separate the various components of a structure.
8. The rules for creating component names are the same as the rules for creating variable names.
9. A major-structure declaration is terminated by a semicolon, the declaration of another structure, or the declaration of a variable (scalar or array).

11.2. STRUCTURE ATTRIBUTES

The elements of a structure can be assigned the same attributes as those assigned to any other variables. This includes FIXED, FLOAT, CHARACTER, INITIAL, and array attributes. This is illustrated by the following declaration of the structure PERSON, which was partially declared in section 11.1.

```
DCL 1 PERSON,
      2 NAME,
          3 LAST CHAR(15),
          3 FIRST CHAR(15),
      2 SSN FIXED,
      2 ADDRESS,
          3 STREET CHAR(25),
          3 CITY CHAR(15),
          3 STATE CHAR(2),
          3 ZIP FIXED;
```

Attribute factoring, including the factoring of level numbers, can be used in structures. For example, the elements LAST and FIRST in the preceding declaration could be declared as

```
3 (LAST,FIRST) CHAR(15),
```

Similarly, the elements in minor structure ADDRESS would be declared as

```
3(STREET CHAR(25), CITY CHAR(15), STATE CHAR(2),
  ZIP FIXED),
```

Unfortunately, attribute and level factoring often obscures the readability of structures. Consequently, structure factoring should be used only when the elements are obviously similar and when factoring does not make the structure less readable.

The INITIAL attribute can be used in the declaration of elements within a structure, as in

```
DCL 1 A,
      2 B FIXED INIT(106),
      2 C,
          3 D CHAR(6) INIT('VALUE='),
          3 E FLOAT INIT(78.6432),
      2 F FIXED INIT(-16);
```

The array attribute is permitted in structures at the major-structure level and at the element level; so both arrays within structures and arrays of structures are possible. The structure declaration

```
DCL 1 A,
      2 B,
          3 C(5) CHAR(10),
          3 D FIXED,
      2 E,
          3 F(25) FLOAT,
          3 G(10) CHAR(2);
```

contains three arrays of elements.

Minor structure B contains six elements: five elements in array C, and the element D. Minor structure E contains 35 elements: 25 elements in array F, and ten elements in array G. There are many useful applications of this concept. For example, consider the minor structure

```
2 CHILDREN,
    3 NUMBER FIXED,
    3 NAME(12) CHAR(15),
```

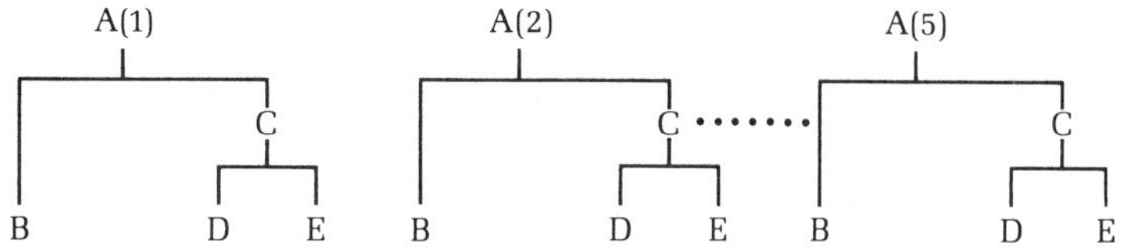

Figure 11.3.

This minor structure would likely be a part of a structure used in a personnel problem. The array in the minor structure permits use of the names of up to 12 children, where the element NUMBER would be an integer value from zero to twelve, indicating the number of children for a particular person. This permits each personnel structure to contain a different number of children's names, although storage space for the 12 elements in array NAME is reserved.

Arrays of structures can be declared by dimensioning the major-structure name. The declaration statement

```
DCL 1 A(5),
      2 B FIXED,
      2 C,
         3 D FLOAT
         3 E CHAR(4);
```

creates five identical structures.

Subscripts are used to specify a particular element or a particular structure. The five structures created here are labeled A(1), A(2), A(3), A(4), and A(5), and are depicted as shown in Figure 11.3.

One possible application for arrays of structures is to store sales information for a 12-month period. In the following declaration, each structure represents sales data for a particular month.

```
DCL 1 SALES(12),
      2 SUMMARY,
         3 TOTAL_SALES FLOAT,
         3 EXPECTED_SALES FLOAT,
         3 NUMBER_OF_UNITS_SOLD FIXED,
      2 TOP_SALESPERSON,
         3 NAME CHAR(20),
         3 SALES_THIS_MONTH FLOAT;
```

This array of structures contains some pertinent sales information over a one-year period. This information is represented in a convenient form and is easily accessed in any type of information-retrieval problem.

11.3. STRUCTURE OPERATIONS*

A good deal of flexibility is allowed in the referencing of structure components. An individual element can be referenced, a minor structure can be referenced, or even a major structure can be referenced. In other words, any of these three structure components can be referenced with one name. The structure

```
DCL 1 A,
      2 B,
         3 C FIXED,
         3 D FLOAT,
         3 E CHAR(2),
      2 F,
         3 C FIXED,
         3 D FLOAT,
         3 E CHAR(2),
      2 G CHAR(2);
```

is used in the following examples of structure referencing.

1. GET LIST (A);	The major-structure name A is referenced in this input statement, and every element in the structure acquires a value in the exact order of declaration. Sample input: 10, 1.5, 'AB', 106, 0.53, 'XY', 'RM'
2. GET LIST (B);	The minor structure B is referenced, and all three elements in B acquire values in the exact order of declaration. Sample input: 403, 196.81, 'CT'
3. GET LIST (G);	The element G is referenced, and it acquires a value. Sample input: 'VL'
4. B = F	The contents of minor structure B are replaced by the contents of minor structure F.
5. A.B.D = 54; or B.D = 54;	This is an example of the use of a qualified name. The name D must be qualified because it is used in two minor structures. Here the qualified name B.D is equivalent to A.B.D, which is a fully qualified name. The element D in minor structure B is assigned a value.

The preceding examples illustrate structure referencing, I/O, and qualified names. The first three examples use a GET statement, but whatever applies to the GET statement also applies to the PUT statement. Similarly, edit-directed I/O could also be used, but data-directed I/O is sometimes not practical, because

*In general, aggregate operations are limited with Subset G. See Appendix G.

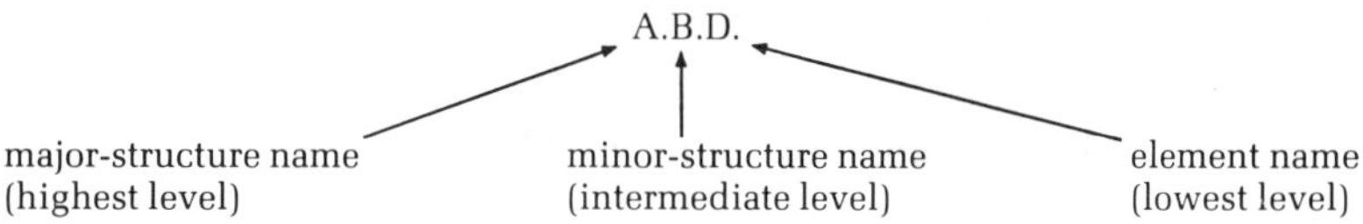

Figure 11.4.

TABLE 11.1. Trace Table for Program 11.1.

Statement	*Elements*					
	B	*D*	*E*	*G*	*I*	*J*
GET LIST(A);	14	5.1	10.3	?	?	?
F = A;	14	5.1	10.3	14	5.1	10.3
H = 2*H;	14	5.1	10.3	14	10.2	20.6
A = A+F;	28	15.3	30.9	14	10.2	20.6

fully qualified element names (which are defined shortly) must appear in the input stream as well as the output stream, even though a major or minor structure name may appear in a GET DATA or PUT DATA statement.

An entire structure is referenced in example 1. This is somewhat analogous to referencing an entire array by referencing the array name only. The minor structure B is referenced in examples 2 and 4, and an element is referenced in example 3. However, all references must be unambiguous, and qualified names are required to eliminate ambiguity. A qualified name is referenced in example 5, because there is an element named D in both minor structures B and F. Here A.B.D is a fully qualified name that references the element D in minor structure B. The term *fully qualified name* simply means that the element is referenced by the structure name, by all minor-structure names that contain the element, and by the element name. The term *qualified name* simply means a name preceded by enough names of a higher level to establish the uniqueness of the element or minor structure referenced. In either case, the names are connected by periods, and the order of the names is always from the higher levels to the lower levels, as illustrated in Figure 11.4.

If A is the name of a structure, then no other variable or array can be named A. If B is the name of an element or a minor structure, the name B can also be used outside the structure as a variable name or as an array name. The name B must then be qualified to avoid any ambiguity with a name B appearing outside the structure. Obviously, if there is only one name B in the entire program, then B does not have to be qualified, because it is unique.

Major structures and minor structures can be used with arithmetic operations or assignment statements if the structures each have the same *relative structure*, i.e., the same form and ordering of minor structures and elements. Program (segment) 11.1 contains several such manipulations, assuming that names A through J are not used elsewhere in the program.

Table 11.1 is a trace table showing the values of the elements in structures A and F that result from execution of the statements in Program 11.1.

PROGRAM 11.1.

Input line: 14 5.1 10.3

```
DCL 1 A,
      2 B FIXED,
      2 C,
        3 D FLOAT,
        3 E FLOAT,
    1 F,
      2 G FIXED,
      2 H,
        3 I FLOAT,
        3 J FLOAT;
            .
            .
            .
            .
            .
GET LIST (A);
F = A;
H = 2*H;
A = A+F;
PUT EDIT ('A=', A, 'F=', F)
         (COL(1), A,X(2), F(2), X(2), (2) F(5,1));
```

Output:

```
A = 28   15.3   30.9
F = 14   10.2   20.6
```

Statements referencing major- or minor-structure names are equivalent to a statement (or statements) referencing only element names. For example, the statement

GET LIST (A);

is equivalent to the statement

GET LIST (B,D,E);

Similarly, the statement

H = 2*H;

is equivalent to the statements

I = 2*I;
J = 2*J;

11.4. EXAMPLES

Complete solutions to two problems are presented in this section. A new attribute is introduced in the first problem, and operations with arrays are amplified in the second problem.

11.4.1. The Top-Salesperson Problem

A wine merchant has decided to implement a new sales incentive by awarding a bonus to the top salesperson of the month. Sales data for each month includes each person's amount of sales and the number of bottles of wine sold. Besides locating the top salesperson and computing the bonus, the wine merchant also wants to know the average sales per salesperson and the average number of bottles sold per salesperson.

The new attribute that is useful for this problem is the LIKE attribute.* The LIKE attribute is used to declare a major structure or a minor structure in the same form as another major or minor structure. Consider the following declaration, which uses the LIKE attribute:

```
DCL 1 A,
        2 B,
           3 C FIXED,
           3 D(4) FLOAT,
        2 E CHAR(10),
     1 F LIKE A,
     1 G LIKE A.B;
```

The structure A is explicitly declared, and the structure F is defined in terms of structure A. That is, structure F has exactly the same form as structure A, including levels, names, and attributes. The major structure G has the same form as minor structure B. Using the LIKE attribute is equivalent to explicitly describing structures F and G as

```
DCL 1 F,
        2B,
           3 C FIXED,
           3 D(4) FLOAT,
        2 E CHAR(10),
     1 G,
           3 C FIXED,
           3 D(4) FLOAT;
```

The LIKE attribute can also be used to declare elements. However, the LIKE attribute must always reference an explicitly declared structure component.

*The LIKE attribute is not available with PL/C or Subset G.

PROGRAM 11.2.

PROBLEM DEFINITION

The input consists of the current month's sales data for each salesperson, and has the following form:

```
NAME
SALES_DATA
   DOLLAR_AMOUNT
   BOTTLES_SOLD
      BURGUNDY
      CHABLIS
```

There are an arbitrary number of salespersons, and the top salesperson is decided solely by DOLLAR_AMOUNT_OF_SALES. The bonus paid is based on NUMBER_OF_BOTTLES_SOLD, i.e., five cents per bottle of BURGUNDY and four cents per bottle of CHABLIS. The output consists of the salesperson's name, the amount of the bonus, the total amount of the sales (for all salespersons), the total number of bottles of Burgundy sold, and the total number of bottles of Chablis sold.

Sample input:

```
'SALLY BONET'   10000   750   1500
'MARK BONVIN'    8000   900    700
        .
        .
        .
        .
        .
        .
```

Sample output:

```
TOP SALESPERSON IS:
      name
BONUS = amount
TOTAL SALES = amount
TOTAL BOTTLES OF BURGUNDY = amount
TOTAL BOTTLES OF CHABLIS = amount
```

ALGORITHM DESIGN

Three structures are useful in the solution to this problem, i.e., one to store data for the top salesperson, one to represent each person in the input stream, and one to store the totals.

Variables to be used:

SALESPERSON	major structure, each person
NAME	element, person's name
SALES_DATA	minor structure
DOLLAR_AMOUNT	element, amount of sales
BOTTLES_SOLD	minor structure
BURGUNDY	element, number of bottles
CHABLIS	element, number of bottles
TOPS	major structure, top salesperson
TOTALS	major structure, grand totals
BONUS-AMOUNT	dollar amount of bonus
EOF	end-of-file flag

PSEUDOCODE

```
Initialize TOPS, TOTALS, EOF
Get first SALESPERSON
Do while input data is available
   IF SALESPERSON.DOLLAR_AMOUNT >
      TOPS.DOLLAR_AMOUNT
      THEN TOPS = SALESPERSON
   Accumulate TOTALS
   GET next SALESPERSON
END
Compute BONUS_AMOUNT
PUT TOPS.NAME,BONUS_AMOUNT,TOTALS
END
```

ALGORITHM IMPLEMENTATION

```
/* COMPUTE BONUS FOR THE TOP WINE SALES PERSON */
BONUS:
    PROC OPTIONS(MAIN);
        DCL 1 SALESPERSON,              /* TYPICAL SALESPERSON */
              2 NAME CHAR(20),
              2 SALES__DATA,
                3 DOLLAR__AMOUNT FLOAT,
                3 BOTTLES__SOLD,
                  4 BURGUNDY FIXED,
                  4 CHABLIS FIXED,
            1 TOPS LIKE SALESPERSON,   /* TOP SALESPERSON */
            1 TOTALS LIKE SALESPERSON.              /* GRAND */
              SALES__DATA,                          /* TOTALS */
            BONUS__AMOUNT FLOAT,                    /* BONUS */
            EOF FIXED INIT(0);                      /* E.O.F. FLAG */
        TOPS.DOLLAR__AMOUNT = 0;
        TOTALS = 0;
        ON ENDFILE(SYSIN) EOF = 1;
        GET LIST(SALESPERSON);
        DO WHILE (EOF = 0);
            IF SALESPERSON.DOLLAR__AMOUNT >
              TOPS.DOLLAR__AMOUNT
              THEN TOPS = SALESPERSON;
            TOTALS = TOTALS + SALESPERSON.SALES__DATA;
            GET LIST(SALESPERSON);
        END;
        BONUS__AMOUNT = TOPS.BURGUNDY * 0.05 +
          TOPS.CHABLIS * 0.04;
        PUT EDIT('TOP SALESPERSON IS:', TOPS.NAME,
                 'BONUS =',BONUS__AMOUNT,
                 'TOTAL SALES =', TOTALS.DOLLAR__AMOUNT
                 'TOTAL BOTTLES OF BURGUNDY =',
                   TOTALS.BURGUNDY,
                 'TOTAL BOTTLES OF CHABLIS =',
                   TOTALS.CHABLIS)
                 (SKIP(5), A, COL(4), A, COL(4), A, X(1), F(9,2),
                 SKIP(2), A, X(1), F(7,2), COL(1), A, X(1), F(7),
                 COL(1), A, X(1), F(7));
    END BONUS;
```

For example, if structure A were explicitly declared, the declaration

```
DCL 1 F LIKE A,
    1 G LIKE F.B;
```

would be in error. The declaration for structure F is valid, but the declaration for structure G is not, because F is not explicitly declared. The LIKE attribute does not provide any new capability, but it does provide a convenient method of describing structure components.

Structure declarations tend to become lengthy, especially when several structures are required. The chief advantage of the LIKE attribute is that it provides a shorthand notation for the declaration of similar major structures, minor structures, or elements. However, extensive use of the LIKE attribute can reduce the readability of programs; so it should be used judiciously and sparingly.

Program 11.2 contains several important structure manipulations, such as the following.

1. Assignment of a constant to a major or a minor structure (every element is assigned that constant).
2. Assignment of one structure to another structure (element-by-element replacement).
3. Addition of a minor structure to a major structure (element-by-element addition).
4. Major structure Input/Output.

Qualified names are also required, because the structures contain identical names (due to the LIKE attribute). However, fully qualified names are not necessary to establish uniqueness for any of the elements.

11.4.2. The Bank-Account Survey Problem

The management of a bank has decided to conduct a survey of its savings accounts. The accounts are selected at random, and account data is stored in an array of structures. The purpose of the survey is to find the following.

1. The average number of years that these accounts have been open.
2. The average balance of these accounts.
3. For each account with an above-average balance, the total amount of deposits and the total amount of withdrawals for the five most recent transactions.

The solution to this problem requires an array of structures as well as an array within a structure. Consequently, a few more comments about arrays and structures are in order before we solve this problem.

Subscripts are used to reference individual elements in an array regardless of how or where that array is used. For example, consider the declaration statement

PROGRAM 11.3.

PROBLEM DEFINITION

The management of a bank has decided to survey 150 savings accounts, which have been randomly selected. The input consists of data for these accounts and has the form

ACCOUNT_NUMBER
CURRENT_BALANCE
NUMBER_OF_YEARS
RECENT_TRANSACTIONS(5)

The RECENT_TRANSACTIONS are either deposits or withdrawals. Deposits are positive numbers, and withdrawals are negative numbers. The output consists of:

1. The average number of years that these accounts have been open.
2. The average current balance of these accounts.
3. The total amount of deposits and withdrawals for the five most recent transactions for the accounts whose current balance is above the average.

Sample input:

```
468931   1862.48   5   26.25   -100
   -200   50   -100
506197   421.63   2   503.19   -200
   -100   -100   25
      .
      .
      .
      .
      .
      .
```

Sample output:

```
SURVEY RESULTS
AVERAGE NUMBER OF YEARS IS ____
AVERAGE CURRENT BALANCE IS ____
FOR ACCOUNTS WITH ABOVE AVERAGE BALANCES
TOTAL AMOUNT OF DEPOSITS IS ____
TOTAL AMOUNT OF WITHDRAWALS IS ____
```

Variables to be used:

ACCOUNT (150)	array of major structures
ACCOUNT_NUMBER	element, account number
CURRENT_BALANCE	element, current balance
NUMBER_OF_YEARS	element, years account opened
RECENT_TRANSACTIONS(5)	array of elements, five most recent transactions
YEARS	total years, average years
BALANCE	total balances, average balance
DEPOSIT	total deposits
WITHDRAW	total withdrawals
I, J	subscripts

ALGORITHM DESIGN

Each account must be referenced twice for this problem to be solved; so the input data must be stored in variables, arrays, or structures. An array of 150 structures is ideally suited to this problem because of the convenience in referencing these accounts.

PSEUDOCODE

```
Initialize YEARS, BALANCE, DEPOSIT, WITHDRAWAL

DO I = 1 TO 150
  GET ACCOUNT (I)
  Accumulate YEARS
  Accumulate BALANCE
END
YEARS = YEARS/150
BALANCE = BALANCE/150

DO I = 1 TO 150
  For each account with a current balance greater than
  BALANCE, accumulate DEPOSIT and WITHDRAW, using the
  five most recent transactions
END
PUT YEARS, BALANCE, DEPOSIT, WITHDRAW
END
```

ALGORITHM IMPLEMENTATION

```
/* THE BANK ACCOUNT SURVEY PROBLEM */
SURVEY:
   PROC OPTIONS(MAIN);
      DCL 1 ACCOUNT (150),            /* ACCOUNTS SURVEYED */
            2 ACCOUNT_NUMBER FIXED,
            2 CURRENT_BALANCE FLOAT,
            2 NUMBER_OF_YEARS FIXED,
            2 RECENT_TRANSACTIONS(5) FLOAT,
          YEARS FLOAT INIT(0),        /* TOTAL & AVERAGE
                                                  YEARS */
          BALANCE FLOAT INIT(0),      /* TOTAL & AVERAGE
                                                BALANCE */
          DEPOSIT FLOAT INIT(0),      /* TOTAL DEPOSITS      */
          WITHDRAW FLOAT INIT(0),     /* TOTAL WITHDRAWALS   */
          (I,J) FIXED;                /* SUBSCRIPTS          */
      DO I = 1 TO 150;
         GET LIST(ACCOUNT (I));
         YEARS = YEARS + ACCOUNT(I).NUMBER_OF_YEARS;
         BALANCE = BALANCE +
           ACCOUNT(I).CURRENT_BALANCE;
      END;
      YEARS = YEARS / 150;               /* COMPUTE AVERAGE */
      BALANCE = BALANCE / 150            /* COMPUTE AVERAGE */
      DO I = 1 TO 150;
         IF ACCOUNT(I). CURRENT_BALANCE > BALANCE
            THEN DO J = 1 TO 5;
                    IF ACCOUNT(I).
                          RECENT_TRANSACTIONS(J)>0
                       THEN DEPOSIT=DEPOSIT
                         + ACCOUNT(I).
                          RECENT_TRANSACTIONS(J);
                       ELSE WITHDRAW=WITHDRAW
                         + ACCOUNT(I).
                          RECENT_TRANSACTIONS(J);
                 END;
      END;
      PUT EDIT('SURVEY RESULTS',
               'AVERAGE NUMBER OF YEARS IS',YEARS,
               'AVERAGE CURRENT BALANCE IS',BALANCE,
               'FOR ACCOUNTS WITH ABOVE AVERAGE
                 BALANCES',
               'TOTAL AMOUNT OF DEPOSITS IS',DEPOSIT,
               'TOTAL AMOUNT OF WITHDRAWALS IS',
                 WITHDRAW)
              (SKIP(5),A,COL(1),A,X(1),F(4,1),
               COL(1),A,X(1),F(8,2),COL(1),A,
               COL(4),A,X(1),F(8,2),COL(4),A,X(1),F(8,2));
   END SURVEY;
```

```
DCL 1 A(10),
      2 B,
        3 C(5) FIXED,
        3 D(10) FLOAT,
      2 E(20) CHAR(5);
```

Ten structures are declared, and each structure can be referenced by a subscript, i.e., A(1), A(2), . . ., A(10). Within each structure are the three arrays C, D, and E. Suppose that the third element of array D in the fifth structure of A were to be assigned the value zero. This would be accomplished by any one of the statements

```
A(5).D(3) = 0;
D(5,3) = 0;                    (if the name D is unique)
A(5,3).D = 0;
A.D(5,3) = 0;
```

A great deal of flexibility is permitted in the construction of subscripts for referencing arrays in structures. An array of structures need not be one-dimensional, but may be multidimensional as well. The flexibility of subscript construction also applies to multidimensional arrays of structures.

The Bank-Account Survey Problem requires an array of structures to store the selected accounts. Each structure contains an array representing the five most recent transactions.

The array of structures used in this program contains no minor structures; only elements are used. Note the use of subscripts in this program to reference an element in an array within a structure. Also note that structural elements can be used in the same manner as scalar variables or array elements.

11.5. SUMMARY

Structures are compared to arrays in terms of data organization and attributes of the data elements. Major structures, minor structures, and structural elements, as well as methods of declaring structures, are discussed. Operations on various levels of structures, including the use of qualified names, are presented. Several complete problems that emphasize the use of structures are solved.

11.5.1. Key Concepts

1. The two types of data aggregates in PL/I are arrays and structures.
2. An array is a collection of homogeneous data elements, but a structure is a collection of heterogeneous data elements.
3. The three components of a structure are:
   major structure
   minor structure
   element

4. A major structure is the entire structure, and a minor structure is a substructure of the major structure.
5. Arbitrarily many minor structures are permitted, and each minor structure may consist of one or more minor structures and/or elements.
6. In a DECLARE statement, level numbers are used to specify relationships between the various components of a structure. The major structure is uniquely assigned level number 1.
7. Level numbers of component names contained in a minor structure must be larger than the level number of the minor-structure name.
8. Only elements have data attributes, which are the same attributes that can be assigned to arrays or scalar variables.
9. Arrays within structures are permitted, as are arrays of structures.
10. A good deal of flexibility is permitted in the referencing of structure components. For example, an entire structure can be referenced in a GET, PUT, or assignment statement.
11. Element names must be qualified if they are referenced but not unique.
12. A fully qualified name includes the major-structure name, all minor-structure names that include the element, and the element name itself. Each name is separated by a period.
13. The LIKE attribute is used to declare a major structure or a minor structure in the same form as another major or minor structure. The LIKE attribute can also be used to declare elements.
14. The LIKE attribute provides a shorthand notation for declaring similar structural components.
15. Much flexibility is permitted in the construction of subscripts for referencing arrays in structures, as well as for referencing arrays of structures.

11.5.2. Terms and Phrases

Write out definitions and/or usage descriptions of these terms. Check yourself against the text.

array
array element
array of structures
element
heterogeneous data
hierarchy
homogeneous data
level factoring
level numbers
LIKE
major structure
minor structure
qualified name
scalar variable
structural element
structure
subscript

PROBLEMS

Problem 11.1. *True or false?*

a. An array is a collection of homogeneous data.

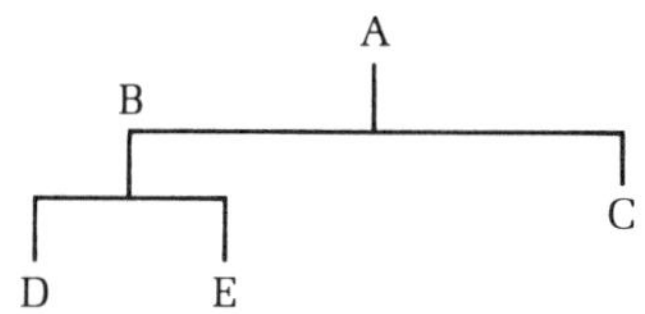

Figure 11.5.

b. A structure is a collection of heterogeneous data.

c. No data attributes can be assigned to major-structure names.

d. Minor-structure names are assigned level 1.

e. Structural elements can be qualified to avoid ambiguity.

Problem 11.2. Write one easy-to-read declaration for the structure in Figure 11.5, in which all elements are FIXED.

Problem 11.3. Using the structure in Problem 11.2, decide which of the following is a properly qualified element name.

a. A.C.E
b. B.E
c. D.E
d. C.A
e. A.B

Problem 11.4. Given the structure declaration

```
DCL 1 A(5),
        2 B FIXED,
        2 C(4) FLOAT,
        2 D CHAR(4);
```

Which of the following is a correct reference to the structure?

a. D = A(1);

b. B.C(2) = A(3).D;

c. C(4) = A(5);

d. D = C;

e. A(3,2).C = 63;

Problem 11.5. Given the structure in Problem 11.4, which of the following cannot be a valid operation?

a. GET LIST(A);

b. B(2) = D(4);

c. A(1).B = A(3).C;

d. A(5).C = 16.5;

e. A.B(4) = A.(4);

Use the problem-solving process to develop a solution for each of the following problems.

Problem 11.6. Computer dating.

Suppose that data for 30 people is to be stored in an array of structures in which each structure contains the following information:

Name (up to 25 characters)
Sex (M or F)
Response Integer array of 20 elements in which each element represents a response to a question in a computer dating questionnaire.

Two people are said to be matched if they have 15 or more identical responses to the questionnaire. The purpose of this problem is to display each person's name, followed by a list of names of all people of the opposite sex who are matched with that person. If a person is not matched with anyone, an appropriate message is displayed.

Sample input: Data for the 30 people

Sample output: LISTING OF ALL MATCHED PERSONS

SALLY ADAMS
  JOHN JONES
  HARVEY SMITH
BOB BEAN
  SORRY—NO MATCHES

Problem 11.7. Computerized test scoring.

The keys to two forms of an examination are to be stored in a structure containing the following information:

Name (up to 30 characters)
Form (the value 1 or 2)
Answers Array of 40 elements that represent correct answers to a multiple-choice examination.

An arbitrary number of students have taken the examination, and data for each student has the same organization as the two keys. The input consists of data for the two keys, followed by data for the students. Each student examination is to be graded with one of the keys, depending on the form number (1 or 2) of each examination. The output consists of each student name and the number of correct answers. After all students are displayed, averages are displayed for all examinations, for all form 1 examinations, and for all form 2 examinations.

Sample input:

```
EXAMINATION KEY 1  43214523 . . . . .
EXAMINATION KEY 2  2135235 . . . . . .
JOHN ADAMS       2  2124235 . . . . . .
```

Sample output:

EXAMINATION RESULTS

NAME	SCORE
JOHN ADAMS	35
.	.
.	.
.	.

12 Complete Data Representation

TABLE 12.1. Attributes for numeric data.

Attribute type	*Attribute possibilities*
Scale	FIXED or FLOAT
Base	DECIMAL or BINARY
Precision	size and decimal position
Mode	REAL or COMPLEX

A working knowledge of the basic data types was presented in earlier chapters. The intention there was to discuss only the essentials, without becoming immersed in details inappropriate for the beginning programmer. However, most details of the major data types are presented in this chapter. In particular, FIXED, FLOAT, and CHARACTER data types are revisited, and there is a presentation of PICTURE and BIT data types.

12.1. NUMERIC DATA

Attributes for numeric data have thus far been restricted to FIXED or FLOAT. However, four attributes are possible for numeric data, as shown in Table 12.1.

The COMPLEX data type is not discussed in this book, so the mode attribute is always assumed to be REAL. The other attributes are illustrated by the following six examples.

1. ```
   DCL  J  FIXED   DECIMAL   (7,2);
              ↑         ↑        ↑
   scale──────┘  base───┘    precision
   ```

   Variable J can contain numbers consisting of seven decimal digits, with two of the digits appearing on the right side of the decimal point. Variable J is thus called a fixed-point variable. For example, the decimal value 64321.89 could be stored in variable J.

2. ```
   DCL  I  FIXED  BINARY  (15);
                or
   DCL  I  FIXED  BINARY  (15,0);
   ```

   Variable I can contain numbers consisting of 15 binary digits (bits), and none of the bits appear to the right of the binary point. For example, the binary value 000001011011011 could be stored in variable I. Binary constants, bit strings, and data conversion are discussed later in this chapter.

3. ```
   DCL  K  FIXED  BINARY  (7,2);
   ```

   Variable K can contain numbers consisting of seven bits, with two of the bits appearing on the right of the binary point. For example, the binary value 00011.01 could be stored in variable K.
   ```

4. DCL X FLOAT DECIMAL (6);

   Variable X can contain floating-point values with up to six significant decimal digits. The size of the exponent is unaffected by a declaration; only the number of significant digits is changed. For example, if variable X were assigned the value 12345689.123, the actual value stored in X would be 1.23456E+07.

5. DCL Y FLOAT BINARY (21);

   Variable Y can contain floating-point values with up to 21 significant bits, or about six decimal digits.

6. DCL Z FLOAT DECIMAL (6,2); /* INVALID */

   This is an invalid declaration, because the precision attribute refers only to the number of significant digits.

The various forms of the precision attribute are:

```
                                DECIMAL
DCL variable name FIXED           or       (W,D);
                                BINARY

                                DECIMAL
DCL variable name FIXED           or       (W);
                                BINARY

                                DECIMAL
DCL variable name FLOAT           or       (W);
                                BINARY
```

where W is the total number of digits and D is the number of digits to the right of the decimal (binary) point.

Except for precision, the order of the data attributes is not important. However, the attributes must be separated by one or more blanks. For example, the statement

```
DCL X DECIMAL FIXED (7,2);
```

is valid, but the statement

```
DCL X FIXEDDECIMAL (7,2);
```

is invalid, because there is no space between two of the attributes. The precision attribute is usually placed immediately after the scale and base attributes to avoid confusion with the array attribute. The statement

```
DCL X (7,2) FIXED DECIMAL;
```

is valid, but no precision attribute is present, because X is declared as a two-dimensional array.

If one or more data attributes are missing in a variable declaration, the compiler assigns default attributes in place of the missing attribute(s). The two most common defaults for data attributes for *undeclared* variables are as follows. In PL/C and IBM PL/I,*

For variable names beginning with the letters I through N	REAL FIXED BINARY (15)
All other variable names	REAL FLOAT DECIMAL (6)

In ANSI Standard PL/I,

All undeclared variable names	REAL FIXED BINARY (15)

If a variable is partially declared (one or more attributes missing), the compiler fully declares that variable with the default attributes. The statement

```
DCL  I  FIXED;
```

is assigned several default attributes and is equivalent to

```
DCL  I  FIXED BINARY (15);
```

Similarly, the statement

```
DCL  X  FLOAT;
```

is assigned several default attributes and is equivalent to

```
DCL X FLOAT DECIMAL (6);
```

although the precision default may vary, depending on which compiler is used.

Variables should always be declared fully rather than by compiler defaults, for several reasons:

1. Programs are not restricted to the characteristics of a particular PL/I compiler.
2. Programs are more readable if variables are declared and appear with brief comments.
3. Programs can be more easily executed on machines that have different PL/I compilers.
4. The defaults may not be as expected.

The FIXED BINARY attribute combination is ideally suited for the representation of integers, and this is how FIXED has been used so far in this book. The FIXED DECIMAL attribute combination is ideally suited for monetary

*For PL/C and IBM PL/I, variables declared with only the FIXED attribute default to REAL FIXED DECIMAL (5).

computations. However, values are not automatically rounded when stored in a FIXED DECIMAL variable. For example, given the statements

```
DCL DOLLAR FIXED DECIMAL (7,2);
   .
   .
   .
   .
   .
DOLLAR = 568.4384;
```

the value 568.43 is stored in variable DOLLAR. The FLOAT DECIMAL and FLOAT BINARY attribute combinations are ideal for mathematical and scientific computations. The abbreviations for DECIMAL and BINARY are DEC and BIN, respectively.

12.2. CHARACTER STRINGS

Character-string data types have been thoroughly covered in previous chapters, but the following examples are presented in the interest of completeness.

1. DCL L CHARACTER (20);

   Variable L contains a character string of 20 characters in length. If a string assigned to L has less than 20 characters, blanks are padded on the right. For example, given

   L = 'THIS IS A STRING';

   The string 'THIS IS A STRINGƀƀƀƀ' is assigned to L; here "ƀ" represents a blank.

2. DCL L CHAR (20) VAR;

   Variable L contains a character string of varying length, i.e., from 0 to 20 characters. Blank padding does not occur. For example, given

   L = 'THIS IS A STRING';

   The string 'THIS IS A STRING' is assigned to variable L. CHAR and VAR are abbreviations for CHARACTER and VARYING, respectively.

3. DCL L CHAR (20) INIT ((3)'ABCDEF');

   This is the same as example 1, except that variable L is initialized to the value

   'ABCDEFABCDEFABCDEFƀƀ'

   If variable L were declared as VARYING in this example, the two blanks would not be padded on the right.

One character-string operation not discussed in previous chapters is the STRING option for GET and PUT statements. The STRING option causes data to be moved internally, instead of performing an input/output operation. The STRING option allows the GET statement to take values from a string, rather than from the input stream, and place these values into specified variables. The PUT statement with the GET option performs a reverse operation; i.e., it places values in a string rather than in the output stream.

The STRING option is particularly useful for handling data with different formats. Suppose that the first value of each input line specifies the type of format for that line, as follows:

```
1 'JONES', 45, 2
2 6289, 503
1 'SMITH', 39, 3
      .
      .
      .
      .
```

The following statements handle these two data formats.

```
DCL TYPE FIXED,                 /* DATA TYPE */
  INFO CHAR(79),                /* DATA      */
  NAME CHAR(20)VAR,             /* FORMAT 1  */
  (AGE,DEP) FIXED,              /* FORMAT 1  */
  (ID,QUANTITY) FIXED;          /* FORMAT 2  */
  .
  .
  .
GET EDIT (TYPE,INFO)(COL(1),F(1),A(79));
IF TYPE = 1
  THEN GET STRING(INFO)
    LIST(NAME,AGE,DEP);
  ELSE GET STRING(INFO)
    LIST(ID,QUANTITY);
```

The STRING option can also be used with edit-directed I/O, but options such as PAGE, COLUMN, LINE, and SKIP may not be used. Following is an example of the PUT statement with the STRING option, assuming that the variables have been declared in the preceding example.

```
NAME = 'MELISSA ANNE';
AGE = 25;
DEP = 1;

PUT STRING(INFO)
  EDIT(NAME,AGE,DEP)
    (A(12),X(1),F(2),X(1),F(1));
```

No output operation occurs as a result of this PUT statement; instead, after it is executed, the character-string variable INFO contains

'MELISSA ANNE 25 0 ƀƀƀƀ . . . . ƀƀƀ'

12.3. PICTURE DATA *

Suppose a variable contains a value such as 8564.73, which is to appear in the output stream as

$8,564.73

This output form can be achieved with the data types discussed previously, but the task would not be easy. However, the PICTURE data type is ideally suited for data-editing problems, such as inserting commas, decimal points, and dollar signs. The PICTURE data type is also used to represent fixed-point, floating-point, and character-string data values. The general form for declaration of PICTURE variables is:

DCL *variable name* PICTURE '*specifications*';

The PICTURE attribute is so named because the specifications resemble a picture of the data being described. There are three types of PICTURE specifications for fixed-point, floating-point, and character-string values. These specifications consist of combinations of picture codes that describe the features of these values. Table 12.2 describes the picture codes used in this chapter

TABLE 12.2. Commonly used picture codes.

		Allowable Specifications		
Picture code	*Description*	*Numeric-fixed*	*Numeric-float*	*Character*
9	decimal digit (0–9)	X	X	X
V	decimal point alignment	X	X	
S	sign (+ or −)	X	X	
Z	zero suppression	X	X	
$	dollar sign	X		
.	decimal-point insertion	X	X	
,	comma insertion	X	X	
*	asterisk fill	X	X	
/	slash insertion	X	X	
A†	characters A–Z and blank			X
X†	any character			X
K†	exponent		X	
E†	exponent, display E		X	

†Not available with Subset G.

*The PICTURE data type is not available with PL/C.

and the specifications in which they can be used. The PICTURE attribute can be used in variable declarations, array declarations, and structure declarations. The following 14 examples illustrate the use of picture codes in creating specifications. The abbreviation for PICTURE is PIC, and the phrase "output value" refers to the output produced by a PUT LIST statement.

1. DCL X PIC '999';

   Variable X contains an unsigned three-digit decimal number, including leading zeros if necessary. The following assignment statements show the various values that can be stored in variable X as a result of this declaration.

X = 5;	output value, 005
X = 192.8;	output value, 192
X = 48.6;	output value, 048
X = 0.9;	output value, 000

2. DCL X PIC 'S999';

X = 5;	output value, +005
X = −47;	output value, −047
X = 19.64;	output value, +019

3. DCL X PIC 'S999V.99';

X = 5;	output value, +005.00
X = −47;	output value, −047.00
X = 19.64;	output value, +019.64
X = −0.643;	output value, −000.64

   The V code specifies the position of the implied decimal point, and the period is an insertion character. In this book, the period is used only when it appears immediately to the right of the V code.

4. DCL X PIC 'S999V99';

X = 5;	output value, +00500
X = −47;	output value, −04700
X = 19.64;	output value, +01964
X = −0.643;	output value, −00064

   The period is not present in this declaration; so it does not appear in the output.

5. DCL X PIC 'SS9V.99';

X = 5;   output value, b̸+5.00

X = −47;   output value, −47.00

X = 19.64;   output value, +19.64

X = −0.643;   output value, b̸−0.64

This example uses the S code in the "drifting" form, but examples 2–4 use the S code in the "static" form.

6. DCL X PIC 'ZZ9S';

X = 5;   output value, b̸b̸ 5+

X = −47;   output value, b̸ 47−

X = 19.64;   output value, b̸ 19−

X = −0.643;   output value, b̸b̸ 0−

The Z code suppresses leading zeros by replacing them with blanks. The S code may optionally be placed on the right side of the specification.

7. DCL X PIC'$$,$$9V.99';

X = 45.6;   output value, b̸b̸b̸ $45.60

X = 7643;   output value, $7,643.00

X = .53;   output value, b̸b̸b̸b̸ $0.53

X = 128.24;   output value, b̸b̸ $128.24

The $ code is used in drifting form here and suppresses leading zeros. Comma insertion is used also.

8. DCL X PIC '*****9V.99';

X = 25;   output value, ****25.00

X = 19.62;   output value, ****19.62

X = 5093;   output value, **5093.00

X = 0.17;   output value, *****0.17

Asterisk fill is often used for check protection; it precedes the dollar amount with asterisks, thereby making it difficult for anyone to tamper with the amount.

9. DCL X PIC '99/99/99';

X = 122584;   output value, 12/25/84

X = 70462;   output value, 07/04/62

The slash-insertion character is useful for separating data fields into month, day, and year portions.

10. DCL X PIC 'AAAAAAAA';

    X = 'MISSY ANNE'; output value, MISSY AN
    X = 'ABCD'; output value, ABCDb̸b̸b̸b̸

    Only the letters A through Z and the blank can be stored in variable X by this declaration. A repetition factor could be used to shorten the picture specification. The specification '(8)A' is equivalent to the above specification. Repetition factors can be used in any picture specification.

11. DCL X PIC '(6)X';

    X = (3)'AB'; output value, ABABAB
    X = 'A1.6B4'; output value, A1.6B4
    X = 'T'; output value, Tb̸b̸b̸b̸b̸

    Any character can be stored in this variable as a result of this declaration, which is equivalent to

    DCL X CHAR(6);

12. DCL X 'AAA999';

    X = 'RSN324'; output value, RSN324
    X = '324RSN'; error

    The X, A, and 9 codes can be intermixed in a character specification. This fact can be used for data verification. For example, here the variable could represent a particular part identification that is supposed to consist of three letters followed by three digits. If any value were placed in variable X that did not meet this requirement, then an error would result.

13. DCL X PIC 'S9V.99KS99';

    X = 46; output value, +4.60+01
    X = −1.5E3; output value, −1.50+03
    X = .0000346; output value, +3.46−05

    The K code is used to specify the exponent for floating-point values.

14. DCL X PIC 'S9V.99ES99';

    X = 46; output value, +4.60E+01
    X = −1.5E3; output value, −1.50E+03
    X = .0000346; output value, +3.46E−05

    The E code is similar to the K code, except that the character "E" appears in the output stream.

Input and output of picture data are performed in the same manner as for the other data types for data-directed and list-directed I/O statements. For example, suppose we are given the input line

```
5  −47  19.64  −0.643
```

and the statements

```
DCL (A,B,C,D) PIC 'SS9V.99';
  .
  .
  .
GET LIST (A,B,C,D);
PUT LIST (A,B,C,D);
```

The output produced by this program segment is

```
+5.00  −47.00  +19.64  −0.64
```

However, edit-directed I/O uses the "P" specification, which indicates picture data format. The form of the P specification for edit-directed I/O is

P '*picture codes*'

The picture codes for the P specification appear in Table 12.2 and are used in the same manner as declarations of picture variables. However, the codes Z, $, comma, *, and / should not be used in GET-statement picture specifications. Only those codes that actually specify the form of the input data should be used in a GET EDIT statement. All the codes may be used in PUT-statement picture specifications. For example, if we are given the input line

```
43.95       3965.27
```

and the statements

```
DCL (A,B) PIC '9999V.99';
  .
  .
  .
GET EDIT (A,B) (COL(1), P'99V.99', X(5), P'9999V.99');
PUT EDIT (A,B) (COL(1), P'***9V.99', X(5), P'$$,$$9V.99');
```

the output produced by this program segment is

```
**43.95       $3,965.27
```

12.4. BIT STRINGS

The character string '10111101' consists entirely of binary digits (bits), i.e., all zeros and ones. If a string consists entirely of bits, a bit string such as

'10111101'B can be used. The character "B" at the end of a bit string distinguishes it from a character string. One advantage of bit strings is that they require only a fraction of the storage required by character strings. Some examples of bit-string constants are

```
'1011'B
'111010111001'B
'110'B
'1'B
'0'B
```

Bit-string variables can be declared with the BIT attribute. The general form for declaration of BIT variables is

DCL *variable name* BIT *(length)*;

number of bits ↗ (pointing to *length*)

The VARYING attribute may be optionally used. If a BIT variable is assigned a bit string that has fewer bits than the declared length of that variable, then zeros are padded on the right. Similarly, bits are truncated on the right if the bit-string length exceeds the BIT variable length to which it was assigned. These truncation and padding features of bit strings are similar to those for character strings. As an example of these features, suppose we are given the input line

```
'1101'B  '11011001100111'B  '1'B
```

and the statements

```
DCL (A,B,C) BIT(6);
  .
  .
  .
GET LIST (A,B,C);
PUT LIST (A,B,C);
```

The output produced by this program segment is:

```
'110100'B  '110110'B  '100000'B
```

Note that the quote marks and the letter "B" appear in both the input and the output. If the variables in this example were declared as

```
DCL (A,B,C) BIT(14) VAR;
```

then the output would be identical to the input, because no truncation or zero padding would result from the VARYING attribute.

Suppose variable X were declared as

```
DCL X BIT(7) VAR;
```

Then each of the following assignment statements would cause the same value to be assigned to variable X.

X = '0101101'B;	bit string assigned to X
X = 0101101B;	binary constant assigned to X
X = '0101101';	character-string constant assigned to X
X = 45;	integer constant assigned to X

The first assignment statement is a straightforward example of assigning a bit string to a BIT variable, but the second example refers to a binary constant, which is the binary representation of the decimal integer 45. A binary constant looks like a bit string, except for the missing quote marks. The third and fourth assignment statements require conversion of a character string and a decimal integer to bit strings. Conversion between data types is discussed in the next section.

Bit strings of length one are of particular interest, because they are used in relational expressions. For example, the condition in a DO WHILE statement or an IF statement is ultimately reduced to a bit string of length one. The bit string '1'B represents "true," and the bit string '0'B represents "false." If FIXED variable X contains the value 10, then the evaluation of the relational expression A > 4 results in the bit string '1'B, which is regarded as true. Actually, any bit string that contains one or more 1s is regarded as true. Consequently, in the statement

```
DCL A FIXED INIT(10);
  .
  .
  .
IF A
  THEN action 1;
  ELSE action 2;
```

the THEN clause would be executed, because the condition in the IF statement is considered true. This occurs because the contents of variable A are equivalent to the bit string '1010'B. Similarly, the statements

```
DO WHILE ('1'B);
END;
```

contain a condition that is always true. This DO loop is actually an "infinite loop," because it loops forever (or until the allocated computer time is completely used).

Bit strings can also be used in the evaluation of expressions. If we are given the statements

```
DCL (B,C) FIXED,
 .     A BIT(1);
 .
 .
B = 10;
C = 15;
```

then given

```
A = B = C;
```

'0'B is stored in A, because variables B and C are not equal. (Note: the first equals sign is a replacement operator, but the other is a relational operator.)

```
A = B < C;
```

'1'B is stored in A, because variable B is less than C.

```
A = B > C;
```

'0'B is stored in A, because variable B is not greater than C.

Bit strings also use the concatenation operator (||), the AND operator (&), the OR operator (|), and the NOT operator (¬). Concatenation of bit strings has the same meaning as concatenation of character strings; given

```
DCL X BIT(10) VAR;
X = '1011'B || '011'B;
```

variable X contains the bit string '1011011'B, and given

```
X = '1'B || '00'B;
```

variable X contains the bit string '100'B.

The NOT operator is a unary operator and works with one bit string. The NOT operator changes all zeros to ones and ones to zeros in a bit string. For example, suppose we are given the statement

```
DCL (A,B) BIT(6) VAR;
```

Table 12.3 gives examples of bit strings that result from applications of the NOT operator.

The AND and OR operators each work with two bit strings and operate on a bit-by-bit basis. Table 12.4 gives examples of AND and OR operations on bit strings of length one. The AND operation results in a 1 bit only if both bits are 1 bits; otherwise a 0 bit results. The OR operation results in a 1 bit if either bit is a 1 bit; only if both bits are 0 bits does a 0 bit result.

The AND and OR operators can operate on two bit strings of any length, by operating on pairs of bits from the two strings. If one bit string is shorter than the other, zeros are padded on the right of the shorter bit string, so that both

TABLE 12.3. NOT operations.

Statements	*Resulting bit string*
A = '0'B; B = ¬ A;	'1'B
A = '100111'B; B = ¬ A;	'011000'B
B = ¬ '010101'B;	'101010'B
A = '101'B; B = ¬ (A || '001'B);	'010110'B
A = '100'B; B = ¬ (A = '101'B);	'1'B

TABLE 12.4. AND and OR operations on one-bit strings.

Expression using AND(&)	*RESULT*	*Expression using OR(|)*	*RESULT*
'0'B & '0'B	'0'B	'0'B | '0'B	'0'B
'0'B & '1'B	'0'B	'0'B | '1'B	'1'B
'1'B & '0'B	'0'B	'1'B | '0'B	'1'B
'1'B & '1'B	'1'B	'1'B | '1'B	'1'B

TABLE 12.5. AND and OR operations on multiple-bit strings.

Operation statements	*Resulting bit string in variable A*
A = '10110111'B & '00100101'B;	'00100101'B
A = '101'B; B = '111111'B; A = A & B;	'10100000'B
A = '11111111'B & '001'B;	'00100000'B
A = '011010'B | '100111'B;	'11111100'B
A = '00'B | (¬ ('010'B & '111'B));	'10100000'B

strings are the same length for the AND and OR operations. Given the statements

```
DCL A BIT(8),
    B BIT(6);
```

Table 12.5 shows the results of several AND and OR operations.

An expression can include arithmetic, logical, relational and character-string operators. However, the rules discussed earlier for evaluating expressions are concerned only with the precedence of arithmetic operators. Table 12.6 gives the precedence levels for all operators; level 1 is the highest precedence and level 7 the lowest.

TABLE 12.6. Precedence of operators.

<table>
<tr><th>Precedence level</th><th>PL/I operators</th></tr>
<tr><td>1</td><td>**, ¬, unary +, unary −</td></tr>
<tr><td>2</td><td>*, /</td></tr>
<tr><td>3</td><td>+, −</td></tr>
<tr><td>4</td><td>||</td></tr>
<tr><td>5</td><td>>=, >, ¬=, =, <, <=, ¬<, ¬></td></tr>
<tr><td>6</td><td>&</td></tr>
<tr><td>7</td><td>|</td></tr>
</table>

The rules for evaluating expressions remain the same, except that more precedence levels need to be considered. Operators are evaluated in the order dictated by the precedence levels, starting with level 1. If two or more operators of the same precedence level appear in an expression, they are evaluated from left to right (except for consecutive exponentiation operators, which are evaluated from right to left). Of course, the use of parentheses can change the order in which operators are evaluated.

Expressions can become quite complex when several of these operators are used. For example, several arithmetic, logical, relational, and character-string operations are used in the following.

```
DCL A FIXED INIT(10),
    B FIXED INIT(5),
    C BIT(8) VAR INIT('1011'B),
    D BIT(20) VAR;
 .
 .
 .
 .
D = (A > 5*B | B <= 10) || C || ¬ (A < 100 & B > 1000);
```

The value stored in variable D as a result of executing this program segment is the bit string '110111'B. Figure 12.1 gives a detailed analysis of how the expression for D is evaluated.

The results are listed in the order in which each operator is evaluated. For example, the first operator evaluated is the multiply operator, which results in a value of 25.

12.5. DATA CONVERSION

Section 12.4 showed that an expression can contain different types of operators. However, an operator cannot directly work with values of unlike data types, such as adding a FIXED value to a FLOAT value. Since many such operations are permitted, conversion from one data type to another is required before the desired operation can be performed. These data conversions are done automatically whenever required by an assignment statement, I/O statement, IF

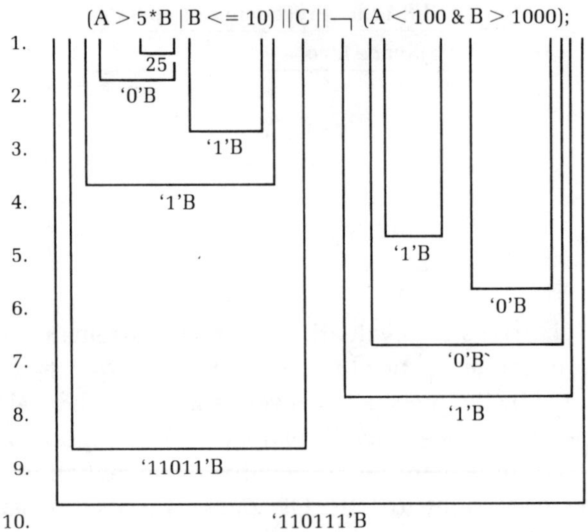

Figure 12.1. *Analysis of precedence evaluation.*

statement, DO statement, etc. One rough guideline for data conversion is that conversion can usually occur if it makes sense. For example, suppose that A is a FLOAT variable in the statement

```
A = 'ABC';                    (error; invalid conversion)
```

The character string 'ABC' needs to be converted to floating-point form before being stored in variable A. This is nonsense, because floating-point values can only be numeric values. However, if A were a FLOAT variable in the statement

```
A = '123';                    (valid conversion)
```

then the character string '123' could be converted to floating-point form, because all the characters in the string are digits. The following examples illustrate valid data conversions.

1. ```
   DCL A FIXED;
   A = '123';
   PUT LIST (A);          /* RESULT: 123 */
   ```

   A character string consisting entirely of digits is assigned to a fixed-point variable.

2. ```
   DCL B FLOAT;
   B = '12.34';
   PUT LIST (B);          /* RESULT: 1.23400E+01 */
   ```

A character string consisting of digits and a period is assigned to a floating-point variable.

3.
```
DCL C FIXED;
C = '1010'B;
PUT LIST (C);            /* RESULT: 10 */
```

A bit string is assigned to a fixed-point variable. Note that 1010_2 is equal to 10_{10}. The subscripts refer to either a binary or a decimal base.

4.
```
DCL D CHAR(9) VAR;
D = 123;
PUT LIST (D);            /* RESULT: b̸b̸b̸123 */
```

A fixed-point constant is assigned to a character variable. The value 'b̸b̸b̸123' is stored in variable D, but the value b̸b̸b̸123 is displayed.*

5.
```
DCL E CHAR (6) VAR;
E = '110111'B;
PUT LIST (E);            /* RESULT: 110111 */
```

A bit string is converted to a character string. The value '110111' is stored in variable E, but the value 110111 is displayed.

6.
```
DCL F BIT (10) VAR;
F = 45;
PUT LIST (F);            /* RESULT: '0101101'B */
```

A fixed-point constant is assigned to a bit variable. Note that 0101101_2 is equal to 45_{10}.

7.
```
DCL G BIT (10) VAR;
G = '10111';
PUT LIST (G);            /* RESULT: '10111'B */
```

A character string is assigned to a bit variable. The character string must consist only of zeros and ones for conversion to take place.

*When a FIXED DECIMAL (*w, d*) value is assigned to a character variable, the resulting string length is *w* + 3. When a FLOAT DECIMAL (*w*) value is assigned to a character variable, the resulting string length is *w* + 6.

8. DCL H PIC '999V.99';
   H = 46.1;
   PUT LIST (H); /* RESULT: 046.10 */

9. DCL I PIC '$$9V.99';
   I = '101101'B;
   PUT LIST (I); /* RESULT: $45.00 */

   A bit string is assigned to a picture variable. Recall that the value 101101_2 is equal to the value 45_{10}.

10. DCL J FLOAT INIT (12.5E0);
    J = J + 1;
    PUT LIST (J); /* RESULT: 1.35000E+01 */

    A fixed-point constant is added to a floating-point variable, which is initialized by 12.5E0 (a floating-point constant). The fixed-point constant 1 is converted to the floating-point value 1E0 before addition is performed.

11. DCL K FIXED INIT (30);
    K = K + '1';
    PUT LIST (K); /* RESULT: 31 */

    A character-string constant is added to a fixed-point variable. The character string cannot contain any nonnumeric characters if conversion to fixed point is to occur.

12. DCL L CHAR (10) VAR INIT ('ABC');
    L = L || 123;
    PUT LIST (L); /* RESULT: ABC 123 */

The automatic data-conversion facility of PL/I permits a great deal of flexibility in data representation. The programmer is thus relieved of many painstaking details, because the conversion is automatic. However, this flexibility must be used wisely to avoid unexpected results. In particular, examples 11 and 12 are valid, but their use can lead to problems. The beginning programmer should avoid using data conversion of the types shown in these last two examples.

12.6. SUMMARY

A working knowledge of FIXED and FLOAT data types was presented in previous chapters, and these data types are covered in greater detail in this chapter. The picture data type is introduced, along with many commonly used picture codes. Bit strings are introduced, and their relationship to relational expressions is illustrated. Conversion of data types is discussed, and several examples are presented that demonstrate allowable conversions.

12.6.1. Key Concepts

1. Numeric variables can have the following attribute types:

Scale	(FIXED or FLOAT)
Base	(DECIMAL or BINARY)
Precision	(W,D) or (W)
MODE	(REAL or COMPLEX)

2. If one or more data attributes are missing in a variable declaration, the compiler assigns default attributes in place of the missing attributes.
3. The FIXED BINARY attribute combination is well suited for the representation of integers.
4. The FIXED DECIMAL attribute combination is well suited for the representation of monetary values.
5. The FLOAT DECIMAL and FLOAT BINARY attribute combinations are quite similar, and both are well suited for mathematical or scientific computations.
6. The STRING option can be used with GET or PUT statements and causes data to be moved internally, instead of performing an I/O operation.
7. The PICTURE attribute is so named because the specifications resemble a picture of the data being described.
8. The PICTURE data type is well suited for data-editing problems, such as inserting commas, decimal points, and dollar signs.
9. The P specification can be used with edit-directed I/O to deal with picture data.
10. Bit strings consist entirely of zeros and ones, and are declared with the BIT attribute.
11. Bit strings require only a fraction of the storage required by corresponding character strings.
12. The value of a relational expression is a bit string of length one, where '0'B represents false and '1'B represents true.
13. Bit strings can be operated on by the AND, OR, and NOT operators.
14. An expression can include arithmetic, logical, relational, and character-string operators. There are seven levels in the complete precedence table for operators.
15. One rough guideline for data conversion is that conversion can usually occur if it makes sense.

12.6.2. Terms and Phrases

Write out definitions and/or usage descriptions of these terms. Check yourself against the text.

AND (&)	NOT (¬)
base	OR (|)
BIT	padding
bit string	PIC
character string	PICTURE
COMPLEX	picture codes
concatenate (||)	picture specification
data conversion	precedence levels
default attributes	precision
false ('0'B)	REAL
FIXED BINARY	scale
FIXED DECIMAL	significant digits
fixed point	STRING
floating point	true ('1'B)
mode	VARYING

PROBLEMS

Use the problem-solving process to develop a solution for each of the following problems.

Problem 12.1. Date representation.

The input consists of arbitrarily many dates in the form

YYYYMMDD

where YYYY represents the year, MM represents the month, and DD represents the day. The output consists of the date in both of these forms:

MM/DD/YYYY   Month Day, Year

For example, if an input data element were 19841025, the corresponding output would be:

10/25/1984   OCTOBER 25, 1984

Problem 12.2. Data editing.

The input consists of monetary quantities, such as 45.68, 8,408.32, or 100. Insert a leading dollar sign and commas as needed, and place five asterisks immediately after the value.

Sample input: 45.68 0.38 8,408.32 100

Sample output:

DATA EDITING	
INPUT	OUTPUT
45.68	$45.68*****
0.38	$0.38*****
8,408.32	$8,408.32*****
100.	$100.00*****

Problem 12.3. Information retrieval.

The input consists of data for an unknown number of persons, in the following form:

Name (up to 25 characters)
Info (a bit string of length 8 that represents sex, age, languages known, and occupation)

The individual bits of the bit string have the meanings shown in Table P12.3.

TABLE P12.3.

Bit number	*Meaning*
1	0 = female, 1 = male
2	0 = under 35 years old, 1 = 35 or older
3	1 = knows French, 0 = does not know French
4	1 = knows Spanish, 0 = does not know Spanish
5	1 = knows Swahili, 0 = does not know Swahili
6	1 = knows Korean, 0 = does not know Korean
7	1 = engineer, 0 = not an engineer
8	1 = salesperson, 0 = not a salesperson

The output consists of the names of all female engineers who speak French and Korean and who are under 35 years of age.

The input data for a person meeting these qualifications could appear as

'SALLY SMITH' '00100110'B

13 Storage Allocation

Two classes of storage allocation have been discussed in previous chapters, AUTOMATIC allocation and STATIC allocation. These two classes are briefly reviewed in this chapter, and two additional storage classes are discussed: CONTROLLED- and BASED-storage allocation.* Problems involving linked lists are solved, and some properties of storage-allocation classes are effectively used.

13.1. STATIC ALLOCATION

The STATIC-storage attribute is used to allocate storage initially and causes that storage to remain allocated as long as the program remains active. The STATIC attribute is used in the DECLARE statement and ensures the continued availability of storage. The statement

```
DCL A(25) FIXED STATIC;
```

forces the allocation of storage for array A when the program is compiled. Storage for array A remains available as long as the program is being executed. The STATIC attribute can be used in the main procedure, external functions, and subroutines to reduce the number of arguments to be passed.

13.2. AUTOMATIC ALLOCATION

AUTOMATIC is the default-storage allocation class.† For this class, storage is automatically allocated and freed as needed. For example, if variables are declared in a BEGIN block, an internal function, or a subroutine, then storage for those variables is allocated when that block is entered, and the storage is released when that block is departed.

The advantage of automatic-storage allocation is that storage is allocated only as long as it is needed, so that the space can be used more efficiently. Variable-size arrays are easily implemented with automatic allocation, but not with static allocation.

13.3. CONTROLLED ALLOCATION§

Controlled-storage allocation is similar to automatic allocation in that both methods allocate and free storage as needed. However, for controlled allocation, the programmer must explicitly allocate and free storage with the ALLOCATE and FREE statements. By contrast, the system automatically allocates and frees storage when blocks are activated and deactivated in automatic allocation.

The CONTROLLED attribute is used in the DECLARE statement to specify controlled status for scalar variables, entire arrays, and major structures. In the statements

*Controlled storage, based storage, and list-processing features are not available with PL/C.

†Except as noted in Chapter 10, the STATIC attribute is the default for EXTERNAL variables.

§Controlled storage allocation is not available with Subset G.

```
DCL X FLOAT CONTROLLED;
ALLOCATE X;
X = 19.25;
PUT LIST (X);
FREE X;
```

the variable X is declared as a controlled variable and X cannot be referenced until storage for X is allocated. In the preceding statements, storage is allocated for X, two statements reference X, and then storage for X is released.

The following statements illustrate how arrays are created with controlled allocation.

```
DCL A(10) FIXED CONTROLLED;
ALLOCATE A;
     .
     .
     .
     .
     .
FREE A;
```

Similarly, structures can be created with controlled allocation, as depicted by the following statements.

```
DCL 1 S CONTROLLED,
      2 A CHAR(10)
      2 B FIXED,
      2 C FLOAT,
      2 D PIC '999';
ALLOCATE S;
     .
     .
     .
FREE S;
```

A *pushdown stack* is formed by allocating the same variable more than once. The statements

```
DCL X FIXED CONTROLLED;
ALLOCATE X;
X = 109;
ALLOCATE X;
X = 13;
ALLOCATE X;
X = 234;
```

234
13
109

Figure 13.1. *A pushdown stack.*

create the stack shown in Figure 13.1. The pushdown stack is so named because each new element is pushed down on top of the existing elements. Only the top element of the stack is accessible and is removed with the FREE statement. The following statements display and remove successive elements from the pushdown stack in Figure 13.1.

```
PUT SKIP LIST (X);          /* RESULT: 234 */
FREE X;
```

The values 13 and 109 remain in the stack.

```
PUT SKIP LIST (X);          /* RESULT: 13 */
FREE X;
```

The value 109 remains in the stack.

```
PUT SKIP LIST (X);          /* RESULT: 109 */
FREE X;
```

The stack is empty.

Controlled-storage allocation is often used in conjunction with based-storage allocation, which is discussed in the next section.

13.4. BASED ALLOCATION*

Based allocation is similar to controlled allocation in that both methods allocate and free storage as needed with the ALLOCATE and FREE statements. However, the location of a based variable depends on a *pointer variable;* it is not the top element of a pushdown stack.

A pointer variable is a special type of variable that can contain the location or address of a scalar variable, an array, or a structure. The POINTER attribute is used to declare a pointer variable in the statement

```
DCL P POINTER;
```

Based allocation can be used for scalar variables, arrays, and structures. However, structures are particularly useful in based allocation, so the only examples given here will be of structures.

The following declaration statement uses the BASED attribute for the structure.

*The SET option is required for the ALLOCATE statement with Subset G; i.e., ALLOCATE *based-variable* SET (*pointer*).

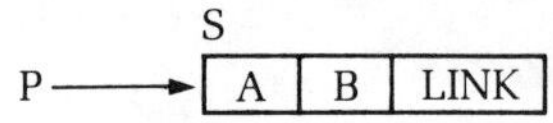

Figure 13.2.

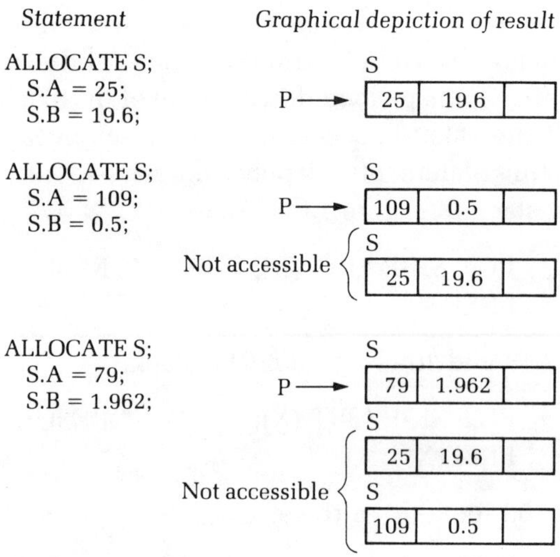

Figure 13.3.

```
DCL P POINTER,
      1 S BASED (P),
          2 A FIXED,
          2 B FLOAT,
          2 LINK POINTER;
```

The pointer variable P can contain only an address; it cannot be used for numeric or character-string operations. Pointer variable P can acquire a value in several ways, two of which are:

1. assignment of another pointer variable to P
2. allocation of a structure S that is based on P

Storage for structure S is not allocated until the statement

```
ALLOCATE S;
```

is executed. When this statement is executed, storage is allocated for structure S, and pointer P is assigned the address of that structure. Graphically, this is depicted as shown in Figure 13.2. Thus, pointer P "points" to structure S, because the address of S is automatically placed in P when the ALLOCATE statement is executed. However, if multiple ALLOCATE statements are executed, pointer P points only to the last structure allocated, as Figure 13.3 shows.

After each ALLOCATE statement in Figure 13.3 is executed, two assignment statements store values in elements of the structure S, which is pointed to by P. In fact, any reference to S is implicitly through P, because S is a based structure (based on P). If multiple ALLOCATE statements are executed, the only structure that can be accessed is the one pointed to by P. The other structures are essentially lost, because there is no way of accessing them. Executing a FREE statement releases storage for the structure currently pointed to by P, but then P does not point to any structure.

One way to prevent these additional structures from becoming inaccessible is to create several pointer variables and to save each value of pointer P for future use. The program segment in Figure 13.4 saves the current value of P in another pointer variable, so that all three of the structures are accessible.

After the third ALLOCATE statement in Figure 13.4, all three structures are accessible, because each is pointed to by a pointer variable. The value of P can be changed to the value of SAVE1 or SAVE2 as needed. The process is reversed by the FREE statements; after the third one, no storage is allocated for structure S.

A special symbol is available to permit easy referencing of based variables. That symbol is composed of the "minus" sign followed by the "greater than" sign (->); they must be adjacent to each other. That compound symbol is interpreted literally as "points to," and the general form of its use is

pointer variable -> based variable

To understand the use of this special symbol, consider this example. Suppose we are given the structure shown in Figure 13.2, in which structure S is based on P. If P points to S, then

```
     S.A = 25;
P -> S.A = 25;
```

are equivalent assignment statements. There can be many occurrences of structure S; the reference P -> S.A refers to an element of the structure currently pointed to by P. Other valid statements using the "points to" symbol are

```
GET LIST (P -> S);
P -> S.A = P -> S.B;
PUT LIST (P -> S.A);
```

Any pointer variable (not just P) can be used with the "points to" symbol; for example, SAVE1, as in Figure 13.5.

Valid statements accessing the structures shown in Figures 13.2 and 13.5 are as follows:

Program segment	*Graphical depiction of result*

DCL (P, SAVE1, SAVE2) POINTER,
  1 S BASED (P),
    2 A FIXED,
    2 B FLOAT,
    2 LINK POINTER;
ALLOCATE S;
S.A = 25;
S.B = 19.6;
SAVE1 = P;
	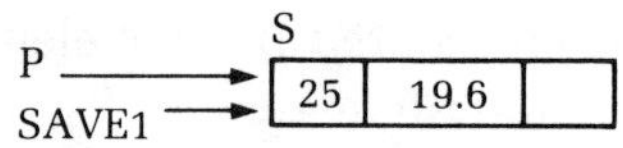
	(Both P and SAVE1 point to S.)

ALLOCATE S; S.A = 109; S.B = 0.5; SAVE2 = P;	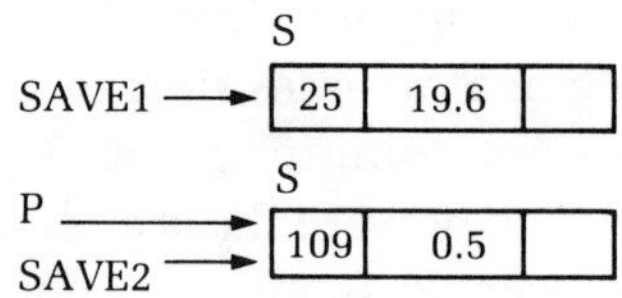
ALLOCATE S; S.A = 79; S.B = 1.962;	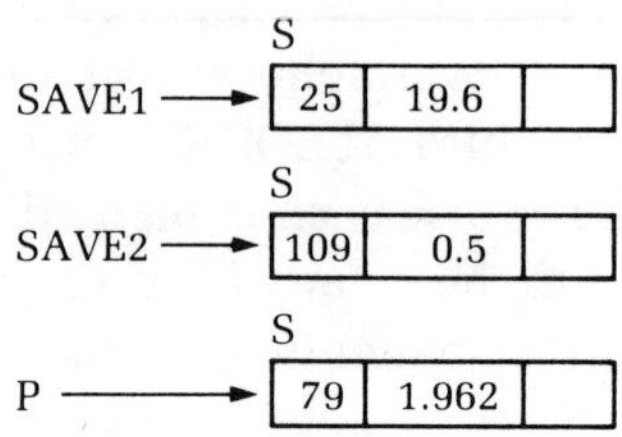
PUT LIST (S.A, S.B); FREE S; P = SAVE1;	/* RESULT: 79, 1.96200E+00 */ 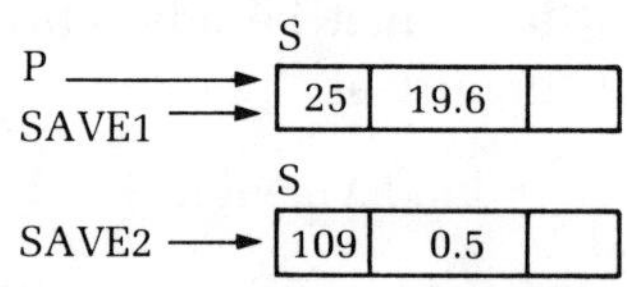
PUT LIST (S.A, S.B); FREE S; P = SAVE2;	/* RESULT: 25, 1.96000E+01 */ 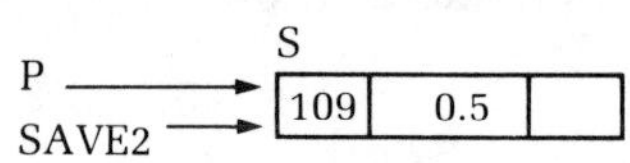
PUT LIST (S.A, S.B);	/* RESULT: 109, 5.00000E−01 */
FREE S;	

Figure 13.4.

```
  P -> S.A = 25;
SAVE1 -> S.A = 64;
SAVE1 -> S.B = P -> S.A;
  GET LIST (SAVE1 -> S.B);
  PUT LIST (SAVE1 -> S);
  P -> LINK = SAVE1;
```

This last statement is noteworthy, because this type of statement is essential for many manipulations of based structures. For example, three structures

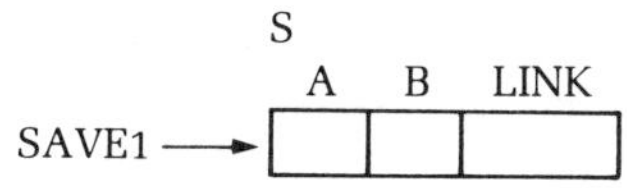

Figure 13.5.

Statement	*Graphical depiction of result*
ALLOCATE S; SAVE1 = P	
ALLOCATE S; P −> LINK = SAVE1; SAVE1 = P;	
ALLOCATE S; P −> LINK = SAVE1; SAVE1 = P;	

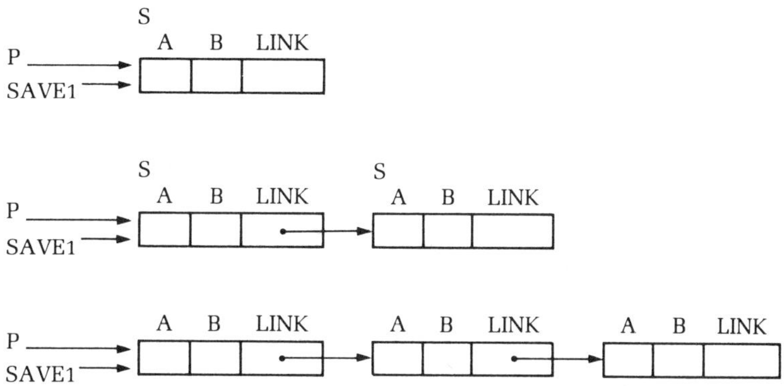

Figure 13.6.

Statement	*Graphical depiction of result*
P = P −> S.LINK;	
P = P −> S.LINK; P −> S.A = 906;	

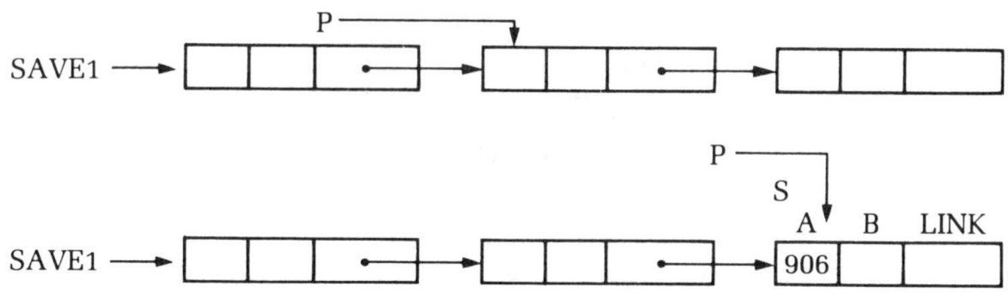

Figure 13.7.

are tied (or linked) together by the statements in Figure 13.6; we are assuming that structure S is based on P, as previously declared, and that SAVE1 is a pointer variable. Notice that the second and third set of statements cause the link field of P −> S to point to another structure.

Arbitrarily, many structures can be linked together in the fashion shown in Figure 13.6. Manipulations of such linked structures are easy to handle. For example, suppose the value 906 is to be placed in element A of the rightmost structure at the bottom of Figure 13.6. Doing so requires moving one of the pointer variables (say, P) to the rightmost structure, as shown in Figure 13.7.

A pointer variable can acquire only an address of a structure, an array, or a variable. A statement such as

```
P -> S.LINK = 45;
```

is invalid, because a data value is assigned to a pointer variable. However, a pointer variable can be assigned the value NULL, which means that it does not point to anything. Actually, the value NULL is a built-in function and is used as follows.

```
DCL NULL BUILTIN;
P -> S.LINK = NULL;
```

The BUILTIN attribute specifies that NULL is a built-in function. It must be declared, because NULL requires no arguments, and the compiler would otherwise regard NULL as a scalar variable. Recall that the BUILTIN attribute is also necessary for such argument-less functions as TIME and DATE. Graphically, the NULL pointer is

```
P -> S.LINK = NULL;
```

as shown in Figure 13.8.

The structure in Figure 13.8 is said to be *grounded;* that is, one of the elements is a pointer variable, and it has the value NULL. A pointer variable can acquire a NULL value only if it is explicitly assigned that value. The NULL value is testable and can appear in relational or logical expressions, such as

```
1. IF P -> S.LINK = NULL
     THEN . . . . .
     ELSE . . . . .
2. DO WHILE (P ¬= NULL);
3. X = P -> S.LINK¬= NULL & P -> S.A > 0;
```

When a group of based structures is tied or linked together by a pointer variable (such as LINK in structure S), the pointer variable in the last structure is often assigned the NULL value, as shown in Figure 13.9. The last structure is grounded so that it can be detected when a problem requires processing of all such linked structures. Otherwise it would be difficult or awkward to detect the last structure in a group of linked structures.

Suppose there exists a group of linked structures, for which pointer variable START points to the first structure and in which the last structure is grounded. Nothing else is known about these structures, and the problem is to count the number of structures in the group. Pictorially, the linked structures are as shown in Figure 13.10. There might not be any structures in this group (i.e., START may be equal to NULL), or there might be many structures. The program segment that will count the number of structures is shown as Program 13.1.

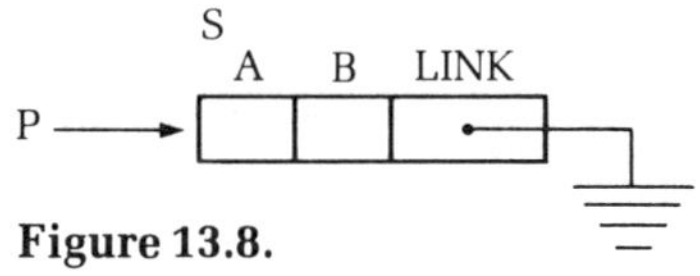

Figure 13.8.

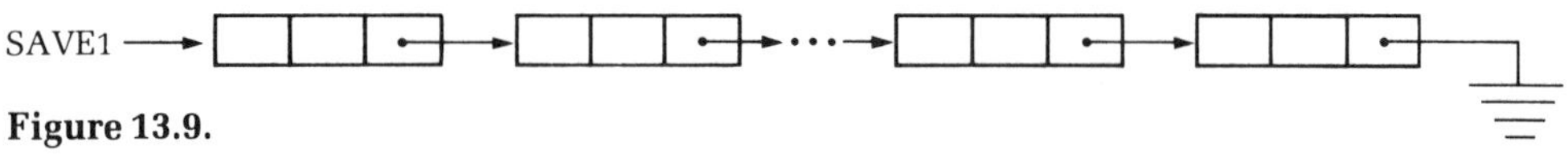

Figure 13.9.

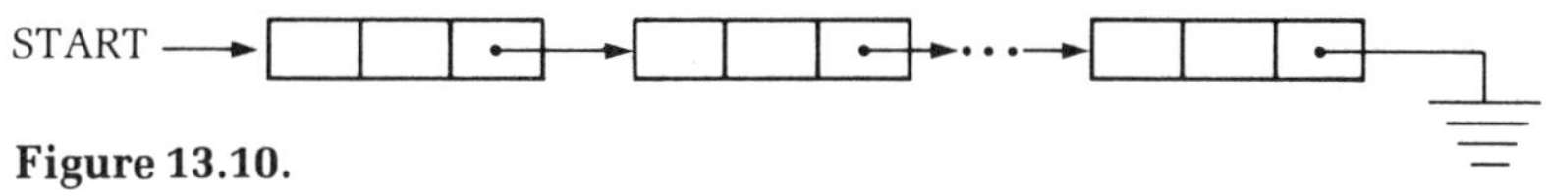

Figure 13.10.

PROGRAM 13.1.

```
DCL (P, START, TEMP) POINTER,
       COUNT FIXED INIT(0),
       NULL BUILTIN,
       1 S BASED (P),
            2 A FIXED,
            2 B FLOAT,
            2 LINK POINTER;
         .
         .
         .
         .
         .
         .
         .
TEMP = START;
DO WHILE (TEMP ¬= NULL);
     TEMP = TEMP -> S. LINK;
     COUNT = COUNT + 1;
END;
PUT LIST ('THE NUMBER OF STRUCTURES IS', COUNT);
```

The pointer variable TEMP is used in Program 13.1 so that pointer variable START is left undisturbed. If the value of pointer variable START were changed, then one or more structures would be inaccessible. Pointer variable TEMP initially points to the first structure but points to the next successive structure with each iteration of the DO loop. Ultimately, pointer TEMP reaches the last structure and acquires the value NULL, thus terminating the loop.

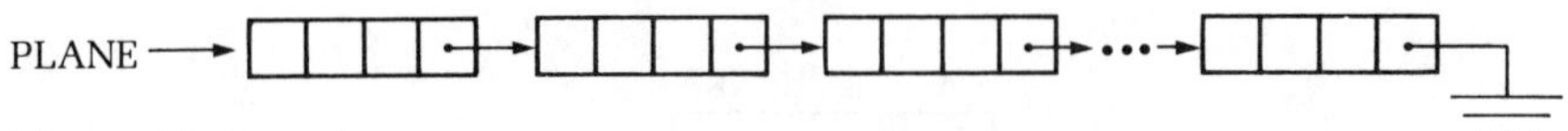

Figure 13.11.

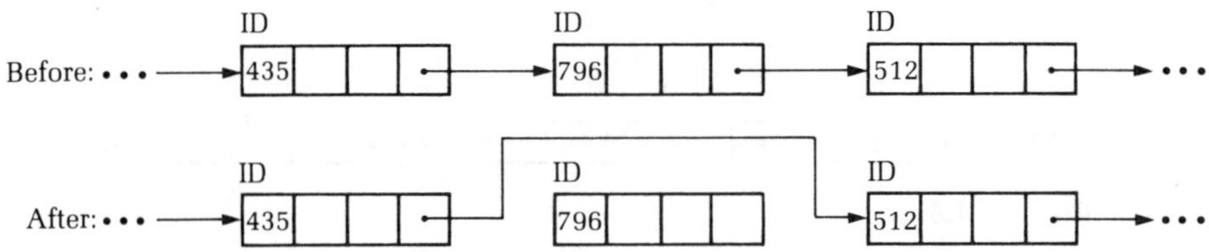

Figure 13.12.

The term *linked structures* is used in this section to describe a collection or group of structures linked together by pointer variables. A linked structure is also called a *linked list*. The focus of the next section is on problem solving by means of linked lists.

13.5. LINKED-LIST PROBLEM

A linked list is a collection of *nodes*, in which each node consists of data and pointer components. In PL/I, a node is typically represented as a based structure in which one of the elements is a pointer variable and the remaining elements are data variables. The first node in a linked list is pointed to by a pointer variable, and the last node is grounded.

Suppose an airport uses a linked list to represent the airplanes currently on the ground. Each node represents an airplane, and the problem is to keep the linked list up to date. Each time an airplane lands, a node is added to the list; and each time an airplane takes off, the corresponding node is removed from the linked list. Each airplane has a unique identification number, which must be used when a node is removed from the list. Nodes are added to the front of the list, at the position indicated by the pointer PLANE in Figure 13.11.

Adding a node to the list is relatively easy, but deleting a node is more complex, because the pointers must be changed. For example, suppose that the node with identification number 796 is to be deleted. Figure 13.12 shows how pointers have to be changed. Storage for the deleted node would be released after the appropriate pointers have been changed.

Subroutine DELETE uses two pointers to locate and remove a specified node from the linked list. Notice how pointer TEMP "follows" pointer P through the list. When the node to be deleted is located, P points to that node. This is important, because when the FREE statement is executed, storage is released for the structure that is being pointed to by P.

One advantage of based storage is that only the storage actually needed is used. There is very little storage waste in applications such as the AIRPORT problem. Furthermore, the storage used does not have to be in consecutive storage locations, because the structures are linked together by pointers.

PROGRAM 13.2.

PROBLEM DEFINITION

Pointer PLANE points to the first node in a linked list, in which each node represents an airplane. Each node contains the following elements:

IDENTIFICATION
TYPE OF AIRCRAFT
CAPACITY
LINK

The input consists of an arbitrary number of data values which specify whether an airplane has landed or has taken off, i.e., whether a node is to be added or deleted. The output consists of an echo check of all input data followed by a summary of all the nodes in the list after all the additions and deletions have been made.

Sample input:

```
'ARRIVAL',     101  DC10  180
'ARRIVAL',     416  B727  120
'ARRIVAL',     724  B747  250
'ARRIVAL',     358  DC10  175
'DEPARTURE',   416  B727  120
'ARRIVAL',     629  B707  110
```

Sample output: echo check of the input

SUMMARY

ID	TYPE	CAPACITY
629	B707	110
358	DC10	175
724	B747	250
101	DC10	180

ALGORITHM DESIGN

A main procedure and two internal subroutines are used. One subroutine adds a node to the list, and the other subroutine deletes a node from the list.

Variables to be used:

P	pointer
S	structure based on P
ID	element of S: identification
TYPE	element of S: aircraft type
CAP	element of S: capacity
LINK	element of S: pointer
PLANE	pointer
TEMP	pointer
COMMAND	arrival or departure
DATA	structure (like data elements of S)
EOF	end-of-file flag
SEARCH	search flag

PSEUDOCODE

Main procedure

```
GET COMMAND, DATA
DO while data is available
    PUT COMMAND, DATA
    IF COMMAND = 'ARRIVAL'
      THEN CALL ADD
      ELSE IF COMMAND = 'DEPARTURE'
              THEN CALL DELETE
              ELSE PUT error message
    GET COMMAND, DATA
END
PUT heading
PUT all nodes in linked list pointed to by PLANE
```

Subroutine ADD

```
Create a node using DATA
Place node at beginning of linked list pointed to by PLANE
```

Subroutine DELETE

```
Search linked list pointed to by PLANE for node specified in
  DATA
IF found
  THEN remove node from list
  ELSE PUT error message
```

ALGORITHM IMPLEMENTATION

```
/* MAINTAIN LINKED LIST REPRESENTING PLANES AT AN
   AIRPORT */

AIRPORT:
   PROC OPTIONS (MAIN);
      DCL (PLANE, P, TEMP) POINTER,     /* POINTERS           */
        EOF FIXED INIT(0),              /* END-OF-FILE FLAG   */
        SEARCH FIXED INIT(0),           /* SEARCH FLAG        */
        1 S BASED (P),                  /* NODE STRUCTURE     */
          2 DATA,                       /* DATA ELEMENTS      */
            3 ID FIXED,                 /* PLANE ID           */
            3 TYPE CHAR(10),            /* PLANE TYPE         */
            3 CAP FIXED,                /* PLANE CAPACITY     */
          2 LINK POINTER,               /* LINK TO NEXT NODE  */
        1 DATA LIKE S.DATA,             /* INPUT DATA         */
        COMMAND CHAR(9) VAR,            /* INPUT COMMAND      */
        NULL BUILTIN;                   /* NULL POINTER       */

/* ASSUME THAT A LINKED LIST EXISTS WHICH CONSISTS OF       */
/* ZERO OR MORE NODES WHERE THE FIRST NODE IS POINTED      */
/* TO BY POINTER PLANE. THE FOLLOWING STATEMENTS           */
/* PROCESS ADDITIONS AND DELETIONS OF NODES FROM           */
/* THAT LIST. IF THE LINKED LIST CONTAINS NO NODES,        */
/* THEN POINTER VARIABLE PLANE IS ASSUMED TO CONTAIN       */
/* THE VALUE NULL                                          */

     ON ENDFILE (SYSIN) EOF = 1;
     PLANE = NULL;
     GET LIST (COMMAND, DATA);
     DO WHILE (EOF = 0);
        PUT SKIP LIST (COMMAND, DATA);
        IF COMMAND = 'ARRIVAL'
          THEN CALL ADD;
          ELSE IF COMMAND = 'DEPARTURE'
                 THEN CALL DELETE;
                 ELSE PUT SKIP LIST ('*** INVALID COMMAND ***');
        GET LIST (COMMAND, DATA);
     END;

     PUT EDIT ('SUMMARY', 'ID', 'TYPE', 'CAPACITY')
              (COL(18),A, COL(10),A, COL(20),A, COL(30),A);
     TEMP = PLANE;
     DO WHILE (TEMP ¬= NULL);
        PUT EDIT (TEMP -> S.DATA)
                 (COL(9),F(4), COL(20),A(4), COL(32),F(3));
        TEMP = TEMP -> S.LINK;
     END;
```

```
ADD:                                         /* SUBROUTINE ADD */
    PROC;
        ALLOCATE S;
        P -> S.DATA = DATA;
        P -> S.LINK = PLANE;
        PLANE = P;
        RETURN;
    END ADD;
DELETE:                                      /* SUBROUTINE DELETE */
    PROC;
        SEARCH = 0;
        TEMP = PLANE;
        P = PLANE -> S.LINK;
        DO WHILE (SEARCH = 0 & P ¬= NULL);
            IF P -> S.ID = DATA.ID
               THEN SEARCH = 1;
               ELSE DO;
                        TEMP = P;
                        P = P -> S.LINK;
                    END;
        END;
        IF SEARCH = 1
           THEN DO;
                    TEMP -> S.LINK = P -> S.LINK;
                    FREE S;
                END;
           ELSE PUT SKIP LIST ('*** INVALID IDENTIFICATION ***');
        RETURN;
END DELETE;
END AIRPORT;
```

13.6. SUMMARY

The four classes of storage allocation are discussed in this chapter, with an emphasis on controlled- and based-storage allocation. The concept of push-down stacks is introduced with controlled-storage allocation. The fundamentals of linked lists are presented with based-storage allocation. A problem is completely solved that effectively uses linked-list techniques.

13.6.1. Key Concepts

1. The STATIC storage attribute causes the initial allocation of storage to occur at compile time, and causes that storage to remain allocated as long as the program remains active.

2. The AUTOMATIC storage attribute causes the automatic allocation of storage when a block is activated, and the release of storage when that block is deactivated. AUTOMATIC is the default-allocation class.
3. The CONTROLLED storage attribute is similar to the AUTOMATIC storage attribute, but for controlled storage the programmer must explicitly allocate and free storage with the ALLOCATE and FREE statements.
4. A pushdown stack is so named because each new data element is pushed down on top of the existing data elements. Data elements can only be removed from the top of the stack. A pushdown stack is sometimes called a LIFO (Last In First Out) list.
5. The ALLOCATE and FREE statements are used to add and delete data elements from a pushdown stack.
6. A pointer variable is a special type of variable that contains the location or address of a scalar variable, an array, or a structure.
7. The BASED-storage attribute causes the allocation of storage to be based on a pointer variable; i.e., the location of a based variable depends on a pointer variable.
8. The ALLOCATE and FREE statements are used to allocate and free based storage.
9. The "points to" symbol (->) permits easy referencing of based variables.
10. Based structures can be linked together by a pointer variable that is a structural element. A collection of linked structures is also called a linked list. A pointer variable is required that points to the first structure (node) in the linked list.
11. The NULL pointer is used to "ground" a linked list.

13.6.2. Terms and Phrases

Write out definitions and/or usage descriptions of these terms. Check yourself against the text.

ALLOCATE
array
AUTOMATIC
BASED
based structure
BEGIN block
BUILTIN
CONTROLLED
FREE
grounded list
linked list
node
NULL
null pointer
POINTER
pointer variable
"points to" symbol (->)
pushdown stack
STATIC
storage allocation
structure

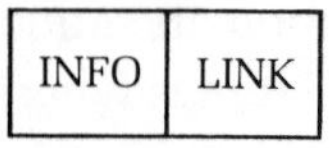

Figure 13.13.

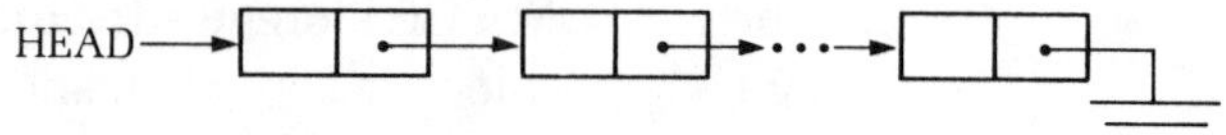

Figure 13.14.

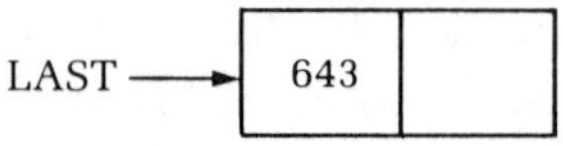

Figure 13.15.

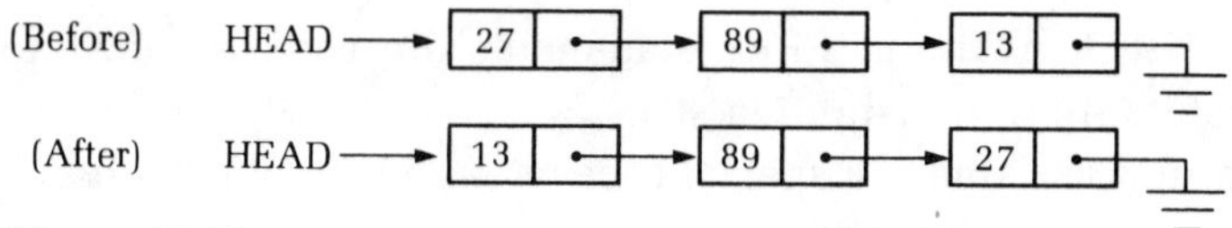

Figure 13.16.

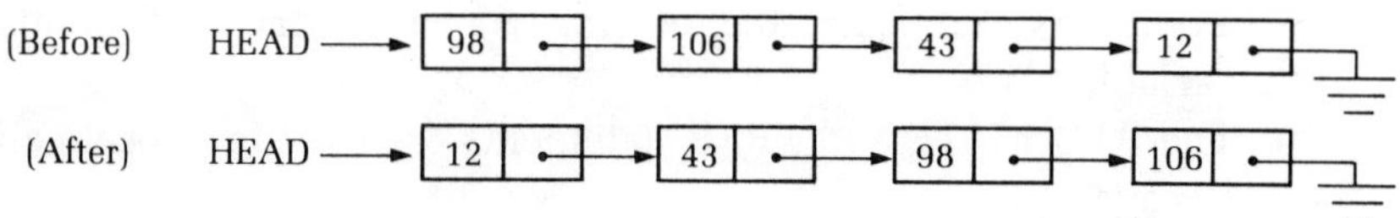

Figure 13.17.

PROBLEMS

Problem 13.1.

```
DCL X FIXED CONTROLLED;
   ALLOCATE X;
   X = 50;
   ALLOCATE X;
   X = 97;
   ALLOCATE X;
   X = 123;
   FREE X;
   PUT LIST (X);
```

The value displayed is ____________

Problem 13.2. Assume here that each node has the form shown in Figure 13.13, where INFO is a FIXED data element and LINK is a pointer. Furthermore, assume the existence of a linked list, as shown in Figure 13.14, in which HEAD is a pointer variable, and the linked list consists of zero or more nodes.

a. Write a series of statements to add the node shown in Figure 13.15 to the rear of the list pointed to by HEAD.

b. Write a series of statements to invert the linked list pointed to by HEAD. An example is shown in Figure 13.16.

c. Write a series of statements to delete every node in the list pointed to by HEAD.

d. Write a series of statements to sort the nodes in the list pointed to by HEAD. The nodes are to be sorted, so that the INFO data elements are in ascending order. An example is shown in Figure 13.17.

Problem 13.3. Subroutine DELETE in section 13.5 is incorrect, because it cannot delete the first node in the list pointed to by PLANE. Modify this subroutine so that it can delete the first node.

14 Stream-File Processing

Filename PEOPLE

'JONES' 46 1976	'SMITH' 23 1978	'BROWN' 33 1972 . . . .

Figure 14.1.

This chapter presents the fundamentals of file manipulation. A *file* is a collection of data stored on a device, such as a magnetic disk, that can store several times as much data as the computer's memory can. Many problems require the processing of large amounts of data, and files are used to store these large quantities of data.

There are several types of PL/I files available, but only *stream files* are considered in this chapter. A stream file is simply one where all stored data is represented as one continuous stream of characters, although the stream can be organized into lines. A typical stream file is shown in Figure 14.1.

In practice, stream files are generally not used for record-keeping and file-handling operations. However, stream files are emphasized here because they are easy to understand and to use, and they embody many fundamental principles of other types of files.

14.1. SYSIN AND SYSPRINT FILES

The concept of stream I/O is discussed in Chapter 4 as a part of understanding the GET and PUT statements. Stream files were actually used there, because SYSIN and SYSPRINT are stream files and are the default I/O files. In other words, SYSIN is the standard file used for input, and SYSPRINT is the standard file used for output. In fact, the pairs of statements

```
GET LIST (A,B,C);
GET FILE (SYSIN) LIST (A,B,C);
```

and

```
PUT LIST (A,B,C);
PUT FILE (SYSPRINT) LIST (A,B,C);
```

are equivalent.

Consequently, the concepts of stream I/O apply directly to stream files. All that is needed is a method to create and manipulate stream files, and that is the topic of the next section.

14.2. STREAM-FILE FUNDAMENTALS*

Several statements are needed to give information to the PL/I compiler about files. For example, a file must have a name and can have various attributes

*Some systems may require additional JCL in order to use existing files or to create new files.

associated with it. Following is a list of the general forms of the statements necessary to create, access, and manipulate stream files.

1. DCL *filename* FILE STREAM;

   The DECLARE statement specifies the name of the file and that it is a stream file. The file name must consist of one to seven characters (letters or digits), and the first character must be a letter. Factoring can be used to declare more than one file.

2. OPEN FILE *(filename) INPUT* or *OUTPUT;*

   This statement establishes a communication path between PL/I and the file. It also specifies the INPUT or OUTPUT attribute for that file. If the attribute is INPUT, then only GET statements can access the file. If the attribute is OUTPUT, then only PUT statements can access the file. The OPEN statement must be placed before GET or PUT statements that access that file. Several files can be opened with one OPEN statement. For example,

   ```
   OPEN FILE (A) INPUT,
        FILE (B) OUTPUT;
   ```

3. GET FILE *(filename) DATA* or *LIST* or *EDIT (variable(s));*

   When executing, this statement copies data from the stream file into the specified variable(s). The term variable(s) here means any combination of scalar variables, arrays, and structures. Data-, list-, and edit-directed* I/O are used for stream files.

4. PUT FILE *(filename) DATA* or *LIST* or *EDIT (expression(s));*

   When executed, this statement copies the value(s) of the expression(s) into the specified stream file.

5. ON ENDFILE *(filename) action;*

   This has the same meaning as before, but any stream file can be specified (including SYSIN).

6. CLOSE FILE *(filename);*

   This statement is used to deactivate a file or to change the INPUT or OUTPUT attribute. For example, if the current file

*Edit-directed I/O statements always require a specification list.

attribute is OUTPUT, it can be changed to INPUT by closing the file and then opening it with the INPUT attribute. This would also "rewind" the file, i.e., reset the stream pointer to the beginning of the file. Several files can be closed with this statement. For example, file A and B are both closed with the statement

```
CLOSE FILE (A),
      FILE (B);
```

Not all the preceding statements are absolutely necessary for stream files, because some of these actions are handled by system defaults. For example, a filename doesn't have to be declared, because the statement

```
GET FILE (SFILE) LIST (A,B,C);
```

implies that SFILE is a stream file and has the default attribute INPUT. This is also true for the PUT FILE statement, except that the default attribute is OUTPUT. If a file is not declared closed when a program terminates execution, then that file is closed automatically. However, these default actions are ignored here, and all actions are explicitly stated so that programs will be more readable.

Stream files are easy to create and easy to use. Consider the following program segment, which creates an output stream file.

```
DCL OUT FILE STREAM,
  X CHAR(1);
OPEN FILE(OUT) OUTPUT;
DO X = 'A', 'B', 'C';
    PUT FILE(OUT) LIST ('IMAGE', X);
END;
CLOSE FILE(OUT);
```

After these statements are executed, stream file OUT would appear as in Figure 14.2.

File OUT could then be opened as an INPUT file and accessed by a GET FILE statement. A stream file can store an arbitrary amount of data obtained from another stream file, such as SYSIN. Consider Program 14.1, in which data is taken from stream file SYSIN, stored in stream file SAVE, retrieved from file SAVE, and then displayed by means of file SYSPRINT.

OUT

```
'IMAGE'  'A'  'IMAGE'  'B'  'IMAGE'  'C'
```

Figure 14.2.

PROGRAM 14.1.

```
DCL SAVE FILE STREAM,              /* STREAM FILE SAVE */
  EOF FIXED INIT(0),               /* END OF FILE FLAG */
      1 INFO,                      /* I/O STRUCTURE    */
        2 A FIXED,
        2 B CHAR(4);

ON ENDFILE (SYSIN) EOF = 1;
OPEN FILE(SAVE) OUTPUT;

GET LIST (INFO);
DO WHILE (EOF = 0);
    PUT FILE(SAVE) LIST(INFO);
    GET LIST(INFO);
END;

CLOSE FILE(SAVE);
OPEN FILE(SAVE) INPUT;
EOF = 0;
ON ENDFILE(SAVE) EOF = 1;
GET FILE(SAVE) LIST(INFO);
DO WHILE (EOF = 0);
    PUT LIST (INFO);
    GET FILE(SAVE) LIST(INFO);
END;

CLOSE FILE(SAVE);
```

Program 14.1 is not very useful, but it does illustrate several interesting features of stream files. File SAVE is opened as an OUTPUT file and then later closed and opened as an INPUT file. There are two occurrences of the ON ENDFILE statement; one detects the end of file for SYSIN, and the other detects the end of file for SAVE. A structure is used to access file SAVE with both GET FILE and PUT FILE statements.

14.3. STREAM-FILE PROCESSING PROBLEM

Many file-processing problems require the maintenance and updating of a *master file,* i.e., a file whose contents are relatively permanent. A master file is updated periodically by means of a *transaction file,* i.e., a file containing changes to be made in the master file.

Suppose an oil company has a master file consisting of data for all its credit-card customers. This master file contains the following data* for each of its customers:

Identification number
Name

*In reality, a typical master file would contain much more data for each customer, but we have used a simplified example to keep our file-processing problem manageable.

MASTER

1623 'JONES' '209 ELMWOOD, CITY' 462.32	1646 'SMITH' • • •

Figure 14.3.

XACT

1646 28.47	1646	1782 9.04	• • •

Figure 14.4.

Address
Current balance

A typical master file (called MASTER) for the problem solved here appears in Figure 14.3. A positive balance indicates the amount owed by the customer, and a negative balance indicates an overpayment by the customer.

The transaction file contains data of the following form for customers who have made payments or charges:

Identification number
Amount of payment or charge

The two types of transactions permitted for this problem are payments and charges, where a payment is a negative number and a charge is a positive number. A typical transaction file called XACT appears in Figure 14.4.

A customer will be represented in the transaction file several times if several payments and charges have been made since the last time the master file was updated. Similarly, if a customer has not made any charges or payments, then no data for that customer will appear in the transaction file. The master file is updated every month, and the transaction file is a collection of all charges and payments made by customers since the last update of the master file. All data on the master file and the transaction file is stored in ascending order according to the customer identification number. That is, data for customers with small identification numbers appears at the beginning of each file, and data for customers with large identification numbers appears at the end of the file. The advantage of dealing with sorted data is that the updating process is performed with one pass through the master and the transaction files. The updating process is depicted in Figure 14.5. Note that a "new" master file is created that is actually the updated "old" master file. The "old" master file and the transaction file are not changed. During the next update, the "new" master file becomes the "old" master file, and the entire process is repeated.

This program is not complete in that statements should be created for the credit-card customers who have a payment due. This could be done in the ELSE portion of the IF statement in the outer DO WHILE loop.

PROGRAM 14.2.

PROBLEM DEFINITION

A master file called MASTER contains data in the following form

Identification number
Name
Address
Current balance

A transaction file called XACT contains data in the following form

Identification number
Amount of payment or charge

The master file is to be updated with the data contained in the transaction file. A new master file called NEW is created; it is the updated file. Files MASTER and XACT remain unchanged. Data in all files is sorted in ascending order by the customer identification number. All data in the master file is assumed to be correct, but the transaction file might contain invalid or nonexistent identification numbers. The input consists of data from files MASTER and XACT. The output consists of data placed in file NEW, as well as zero or more error messages that are displayed.

ALGORITHM DESIGN

Three stream files are required in the solution to this problem, and *most* of the I/O uses these files. Two structures are useful in accessing these files.

Variables to be used:

MASTER	master file
XACT	transaction file
NEW	new master file
CUSTOMER	structure for master file
M_ID	element: identification
NAME	element: name
ADDRESS	element: address
BALANCE	current balance
ACTIVITY	structure for transaction file
T_ID	element: identification
AMOUNT	element: charge or payment
EOF_M	MASTER end-of-file flag
EOF_X	XACT end-of-file flag

PSEUDOCODE

```
OPEN files
GET customer data from MASTER
GET activity data from XACT
DO while data in MASTER is available
   IF T_ID < M_ID and data in XACT is available
      THEN PUT error message
           GET activity data from XACT
      ELSE DO while data in XACT is available and
                 T_ID = M_ID
              Add AMOUNT to BALANCE
              GET activity data from XACT
           END
           PUT customer data in NEW
           GET customer data from MASTER
END
CLOSE files
END
```

ALGORITHM IMPLEMENTATION

```
UPDATE:
  PROC OPTIONS (MAIN);
      DCL (MASTER, XACT, NEW) FILE STREAM,
          1 CUSTOMER,                     /* MASTER/NEW FILE
                                             STRUCTURE      */
            2 M_ID FIXED,                 /* IDENTIFICATION
                                             NUMBER         */
            2 NAME CHAR(20) VAR,          /* CUSTOMER NAME  */
            2 ADDRESS CHAR(30) VAR,       /* CUSTOMER
                                             ADDRESS        */
            2 BALANCE FIXED DECIMAL (7,2), /* CURRENT
                                             BALANCE        */
          1 ACTIVITY,                     /* TRANSACTION
                                             STRUCTURE      */
            2 T_ID FIXED,                 /* IDENTIFICATION
                                             NUMBER         */
            2 AMOUNT FIXED DECIMAL (6,2), /* CHARGE OR
                                             PAYMENT        */
          EOF_M FIXED INIT(0),            /* EOF FLAG FOR
                                             MASTER FILE    */
          EOF_X FIXED INIT(0);            /* EOF FLAG FOR
                                             XACT FILE      */
      ON ENDFILE (MASTER) EOF_M = 1;
      ON ENDFILE (XACT) EOF_X = 1;
      OPEN FILE (MASTER) INPUT,
        FILE (XACT) INPUT,
        FILE (NEW) OUTPUT;
      GET FILE (MASTER) LIST (CUSTOMER);
      GET FILE (XACT) LIST (ACTIVITY);
      DO WHILE (EOF_M = 0);
          IF T_ID < M_ID & EOF_X = 0
            THEN DO;
                     PUT SKIP LIST ('ERROR', ACTIVITY);
                     GET FILE (XACT) LIST (ACTIVITY);
                 END;
            ELSE DO;
                     DO WHILE (EOF_X = 0 & T_ID = M_ID);
                         BALANCE = BALANCE + AMOUNT;
                         GET FILE (XACT) LIST (ACTIVITY);
                     END;
                     PUT FILE (NEW) LIST (CUSTOMER);
                     GET FILE (MASTER) LIST (CUSTOMER);
                 END;
      END;
      CLOSE FILE (MASTER),
        FILE (XACT),
        FILE (NEW);
  END UPDATE;
```

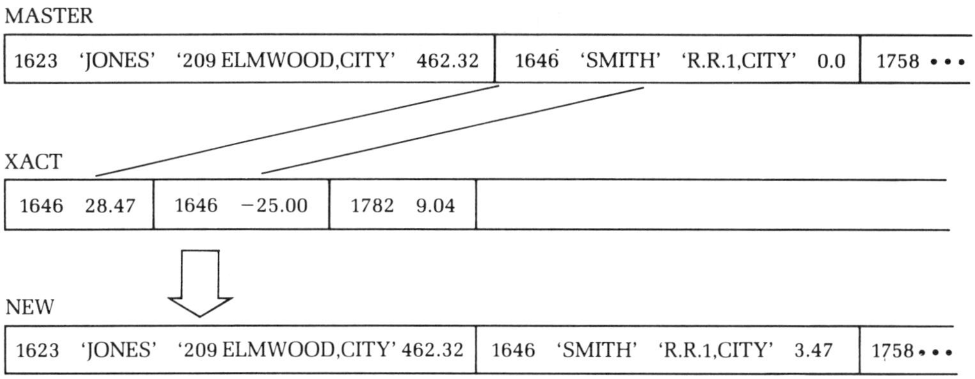

Figure 14.5.

This problem is also known as a sequential file-processing problem. Data is organized in sequential order on the three files, and data is processed sequentially from the beginning to the end of the file.

This is only one example of many types of problems that can be solved by a sequential file-processing technique. Payroll processing, customer billing, and student-grade processing are problems that are generally solved by sequential file processing.

14.4. SUMMARY

This chapter deals only with stream files. The default I/O files of SYSIN and SYSPRINT are discussed and related to stream files in general. The declaration, opening, and closing of stream files are discussed, as well as manipulation of stream files. A problem that uses several features of stream files is completely solved.

14.4.1. Key Concepts

1. Data stored on a stream file is represented as one continuous stream of characters, which can be organized into lines by the SKIP option of the PUT FILE statement.
2. SYSIN and SYSPRINT are stream files and are the default I/O files.
3. Stream files can be declared with the FILE and STREAM attributes.
4. The OPEN statement establishes a communication path between the PL/I program and the stream file. It also specifies whether that file is to be used for INPUT or for OUTPUT.
5. The GET FILE statement retrieves data from the stream file and places it into specified variables.
6. The PUT FILE statement stores the value(s) of the expression(s) into the stream file.
7. The ON ENDFILE statement is used to detect the end-of-file condition for any specified stream file.

8. The CLOSE statement is used to deactivate a stream file or to allow the changing of the INPUT or OUTPUT attribute with a subsequent OPEN statement.
9. The contents of a master file are relatively permanent. However, the contents of a transaction file consist entirely of changes in the master file. The transaction file is used to update the master file periodically.

14.4.2. Terms and Phrases

Write out definitions or usage descriptions of these terms. Check yourself against the text.

FILE
CLOSE
GET FILE
INPUT
master file
ON ENDFILE
OPEN
OUTPUT
PUT FILE
sequential file processing
STREAM
stream file
SYSIN
SYSPRINT
transaction file

PROBLEMS

Use the problem-solving process to develop a solution for each of the following problems.

Problem 14.1. Merging files.

Suppose stream files A and B contain information of the form

Identification number
Amount

Suppose that each file is sorted to put the identification numbers in ascending order. Given stream files A and B in Figure 14.6, stream file C is created by "merging" stream files A and B, and appears as shown. The input consists of data in stream files A and B. The output consists of data in stream file C obtained by merging stream files A and B.

A	142 8.56	193 12.45	245 7.35	...
B	155 43.86	184 28.92	349 12.45	...
C	142 8.56	155 43.86	184 28.92	193 ...

Figure 14.6.

Problem 14.2. File searching.

The input consists of the MASTER stream file discussed in section 14.3 and used in the file-processing problem. Check the current balance of each customer in the MASTER file. The output consists of the names of all customers whose current balance exceeds $200.

Problem 14.3. File operations.

The input consists of the XACT stream file discussed in section 14.3, which contains data of the form

Identification number
Amount of payment or charge

The output consists of a stream file called XACT2, which contains data of the form

Identification number
Total amount of all payments and all charges

An identification number appears only once in file XACT2, and the value associated with each identification number is the total of all payments and charges, as illustrated in Figure 14.7.

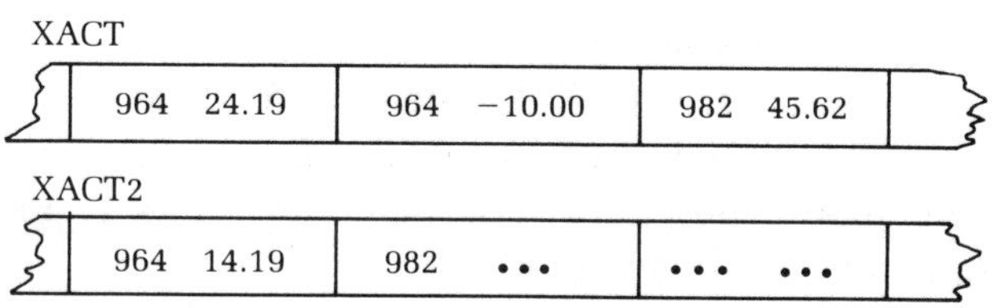

Figure 14.7.

Appendix A

Sample Job Control Language (JCL) Statements for Selected Computers

This appendix contains sample JCL statements necessary to run PL/I programs for several different computers. Additional information must be obtained from the local computer installation in order to run programs. For example, a charge number, a user name, or a password may be required.

JCL statements, unlike PL/I statements, are not written in free form. JCL statements must be written in the exact order indicated. Sometimes the absence of a blank or the presence of an additional blank is sufficient to halt processing of the program. Most JCL statements start in column 1.

A.1. PL/C COMPILER

The Cornell University PL/C compiler is available on many IBM and Amdahl computers.

```
*PL/C ID='LAMIE'                     *DATA
  ____                                 ____
  ____                                 ____
  ____                                 ____
  ____                                 ____
  ____  PL/I program                   ____
  ____                                 ____  data (if any)
                                       ____
```

A.2. IBM

JCL statements for three IBM compilers follow. Of these three, the checkout compiler is best-suited for most student programs. On some IBM compilers, the last line is // rather than /*, which appears in the following three examples.

A.2.1. PL/I F compiler

```
//ED JOB 1234, LAMIE
// EXEC PL1FCG
//SYSIN DD *
 ____
 ____  PL/I program
 ____
/*
//GO.SYSIN DD *
 ____
 ____  data (if any)
 ____
/*
```

A.2.2. PL/I checkout compiler

```
//ED JOB 1234,LAMIE
// EXEC PLICKR
//GO.SYSCIN DD *
 ____
 ____  PL/I program
 ____
* DATA
 ____
 ____  data (if any)
 ____
/*
```

A.2.3. PL/I Optimizing compiler

```
//ED JOB 1234,LAMIE
// EXEC PLIXCLG
//PLI.SYSIN DD *
 ____
 ____  PL/I program
 ____
/*
//GO.SYSIN DD *
 ____
 ____  data (if any)
 ____
/*
```

A.3. BURROUGHS PL/I (B6700/B7700 computers)

```
BEGIN JOB ED/ELAMIE;
  COMPILE ED/ELAMIE/OBJECT WITH PL/I LIBRARY GO;
  COMPILER DATA CARD
           .
           .
           .
      PL/I program
           .
           .
           .
⊕ [a special symbol representing multiple punches in the same
  column of a punched card; also used for CDC PL/I]
END JOB.
```

This JCL is for a simple compile job only.

Burroughs PL/I is closer to IBM PL/I than ANSI PL/I.

A.4. CDC PL/I (Cyber 70, 170, and 6000 computers)

```
JOB.
USER(LAMIE,PWORD)
CHARGE(CPS,D0001)
PLI,GO.
⊕
  ____
  ____  PL/I program
  ____
⊕
  ____
  ____  data (if any)
  ____
⊕
```

CDC PL/I is a subset of ANSI PL/I. CDC PL/I programs can be compiled and executed from an interactive terminal with the statement

```
PLI(I = NAME, GO)
```

where NAME is the name of a file containing the source program.

A.5. DATA GENERAL PL/I (Eclipse minicomputer)

```
X PL1/L/S/B NAME
```

where NAME is the name of a file containing the source program.

Operating-system control statements are not included here. The preceding statement is used to compile and execute a PL/I program interactively or in batch.

Data General PL/I is a subset of ANSI PL/I.

A.6. DEC CPL (DEC System 10 and 20 computers)

```
      ____
      ____  PL/I program
      ____
      ____
    XEQ
```

Operating-system control statements are not included here. Each statement in a CPL (Conversational Programming Language) program is preceded by a line number and a period.

CPL is intended for interactive terminal use. XEQ is a terminal command to compile and execute the preceding program.

CPL is a subset of ANSI PL/I.

A.7. HONEYWELL PL/I (Honeywell Series 60 computers)

To compile and execute from an interactive terminal, the source program being stored in file NAME.PL1, the commands

```
PL1     NAME.PL1
NAME
```

are entered. The terminal serves as both SYSIN and SYSPRINT. The source program can be listed with the command

```
PRINT     NAME.PL1
```

Honeywell PL/I is based on ANSI PL/I. Most of the MULTICS operating system is written in PL/I.

A.8. Q1/LMC AND Q1/LITE (Q1 microcomputer)

```
EDIT,N NAME
  ____
  ____
  ____  PL/I program
  ____
  (depress the F7 function key)
PRINT NAME
PL1 NAME
  ____
  ____
  ____  data (if any)
  ____
```

Q1 PL/I is a subset of PL/I. The Q1 microcomputer is based on the 8080 microprocessor.

A.9. SP/K COMPILERS (IBM, DEC PDP-11, Univac 90/30 computers)

```
$JOB ID
 ____
 ____
 ____  PL/I program
$DATA
 ____
 ____  data (if any)
 ____
 ____
```

SP/K compilers are subsets of PL/I. Structured programming is emphasized; e.g., the GO TO statement is not available.

A.10. UNIVAC PL/I (Univac 1100 series computers)

```
@RUN LAMIE,123456,123456789
@PL1,ISE
 ____
 ____  PL/I program
 ____
@LOADER
 ____
 ____  data (if any)
 ____
@FIN
```

Univac PL/I is based on ANSI PL/I. PLUM (University of Maryland PL/I) is also available on Univac 1100 series computers. PLUM is a subset of ANSI PL/I.

Appendix B

Reading a Program Listing

Program B.1 is a source program produced by a PL/I compiler. The listing consists of four parts: STMT, BLK, DO, and SOURCE.

PROGRAM B.1.

```
STMT  BLK  DO  SOURCE
               /* NONSENSE PROGRAM TO ILLUSTRATE
                  SOURCE LISTING */
  1    0       TEST: PROC OPTIONS(MAIN);
                          /* THIS LINE HAS NO 'STMT'
                             NUMBER */
  2    1                  DCL (SUM, I, J) FIXED INIT(0);
  3    1                  GET LIST (J);
  4    1                  IF J > 5
  5    1                    THEN BEGIN;
  6    2                                IF J = 10
  7    2                                  THEN DO;
  8    2    1                                         DO I = 1
                                                         TO 10;
  9    2    2                                            SUM =
                                                         SUM + I;
 10    2    2                                         END;
 11    2    1                                     END;
 12    2                                  ELSE;
 13    2                          END;
 14    1                 ELSE;
 15    1               PUT LIST (J, SUM);
 16    1            END TEST;
```

The meaning of each of the four parts is as follows.

1. STMT — The number of the first source statement that begins on that line. A line may contain more than one statement, or it may not contain any statements at all; i.e., it might be a comment or blank line.
2. BLK — The level of block nesting for that statement. Note the level number for statements in the BEGIN block.
3. DO — The level of DO loop or DO group nesting for that statement. Note the level number for statements in the DO loop. A level number of zero or blank indicates that this statement is not nested in any DO loop or DO group.
4. SOURCE — The actual PL/I statements.

Appendix C

Skeleton Syntax for PL/I Statements

This appendix contains the general form, or skeleton syntax, for every statement type discussed in this book. The statements appear in alphabetical order and are executable unless stated otherwise.

1. ALLOCATE *controlled-variable or based-variable;*
   Abbreviation: ALLOC
2. Assignment statement *variable = expression;*
   If more than one variable appears on the left side of the equals sign, each variable must be separated by a comma.
3. BEGIN; . . . . END;
4. CALL *subroutine name;*
   CALL *subroutine name (argument(s));*
5. CLOSE FILE *(filename);*
6. DECLARE *variable(s) attribute(s);*
   This is a nonexecutable statement.
7. DO;
   DO *index variable = expression 1* TO *expression 2* BY *expression 3;*

For the remaining examples of the DO statement, assume that I is an index variable, and that E_i is an expression.

DO I = E1 TO E2;
DO WHILE (E1);
DO I = E1 TO E2 WHILE (E3);
DO I = E1, E2, E3, E4;
DO I = E1 TO E2, E3 TO E4 WHILE (E5);
DO I = E1 BY E2 WHILE (E3);

8. END;
   END *label;*
9. *label:* FORMAT *(specification(s));*
   This is a nonexecutable statement.
10. FREE *controlled-variable or based-variable;*
11. GET DATA;
    GET DATA *(variable(s));*
    GET EDIT *(variable(s)) (specification(s));*
    GET LIST *(variable(s));*
12. GET FILE *(filename)* EDIT *(variable(s)) (specification(s));*
    GET FILE *(filename)* LIST *(variable(s));*
13. GO TO *label;*
14. IF *expression* THEN *action 1;* ELSE *action 2;*
    IF *expression* THEN *action 1;*
15. ON *condition action;*
16. OPEN FILE *(filename) INPUT or OUTPUT;*
17. PROCEDURE;
    PROCEDURE *(parameter(s) and option(s));*
    PROCEDURE OPTIONS (MAIN);
    Abbreviation: PROC (This is a nonexecutable statement.)
18. PUT DATA;
    PUT DATA *(variable(s));*
    PUT EDIT *(expression(s)) (specification(s));*
    PUT LIST *(expression(s));*
19. PUT FILE *(filename)* EDIT *(expression(s)) (specification(s);*
    PUT FILE *(filename)* LIST *(expression(s));*
20. RETURN;
    RETURN *(expression);*
21. SIGNAL *condition;*

Appendix D

Keywords

This appendix contains an alphabetical list of all PL/I keywords used in this book. These keywords are not reserved words and are recognized as keywords only if they appear in the appropriate context.

Keyword	*Abbreviation*	*Appropriate context*
A		format item
ABS		built-in function
ACOS		built-in function
ALLOCATE	ALLOC	statement
ASIN		built-in function
ATAN		built-in function
ATAND		built-in function
AUTOMATIC	AUTO	attribute
B		format item
BASED		attribute
BEGIN		statement
BINARY	BIN	attribute
BIT		attribute
BUILTIN		attribute
BY		option in DO specification in GET or PUT statement
BY		statement option (DO)
CALL		statement
CHARACTER	CHAR	attribute
CLOSE		statement
COLUMN	COL	format item
CONDITION	COND	condition
CONTROLLED	CTL	attribute
CONVERSION	CONV	condition
COS		built-in function
COSD		built-in function
DATA		statement option (GET or PUT)

Keyword	*Abbreviation*	*Appropriate context*
DATE		built-in function
DECIMAL	DEC	attribute
DECLARE	DCL	statement
DO		statement option (GET or PUT)
DO		statement
E		format item
EDIT		statement option (GET or PUT)
ELSE		statement option (IF)
END		statement
ENDFILE		condition
ENDPAGE		condition
ENTRY		attribute
ERROR		condition
EXP		built-in function
EXTERNAL	EXT	attribute
F		format item
FILE		attribute
FILE		statement option (GET or PUT)
FIXED		attribute
FIXEDOVERFLOW	FOFL	condition
FLOAT		attribute
FORMAT		statement
FREE		statement
GET		statement
GOTO		statement
GO TO		statement
IF		statement
INDEX		built-in function
INITIAL	INIT	attribute
INPUT		attribute
INPUT		statement option (OPEN)
INTERNAL	INT	attribute
LIKE		attribute
LINE		format item
LINE		statement option (PUT)
LIST		statement option (GET or PUT)
LOG		built-in function
LOG10		built-in function
LOG2		built-in function
MAIN		option in OPTIONS option (PROCEDURE)
MOD		built-in function
NULL		built-in function
ON		statement
ONCHAR		built-in function
ONCODE		built-in function
ONLOC		built-in function
ONSOURCE		built-in function
OPEN		statement
OPTIONS		statement option (PROCEDURE)
OUTPUT		attribute
OUTPUT		statement option (OPEN)
OVERFLOW	OFL	condition
P		format item
PAGE		format item

Keyword	*Abbreviation*	*Appropriate context*
PAGE		statement option (PUT)
PICTURE	PIC	attribute
POINTER	PTR	attribute
PRINT		attribute
PROCEDURE	PROC	statement
PUT		statement
R		format item
REAL		attribute
RECURSIVE		statement option (PROCEDURE)
RETURN		statement
RETURNS		attribute
RETURNS		statement option (PROCEDURE or ENTRY)
ROUND		built-in function
SET		statement option (ALLOCATE)
SIGN		built-in function
SIGNAL		statement
SIN		built-in function
SIND		built-in function
SIZE		condition
SKIP		format item
SKIP		statement option (GET or PUT)
SNAP		statement option (ON)
SQRT		built-in function
STATIC		attribute
STOP		statement
STREAM		attribute
STREAM		statement option (OPEN)
STRING		statement option (GET or PUT)
STRINGRANGE	STRG	condition
SUBSCRIPTRANGE	SUBRG	condition
SUBSTR		built-in function
SUBSTR		pseudovariable
SYSTEM		statement option (ON)
TAN		built-in function
TAND		built-in function
THEN		statement option (IF)
TIME		built-in function
TO		option in DO specification in GET or PUT statement
TO		statement option (DO)
TRUNC		built-in function
UNDERFLOW	UFL	condition
VARYING	VAR	attribute
VERIFY		built-in function
WHILE		option in DO specification in GET or PUT statement
WHILE		statement option (DO)
X		format item
ZERODIVIDE	ZDIV	condition

Appendix E
IBM PL/I

This book contains a subset of PL/I that is very similar to the following IBM compilers.

PL/I-F
DOS PL/I Optimizer
OS PL/I Optimizer
PL/I Checkout

The primary differences between these IBM compilers and the subset of ANSI PL/I that appears in this book are summarized in this appendix.

E.1. IDENTIFIERS AND VARIABLES

An identifier (or variable name) consists of one to 31 characters, where the first character must be a letter (A–Z) or one of the special characters $, @, or #. The remaining characters must consist of letters (A–Z), digits (0–9), or the special characters $, @, #, or _. Embedded blanks are not permitted within an identifier.

E.2. PROCEDURE AND FILENAMES

A procedure name or a filename is an identifier consisting of one to seven characters but not containing the characters _, #, $, or @. However, internal procedure names may contain up to 31 characters.

E.3. RESERVED KEYWORDS

Reserved keywords exist only in the 48-character set. Table E.1 lists the reserved keywords in the 48-character set, compared to their counterparts in the 60-character set.

Some observations on Table E.1 are needed.

TABLE E.1.

<table>
<tr><th>48-character set</th><th>60-character set</th></tr>
<tr><td>NOT</td><td>¬</td></tr>
<tr><td>AND</td><td>&</td></tr>
<tr><td>OR</td><td>|</td></tr>
<tr><td>CAT</td><td>||</td></tr>
<tr><td>LT</td><td><</td></tr>
<tr><td>GT</td><td>></td></tr>
<tr><td>NG</td><td>¬></td></tr>
<tr><td>GE</td><td>>=</td></tr>
<tr><td>NE</td><td>¬=</td></tr>
<tr><td>LE</td><td><=</td></tr>
<tr><td>NL</td><td>¬<</td></tr>
<tr><td>PT</td><td>-></td></tr>
</table>

1. One or more blanks must precede and follow each of the above reserved keywords.
2. In the 48-character set, the semicolon (;) is represented by the characters ",." and the characters ".." are used to represent a colon (:).
3. There are no reserved keywords in the 60-character set.
4. All the keywords in Appendix D are available with IBM PL/I.

E.4. SOURCE PROGRAM STATEMENTS

Cardpunch machines and interactive terminals are commonly used to prepare IBM PL/I programs. In either case, each PL/I statement must appear within columns 2 through 72, inclusive. Column 1 is not used, and columns 73 through 80 are reserved as an optional identification or sequencing field.

E.5. DEFAULTS

IBM PL/I compilers observe the "I through N" rule for undeclared variables. That is, for an undeclared variable name that begins with a letter I through N, inclusive, the default attributes for that variable are

FIXED BINARY (15, 0) REAL AUTOMATIC

All other undeclared variables have the default attributes

FLOAT DECIMAL (6) REAL AUTOMATIC

However, if a variable is partially declared, the default attributes may not be as expected. For example, if the scale attribute is declared as either FIXED or FLOAT, the default base attribute is DECIMAL. If the base attribute is declared as either BINARY or DECIMAL, the default scale attribute is FLOAT.

E.6. RESTRICTIONS

The IBM optimizing compilers handle arrays somewhat differently than ANSI PL/I compilers. Suppose variable B is declared as a singly dimensioned array in the following statement.

```
B = B + B(6);
```

In ANSI PL/I, the same value is added once to each element of array B. However, in the IBM optimizing compilers, each element is essentially incremented twice for elements B(7) and beyond.

Appendix F
PL/C

This book contains a subset of PL/I that is compatible with PL/C. However, there are a few restrictions and differences between PL/C and this book, and these are summarized in this appendix.

F.1. IDENTIFIERS AND VARIABLES

An identifier (or variable name) consists of one to 31 characters, of which the first must be a letter (A–Z) or one of the special characters $, @, or #. The remaining characters must consist of letters (A–Z), digits (0–9), or the special characters $, @, #, or _. Embedded blanks are not permitted within an identifier.

F.2. PROCEDURE NAMES AND FILENAMES

An external procedure name or a filename is an identifier that consists of one to seven characters, but may not contain the characters _, #, or @.

F.3. RESERVED KEYWORDS

The following PL/C reserved keywords cannot be used as identifiers or variables.

ALLOCATE		END
BEGIN		ENTRY
BY		EXIT
CALL		FLOW
CHECK		FORMAT
CLOSE		FREE
DECLARE	DCL	GET
DELETE		GO
DO		GO TO
ELSE		GOTO

IF		RETURN
NO		REVERT
NOCHECK		REWRITE
NOFLOW		SIGNAL
ON		STOP
OPEN		THEN
PROCEDURE	PROC	TO
PUT		WHILE
READ		WRITE

F.4. SOURCE PROGRAM STATEMENTS

Cardpunch machines and interactive terminals are commonly used to prepare PL/C programs. In either case, each PL/C statement must appear within columns 2 through 72, inclusive. Column 1 is not used, and columns 73 through 80 are reserved as an optional identification or sequencing field.

PL/C statements may be continued from one line to the next, but every identifier or variable name must appear in one source line; i.e., they cannot be split between two lines.

F.5. COMMENTS

Some PL/C compilers require each comment to begin and to end on the same source line.

F.6. DEFAULTS

The default attributes for PL/C variables are essentially the same as those for IBM PL/I. That is, if the attributes for a variable are not declared, the "I through N" rule is used. That is, if a variable name begins with a letter I through N, inclusive, the default attributes for that variable are

FIXED BINARY (15, 0) REAL AUTOMATIC

Variable names beginning with letters other than I through N have the default attributes

FLOAT DECIMAL (6) REAL AUTOMATIC

However, if a variable is partially declared, the default attributes may not be as expected. For example, if the scale attribute is declared as either FIXED or FLOAT, the default base attribute is DECIMAL. If the base attribute is declared as either BINARY or DECIMAL, the default scale attribute is FLOAT.

F.7. ON STATEMENTS

The general form for a PL/C ON statement is

TABLE F.1.

Declared attributes	*Comments*
FIXED BINARY (15)	$-32768 \leq$ stored value $\leq +32767$
FIXED DECIMAL (5)	$-99999 \leq$ stored value $\leq +99999$
FLOAT DECIMAL (6)	stored value contains a six-place decimal with an exponent between -78 and $+75$.
CHARACTER (n) VARYING	$1 \leq n \leq 256$
BIT (n) VARYING	$1 \leq n \leq 256$

ON condition on-unit

The "on-unit" can be any unlabeled statement except for DO loops, DO groups, IF statements, RETURN statements, or ON statements. An unlabeled BEGIN block is permitted. The following conditions are permitted:

CONVERSION	data-conversion error
ENDFILE	end of file
ENDPAGE	end of page on a print file
FIXEDOVERFLOW	fixed-point arithmetic overflow
OVERFLOW	floating-point arithmetic overflow
SUBSCRIPTRANGE	subscript out of range
UNDERFLOW	floating-point arithmetic underflow
ZERODIVIDE	division by zero

F.8. STORAGE CONSIDERATIONS

All floating-point arithmetic is performed with double precision and generally produces more precise results than IBM PL/I. Regardless of programmer declarations, PL/C assigns a full word for each FIXED BINARY variable and two words of storage for each FIXED DECIMAL variable. In general, PL/C also consumes more storage for character strings than does IBM PL/I. Table F.1 shows the range of possible values for stored values.

F.9. RESTRICTIONS

1. The 48-character set is not available; consequently only the 60-character set may be used.
2. The topics in Chapter 13 dealing with controlled storage, based storage, and list processing are not available in PL/C.
3. String constants may not have replication factors; i.e., the string constant (5) 'ABCDEF' is not permitted.
4. PICTURE data types (Chapter 12) are not available.
5. The LIKE attribute (Chapter 11) is not available.

There are other differences between PL/C and ANSI PL/I, but only the differences between PL/C and the topics discussed in this book are considered.

Appendix G

ANSI Subset G

Subset G is a proper subset of ANSI PL/I. This subset is implemented on small and medium-size computer systems, including many microcomputer- and microprocessor-based systems. This book contains a subset of ANSI PL/I that is quite similar to Subset G. This appendix contains a summary of the differences between the PL/I in this book and Subset G.

G.1. FEATURES NOT AVAILABLE

1. Binary constants, e.g., 10110B.
2. Replicated string constants, e.g., (4)'ABCD'.
3. COMPLEX data type.
4. BIT VARYING is not permitted, but the BIT data type remains.
5. The following PICTURE codes: A E K X.
6. Data-directed stream I/O.
7. The LIKE attribute for structure declaration.
8. CONTROLLED storage (considered redundant with BASED).
9. Aggregate assignment is limited to scalars and aggregates with identical data attributes.
10. Expressions containing data aggregates.
11. Programmer-defined conditions, i.e., CONDITION.
12. The division operator (/) may not be used with fixed-point binary operands.
13. Multiple-target variables in assignment statements, e.g.,

    A, B, C = 0;

G.2. RESTRICTIONS OR DIFFERENCES

1. All variable names must be explicitly declared.
2. The characters /* must not appear within the body of a comment.

3. Only STATIC variables and members of STATIC structures can be initialized with the INITIAL attribute.
4. Only constant values can appear in format lists; i.e., variables or expressions are not permitted in format lists.
5. Operands of arithmetic operations must be either arithmetic or pictured.
6. Operands of relational operations must be either arithmetic or pictured, or both operands must be the same type.
7. Arguments to arithmetic functions must be either arithmetic or pictured.
8. GET and PUT statements may not contain more than one I/O list or more than one format list.
9. The conditional expression in an IF statement or WHILE clause must reduce to a big string of length one.
10. The index variable of an iterative DO statement must be an integer or a pointer. Only integer values are permitted in the TO and BY options.
11. All operators must yield scalar values.
12. All functions must return scalar values.
13. All subscripts must be integers.
14. Only the following PICTURE codes are permitted:

    S V Z 9 − + $ * . , /

15. An ALLOCATE or FREE statement can refer to only one item.
16. The SET option is required for the ALLOCATE statement, i.e.,

    ALLOCATE based-variable SET (pointer);

17. An OPEN or CLOSE statement can refer to only one file.

G.3. KEYWORDS

There are no reserved keywords in Subset G. All the keywords that appear in Appendix D are available with Subset G, except for the following:

CONDITION	COND	ONSOURCE	
CONTROLLED	CTL	REAL	
CONVERSION	CONV	SIZE	
DATA		SNAP	
LIKE		STRINGRANGE	STRG
ONCHAR		SUBSCRIPTRANGE	SUBRG
ONLOC		SYSTEM	

G.4. IMPLEMENTATIONS

An increasing number of PL/I compilers are based on Subset G. Some of the compilers that are currently available are

Digital Research PL/I-80
DEC VAX-11 PL/I
Prime PL/I
Data General PL/I
Wang VS PL/I

G.5. OTHER POINTS

1. This appendix does not summarize all the differences between ANSI PL/I and Subset G. Rather, it summarizes the differences between Subset G and the subset of ANSI PL/I presented in this book. These differences are also cited throughout this book with footnotes or other discussion.
2. There are several PL/I-like compilers currently available on microprocessor-based systems, including the following:

   Intel PL/M
   Intel PL/M-86
   Motorola MPL
   Signetics PLuS

   These languages are similar to PL/I, but are not based on any particular version of PL/I.

Appendix H
DEC CPL

Digital Equipment Corporation's Conversational Programming Language (DEC CPL, or simply CPL) is a subset of ANSI PL/I and is a smaller subset than Subset G, which is discussed in Appendix G. CPL was designed for use with interactive terminals on DECSYSTEM 10/20 computer systems. CPL can be used in "direct" or "collect" mode. In direct mode, each statement is immediately executed when entered at the terminal. In collect mode, statements are collected to form a program, and that program is then executed. Only collect mode is considered, because it is similar to the compilation* process used throughout this book. The differences between CPL and the PL/I used in this book are summarized in this appendix.

H.1. CHARACTER SET

Letters: A–Z and a–z (upper- and lower-case letters)
Digits: 0–9
Characters: b̸ (blank) = + − * / ( ) , . : ; ? _ ' < > ∧ (not) ! (or) & (and)

H.2. IDENTIFIERS AND VARIABLES

An identifier or a variable name consists of one to 31 characters, of which the first must be a letter (upper- or lower-case). The remaining characters must be letters (upper- or lower-case), digits, or the underscore (_). Note that the following are eight *different* identifiers:

NAM NaM nAm nam Nam nAM NAm naM

*CPL actually functions as an "interpreter," rather than as a compiler. That is, each statement is interpreted and executed each time it is encountered. There is no object program generated by a CPL source program.

H.3. SOURCE PROGRAM STATEMENTS

1. Each statement must be preceded with a line number from 1. to 9999.99 (the period is required). The order of the line numbers is important.
2. A semicolon is automatically inserted at the end of each line.
3. A statement with a "&" as the last character is continued to the next line (no semicolon is inserted).
4. The available 2-character operations are:

```
** >= <= ∧= ∧> ∧< -> !! /* */
```

H.4. DATA TYPES

The only data tapes available with CPL are

FIXED
FLOAT
CHARACTER(*n*)
CHARACTER(*n*) VARYING
BIT(n)
BIT(n) VARYING
POINTER

Variables cannot be declared as FIXED DECIMAL, FIXED BINARY, FLOAT DECIMAL, or FLOAT BINARY. The FIXED data type permits only integer values, and is logically equivalent to

FIXED BINARY(35)

The FLOAT data type is logically equivalent to

FLOAT BINARY(27)

The ranges of values that can be stored in FIXED and FLOAT variables are

$-34359738368 \leqslant \text{FIXED value} \leqslant +34359738367$
$-1.7014118\text{E}-38 \leqslant \text{FLOAT value} \leqslant +1.7014118\text{E}+38$

H.5. DEFAULTS

All undeclared variables default to FLOAT.

H.6. ON STATEMENTS

The conditions available with the ON statement are

SUBSCRIPTRANGE	SUBRG	ENDFILE
STRINGRANGE	STRG	RECORD
ZERODIVIDE	ZDIV	ERROR
		CONDITION

H.7. KEYWORDS

There are no reserved keywords in CPL. All the keywords in Appendix D are recognized by CPL, except for the following:

BINARY	BIN	INITIAL	INIT	P	
DATA		INTERNAL	INT	PICTURE	PIC
DECIMAL	DEC	LIKE		REAL	
ENDPAGE		LINE		RECURSIVE	
ENTRY		MAIN		ROUND	
EXTERNAL		OPTIONS		TAN	
				TAND	

Either upper- or lower-case letters can be used for any of the keywords. For example, "DECLARE" is equivalent to "declare." SYSIN and SYSPRINT should be treated as reserved words to avoid problems with GET/PUT statements without the FILE option.

H.8. SAMPLE CPL PROGRAM

Program H.1. is a complete CPL program that computes and prints the squares and cubes of integers from 1 to 20.

PROGRAM H.1.

```
100.    /* PRINT SQUARES AND CUBES */ ;
110.    /* OF INTEGERS FROM 1 TO 20 */ ;
120.    DCL (A,B,C) FIXED;
130.    PUT EDIT ('INTEGER','SQUARE','CUBE') &
140.             (COL(10),A,COL(20),A,COL(30),A);
150.    DO A = 1 TO 20;
160.       B = A**2;
170.       C = A**3;
180.       PUT EDIT (A,B,C) &
190.                (COL(13),F(2),COL(21),F(3),COL(30),F(4));
200.    END;
```

H.9. FEATURES NOT AVAILABLE

1. There is no PROCEDURE OPTIONS(MAIN) statement. The main procedure is an undeclared procedure (see the preceding CPL program, which is a main procedure).
2. Structures are not available.

3. The following items are not available:

   PICTURE data type
   COMPLEX data type
   LINE format item
   LIKE attribute
   EXTERNAL attribute
   DATA option for GET/PUT statements

4. The RECURSIVE attribute is not available, because all function and subroutine procedures are automatically recursive.

H.10. RESTRICTIONS OR DIFFERENCES

1. The default for undeclared variables and the output produced by the PUT LIST statement differs from ANSI PL/I. To make CPL compatible with ANSI PL/I for these items, place the following at the beginning of a CPL program:

   1. DCL SYSPRINT PRINT; (RANGE(*)) FIXED;

2. Comments should begin and end on the same line.
3. Division of one FIXED value by another FIXED value is not permitted.
4. Aggregate assignments are not permitted.
5. Aggregates and DO options are not permitted in GET/PUT statements.
6. The PUT EDIT statement is permitted, but the GET EDIT statement is not permitted.
7. A FORMAT statement must be within the same block as the PUT EDIT statement which references it.

H.11. OTHER POINTS

1. Null statements are permitted; see the comments in the sample CPL program.
2. CPL was developed by one person within an eight-month period.
3. This appendix does not summarize all the differences between ANSI PL/I and CPL. Rather, it summarizes the differences between CPL and the subset of ANSI PL/I presented in this book.

Appendix I
DEC VAX-11 PL/I

DEC VAX-11 PL/I contains the features of Subset G as well as several extensions. The extensions and features unique to DEC VAX-11 PL/I are outlined in this appendix.

I.1. DEFAULT PRECISION FOR ARITHMETIC DATA

FIXED BINARY (31)
FIXED DECIMAL (10)
FLOAT BINARY (24)
FLOAT DECIMAL (7)

I.2. MAXIMUM PRECISION FOR ARITHMETIC DATA

FIXED BINARY (31)
FIXED DECIMAL (31)
FLOAT BINARY (113)
FLOAT DECIMAL (34)

I.3. CONDITIONS AVAILABLE WITH THE ON STATEMENT

ERROR	OVERFLOW
ENDFILE	UNDERFLOW
ENDPAGE	ZERODIVIDE
FIXEDOVERFLOW	

I.4. CHARACTER SET

The full 256-character ASCII character set is supported.

I.5. EXTENSIONS

1. The ON statement supports the programmer-defined VAX-CONDITION condition.
2. The expression in a WHILE clause or in an IF statement may be a bit string of any length.
3. The index variable and the expressions in the TO and BY options of the DO statement are not restricted to integers and pointers.
4. The picture codes Y, T, I, and R are supported.
5. RETURNS CHARACTER (*) is valid.
6. Automatic variables may be initialized. The INITIAL attribute may contain scalar expressions and asterisks.
7. The SET option is optional on the ALLOCATE statement if the allocated variable is declared as BASED.
8. The character pair /* may be embedded in a comment.
9. This appendix does not contain all the differences between Subset G and VAX-11 PL/I. Rather, it contains the differences between VAX-11 PL/I and that portion of Subset G described in Appendix G.

Appendix J
Digital Research PL/I-80*

Digital Research PL/I-80 contains most of the features of Subset G and several extensions. The limitations and features unique to PL/I-80 are outlined in this appendix.

J.1. LIMITATIONS

The following attributes are not included:

DEFINED
LIKE
PICTURE (allowed only as an output edit format item)
FILE (allowed only in an OPEN statement)
Asterisk extents and dynamic arrays

The following built-in functions are not included:

DATE
STRING
TIME

J.2. IDENTIFIERS

Identifiers can consist of one to 31 characters, i.e., letters, digits, or the underscore, but the first character must be a letter. Upper- and lower-case letters can be used, but lower-case letters are always represented internally as upper-case letters; e.g., variables abc and ABC are regarded as the same.

*PL/I-80 is a trademark of Digital Research.

J.3. CONDITIONS AVAILABLE WITH THE ON STATEMENT

ENDFILE
ENDPAGE
ERROR
FIXEDOVERFLOW
OVERFLOW
UNDERFLOW
ZERODIVIDE

J.4. DEFAULT PRECISION FOR ARITHMETIC DATA

FIXED BINARY (15)
FIXED DECIMAL (7)
FLOAT BINARY (24)

J.5. MAXIMUM PRECISION FOR ARITHMETIC DATA

FIXED BINARY (15)
FIXED DECIMAL (15)
FLOAT BINARY (24)

J.6. MAXIMUM STRING LENGTHS

CHARACTER (254)
BIT (16)

J.7. OTHER POINTS

1. All variables must be declared.
2. An array can be assigned to another array, without subscripts, only if both arrays are declared with the same data type, dimension, and subscript ranges.
3. An array, major structure, or minor structure can be assigned a compatible scalar expression.
4. Only STATIC variables can have the INITIAL attribute.
5. This appendix does not contain all the differences between PL/I-80 and Subset G. Rather, it contains the differences between PL/I-80 and that portion of Subset G described in Appendix G.

Appendix K
CDC PL/I

CDC PL/I is a subset of ANSI PL/I and is similar to Subset G in many respects. However, all comparisons of CDC PL/I in this appendix are with ANSI PL/I.

K.1. DEFAULT PRECISION FOR ARITHMETIC DATA

FIXED BINARY (15)
FIXED DECIMAL (5)
FLOAT BINARY (48)
FLOAT DECIMAL (14)

K.2. MAXIMUM PRECISION FOR ARITHMETIC DATA

FIXED BINARY (48)
FIXED DECIMAL (14)
FLOAT BINARY (48)
FLOAT DECIMAL (14)

K.3. MAXIMUM STRING LENGTHS

CHARACTER (131071)
BIT (131071)

K.4. IDENTIFIERS

Identifiers can consist of one to 40 characters, i.e., letters, digits, the underscore, and the special characters @, #, and $, but the first character must be a letter or one of the special characters @, #, and $.

K.5. OTHER POINTS

1. Data-directed I/O is not available.
2. Aggregate operations are not supported in any way; i.e., only subscripted variables or structural elements can appear in any executable statement.
3. The TIME built-in function returns six characters, hhmmss.
4. The exponent range for floating point values is about −294 to +322.
5. All the keywords in Appendix D are available with CDC PL/I.
6. This appendix does not contain all the differences between ANSI PL/I and CDC PL/I. Rather, it contains the differences between CDC PL/I and the subset of ANSI PL/I presented in this book.

Index